Cinematic Style

Also by Jess Berry and also by Bloomsbury

House of Fashion: Haute Couture and the Modern Interior

Cinematic Style

Fashion, Architecture and Interior Design on Film

Jess Berry

BLOOMSBURY VISUAL ARTS
LONDON • NEW YORK • OXFORD • NEW DELHI • SYDNEY

BLOOMSBURY VISUAL ARTS
Bloomsbury Publishing Plc
50 Bedford Square, London, WC1B 3DP, UK
1385 Broadway, New York, NY 10018, USA
29 Earlsfort Terrace, Dublin 2, Ireland

BLOOMSBURY, BLOOMSBURY VISUAL ARTS and the Diana logo
are trademarks of Bloomsbury Publishing Plc

First published in Great Britain 2022

Copyright © Jess Berry, 2022

Jess Berry has asserted her right under the Copyright, Designs and
Patents Act, 1988, to be identified as Author of this work.

For legal purposes the Acknowledgements on pp. x–xi constitute an
extension of this copyright page.

Cover design: Charlotte Daniels
Cover image: Joan Crawford (1908–1977) as Diane Lovering in Chained,
directed by Clarence Brown and costumes by Adrian. (© George Hurrell/John
Kobal Foundation/Getty Images)

All rights reserved. No part of this publication may be reproduced or
transmitted in any form or by any means, electronic or mechanical, including
photocopying, recording, or any information storage or retrieval system,
without prior permission in writing from the publishers.

Bloomsbury Publishing Plc does not have any control over, or responsibility for,
any third-party websites referred to or in this book. All internet addresses given
in this book were correct at the time of going to press. The author and publisher
regret any inconvenience caused if addresses have changed or sites have
ceased to exist, but can accept no responsibility for any such changes.

A catalogue record for this book is available from the British Library.

A catalog record for this book is available from the Library of Congress.

ISBN:	HB:	978-1-3501-3761-5
	PB:	978-1-3501-3762-2
	ePDF:	978-1-3501-3760-8
	eBook:	978-1-3501-3763-9

Typeset by Integra Software Services Pvt. Ltd.

To find out more about our authors and books visit www.bloomsbury.com
and sign up for our newsletters.

Contents

Illustrations	vi
Acknowledgements	x
Introduction: Cinematic style – fashion, architecture and interior design on film	1
1 Bedrooms, boudoirs and bathrooms: Modern women, seductive spaces and spectacular silhouettes	13
2 Evil lairs and bachelor dandies: Modernist architecture, spies and the suit	41
3 Luxurious longings: Queer heterotopias in décor and dress	63
4 Grand entrances: Staircases, stages and fashion parades	85
5 Windows and screens: Cinema, department stores and boutique display	107
6 Dream spaces: Film sets as fashion flagships and experiential retail environments	129
Conclusion	151
Notes	158
Filmography	180
Bibliography	188
Index	203

Illustrations

1.1 Greta Garbo as Arden in *The Single Standard* (1929). Credits: John S. Robertson (Director), Metro-Goldwyn-Mayer (MGM) (Film Production). Photo: ullstein bild via Getty Images. 17
1.2 Laure Maresco as Nathalie Lissenko in *Le Double Amour* (1925). Credits: Jean Epstein (Director). Films Albatros (Film Production). Screen still. 19
1.3 Doris Day as Jan Morrow and Thelma Ritter as Alma in *Pillow Talk* (1959). Credits: Michael Gordon (Director). Photo: Silver Screen Collection/Getty Images. 23
1.4 Maggie Cheung as Su Lizhen *In the Mood for Love* (2000). Credits: Wong Kar-Wai (Director), Jet Tone Productions and Paradise Films (Film Production), Screen still. 26
1.5 Jean Harlow as Kitty Packard in *Dinner at Eight* (1933). Credits: George Cukor (Director) Metro-Goldwyn-Mayer (MGM) (Film Production). Photo Credit: John Springer Collection/ CORBIS via Getty Images. 29
1.6 Rita Hayworth as Gilda and George Macredy as Ballian Mudson in *Gilda* (1946). Credits: Charles Vidor (Director), Columbia Pictures (Film Production). Photo Credits: Columbia/Getty Images. 31
1.7 Joan Crawford as Crystal Allen in the bath and Rosalind Rusell as Sylvia in *The Women* (1939). Credits: George Cukor (Director), Metro-Goldwyn-Mayer (MGM) (Film Production). Photo Credits: Metro-Goldwyn-Mayer/Getty Images. 35
1.8 Julia Roberts as Vivian Ward and Richard Gere as Edward Lewis in *Pretty Woman* (1990). Credits: Garry Marshall (Director), Touchstone Pictures (Film Production). Screen still. 38
2.1 Vandamm House in *North By Northwest* (1959). Credits: Alfred Hitchcock (Director), Metro-Goldwyn-Mayer (MGM) (Film Production). Screen still. 45
2.2 Interior of Vandamm House, *North by Northwest* (1959). Credits: Alfred Hitchcock (Director), Metro-Goldwyn-Mayer (MGM) (Film Production). Screen still. 46

Illustrations vii

2.3 Cary Grant as Roger Thornhill in *North by Northwest* (1959). Credits: Alfred Hitchcock (Director), Metro-Goldwyn-Mayer (MGM) (Film Production). Photo Credit: Sunset Boulevard/ Corbis via Getty Images. 49

2.4 Sean Connery as James Bond and Jack Lord as Felix Leiter in *Dr. No* (1962). Credits: Terrance Young (Director), Eon Productions (Film Production). Photo Credit: United Artist/Getty Images. 51

2.5 Daniel Craig as James Bond wearing Tom Ford in *Spectre* (2015). Credits: Sam Mendes (Director), Eon Productions (Film Production). Screen still. 52

2.6 Adolf Loos interior design for the gentleman's outfitters Knize, Vienna (1910–1913). Photography by Photo Studio Gerlach. Photo Credit: Imagno/Getty Images. 56

2.7 Lola Larson as Bambi, Elrod House interior, *Diamonds Are Forever* (1971). Credits: Guy Hamilton (Director), Eon Productions (Film Production). Screen still. 59

3.1 Contrasting textures. Rooney Mara as Therese and Cate Blanchett as Carol in *Carol* (2015). Credits: Todd Haynes (Director), Number 9 Films, Film 4, Killer Films (Film Production). Screen still. 66

3.2 Attention to fabric. Rooney Mara as Therese and Cate Blanchett as Carol in *Carol* (2015). Credits: Todd Haynes (Director), Number 9 Films, Film 4, Killer Films (Film Production). Screen still. 67

3.3 Surface style. Colin Firth as George and Julianne Moore as Charlie in *A Single Man* (2009). Credits: Tom Ford (Director), Artina Films, Depth of Field and Fade to Black (Film Production). Screen still. 69

3.4 John Lautner Schaffer Residence. Colin Firth as George in *A Single Man* (2009). Credits: Tom Ford (Director), Artina Films, Depth of Field and Fade to Black (Film Production). Screen still. 70

3.5 The intimate interior. Colin Firth as George and Nicolaus Hoult as Kenny in *A Single Man* (2009). Credits: Tom Ford (Director), Artina Films, Depth of Field and Fade to Black (Film Production). Screen still. 71

3.6 The Presidential Suite. Rooney Mara as Therese and Cate Blanchett as Carol in *Carol* (2015). Credits: Todd Haynes (Director), Number 9 Films, Film 4, Killer Films (Film Production). Screen still. 73

3.7 Mirror as queer heterotopia. Rooney Mara as Therese and Cate Blanchett as Carol in *Carol* (2015). Credits: Todd Haynes (Director), Number 9 Films, Film 4, Killer Films (Film Production). Screen still. 74

3.8 Melvin Poupaud as Laurence Alia in *Laurence Anyways* (2012). Credits: Xavier Dolan (Director), Layla Films and MK2 (Film Production). Screen still. 77
3.9 The Five Roses in *Laurence Anyways* (2012). Credits: Xavier Dolan (Director), Layla Films and MK2 (Film Production). Screen still. 78
4.1 Fashion designer Gabrielle Coco Chanel sitting on the stairs in her atelier. Photo Credit: Photo by Photo 12/UIG/Getty Images. 90
4.2 Model standing on staircase wearing a white organdie dress by Dior, Paris, March 1956. Publication: Picture Post. Photo Credit: Savitry/Picture Post/Hulton Archive/Getty Images. 93
4.3 *Ziegfeld Follies* performers dressed by Lucile (Lady Duff Gordon) (1917). Photo Credit: Bettmann/Getty Images. 95
4.4 Hedy Lamarr, Judy Garland and Lana Turner as chorus girls wearing Adrian designed gowns in *Ziegfeld Girl* (1941). Credits: Busby Berkeley and Robert Z. Leonard (Director) Metro-Goldwyn-Mayer (Film Production). Photo Credit: Bettmann/Getty Images. 97
4.5 Audrey Hepburn descends the Daru Staircase at the Louvre in Paris, in a scene from *Funny Face* (1957). Credits: Stanely Donen (Director), Paramount Pictures (Film Production). Photo Credit: Archive Photos/Getty Images. 98
4.6 Tilda Swinton as Emma Recchi in *I Am Love (Io sonno l'amore)* (2009). Credits: Luca Guadagnino (Director), First Sun (Film Production). Screen still. 100
4.7 Oki Sato, Nendo Studio *Ame Nochi Hana-Rain Flowers* at Le Bon Marche department store (2020). Photo Credit: Chesnot/Getty Images. 102
4.8 Prada Epicentre staircase designed by architect Rem Koolhaas (2001). Photo credit: David LEFRANC/Gamma-Rapho via Getty Images. 104
5.1 Selfridges windows lit up at night (1935). Photo Credit: David Savill/Topical Press Agency/Getty Images. 110
5.2 Recreation of Sonia Delaunay's Boutique Simultanée at the Museum of Modern Art, Paris, 2014. The original shopfront was first presented at the 1924 Salon d'Automne. Photo Credit: Chesnot/Getty Images. 113
5.3 Robert Mallet-Stevens' set design for *L'Inhumaine* (1924). Marcel L'Herbier (Director). Credit: *Art et Decoration* July 1926: 134. 115
5.4 Robert Mallet-Stevens' residence at rue Mallet-Stevens Paris (1927). Photo Credit: Jess Berry. 116

5.5	Interior design by Robert Mallet-Stevens and Sonia Delaunay, *Le P'tit Parigot* (1926). Credits: René Le Somptier (Director), Luminor (Film Production) Photo Credit: ullstein bild/ullstein bild via Getty Images.	118
5.6	René Herbst, Hall of Windows, Studio Siegel. *Art et Decoration* 1927: 199.	120
5.7	Sam Hood, *Ziegfeld Girl* display window using MGM promotional material (1941). Photo Credit: State Library of New South Wales.	123
5.8	Baz Luhrmann (Director) and Catherine Martin (Production Designer) at the unveiling of Tiffany's Fifth Avenue windows inspired by their adaptation of *The Great Gatsby* (2013). Photo Credit: Andrew H. Walker/Getty Images for Tiffany & Co	124
6.1	Cinema da Camera, Gucci Gardens, Florence. Photo Credit: Jess Berry (2019).	133
6.2	*Italy in Hollywood* exhibition Museum Salvatore Ferragamo (2018). Photo Credit: Jess Berry.	135
6.3	Bedroom decorated by Ralph Lauren as part of his new Home Collection New York. LIFE 1986. Photo Credit: Dirck Halstead/The LIFE Images Collection via Getty Images/Getty Images.	138
6.4	Catherine Martin and Miuccia Prada Dress Gatsby at Prada Epicentre, New York (2013). Photo Credit: Dimitrios Kambouris/ Getty Images for Prada.	140
6.5	Wes Anderson, Bar Luce at Fondazione Prada, Milan. Photo Credit: Jess Berry (2018).	141
6.6	Anita Eckberg on the set of *Boccaccio '70* segment 'Le tentazioni del dottor Antonio'(1961) against the backdrop of Palazzo Civiltà Italiana, directed by Fedrico Fellini. Photo Credit: Vittoriano Rastelli/Corbis via Getty Images.	145
6.7	Fendi New York Flagship Boutique, Madison Aveue (2015). Photo Credit: Gilbert Carrasquillo/GC Images via Getty Images.	147
6.8	India Mahdavi interior for RED Valentino London Flagship store, 2016. Photo Credit: David M. Benett/Getty Images for Red Valentino.	149

Acknowledgements

Much of this book was written while I was on study leave during a year of great upheaval in the Australian university sector as a result of the global pandemic. The significant opportunity to dedicate time to research and writing was made possible due to the support of my colleagues at Monash University. Dean of Art, Design and Architecture, Professor Shane Murray and Associate Dean Research, Professor Melissa Miles deserve my deep gratitude for their support of this project. My sincere appreciation also goes to Associate Professor Gene Bawden, Associate Professor Nicole Kalms, Professor Lisa Grocott and Sarah Stratton who all provided stimulating discussion, guidance, mentorship and friendship in one way or another that has not only sustained me through the challenging year that was 2020, but throughout my time at Monash. The entire XYX Gender + Place research lab team similarly deserve my grateful thanks as a dedicated, ambitious, inspiring and supportive group of people to work with on projects at the intersection of gender, identity and spatial practice. Thank you also to the intelligent women of the Orbital reading group – Dr Alex Brown, Charity Edwards, Dr Helen Hughs and Dr Anna Parlane – who provided insightful discussion and thoughtful feedback on elements of the manuscript.

I owe an ongoing debt to Professor Susan Best. Her encouragement and mentorship over many years, along with generous reading of the manuscript and insightful critique, have been invaluable. Sue is also a dear friend; her patience and humour for problem solving Zoom calls is a further kindness that I much appreciate. Stimulating conversations and opportunities emerging from conferences helped hone many of the ideas in this book. I am grateful to Sarah Gillan for the opportunity to share my work at Fashion, Costume and Visual Cultures with colleagues in Zagreb. I would especially like to thank Professor Pamela Church Gibson who encouraged me to write this book at a conference organized by Professor Vicki Karaminas in New Zealand, her assurance that there was something in it was the catalyst for this project.

My deep gratitude to my brilliant editor at Bloomsbury, Frances Arnold, this is my second book with her, and her interest and enthusiasm for my work are much appreciated. Rebecca Hamilton and the rest of the team at Bloomsbury are incredibly helpful and make the publishing process a pleasure. I also thank the anonymous reviewers for their helpful comments on the proposal and manuscript.

Lastly, thank you and love to my friends and family, especially Ruth and Wolfgang, Dale and Gary, Andrea, and Tori who have always been there when I needed them. Taco and The Dude Lebowski also deserve my thanks as borrowed fur friends who were great company while writing this book.

Introduction: Cinematic style – fashion, architecture and interior design on film

From cinema's silent beginnings the spectacular visual pleasures of fashion, interior design and architecture have enthralled audiences. Take for example Cecil B. DeMille's productions from the 1920s, in which 'sex, sets and costumes' were the secret to the director's success.[1] DeMille was amongst early pioneers who brought architects, designers, artists and costumers to screen-production paving the way for cinematic style to penetrate the imagination of a receptive cinema-going public. The extravagant and ornate mise-en-scène of films such as *The Affairs of Anatol* (1921) introduced audiences to the Art Nouveau designs of the celebrated French fashion illustrator, Paul Iribe.[2] It is clear that from very early on, cinema cultivated consumer culture through fashions and furnishings, where *Theatre* magazine claimed that: 'more women see DeMille's pictures than read fashion magazines ... and then there are the tips on interior decoration and house furnishing ... [educating] the taste of the masses.'[3] Iribe's visually arresting patterned fabrics for evening dresses and coats coupled with the alluring curvilinear décor of boudoirs and bedrooms were certainly glamorous images that portrayed an alignment between style, sexuality, luxury and pleasure. Yet, they conveyed more than just a glimmer of sexual impropriety. Just as design discourse of the time designated decorative coherence between fashion and the interior as an extension of women's psychological interiority, sets and costumes on screen revealed a character's personality, desires and arc of transformation.

Through the aesthetics of Art Nouveau in *The Affairs of Anatol* – as well as in the Natacha Rambova designed films *Camille* (1921) and *Salomé* (1923) – audiences soon became acquainted with a prevailing cinematic trope that saw sexually liberated, femme fatale figures represented by the glamorous clothes they wore, and the luxurious rooms they inhabited. Women were cast in a decorative mode, confirming links between interior, dress and lifestyle. As Louise Wallenberg summarizes in *Fashion and Modernity*, film's growing popularity as a medium in the 1920s coincided with women's increased sexual, social and economic emancipation leading to archetypal representations that circumscribed coherence between the 'sexual woman' and consumption.[4] These themes resurfaced continually in design and cinema discourses throughout the twentieth and twenty-first centuries, and herein lies a problem that has long-lasting effects.

The gendered perception of glamorous and fashionable design modes marks them as lacking in substance. The film theorist Rosalind Galt describes how these types of screen surfaces trouble cinematic value by complying with qualities that are: 'carefully composed ... richly textured ... ornamental ... [comprised of] detailed *mise-en-scène,* and an emphasis on [a self-evidently designed] cinematographic surface'.[5] She reminds us that: 'the rhetoric of cinema has consistently denigrated surface decoration, finding the attractive skin of the screen to be false, shallow, feminine or apolitical.'[6] In other words, while audiences may well be enamoured with the surfaces of cinematic style, fashion and the interior share a long association with social, cultural and psychological aspects of feminine and queer identities, resulting in their neglect within the broader histories of design and cinema.

Despite the spectacular technological advancements of twenty-first century cinema, stunning silhouettes and striking spaces still have the ability to dazzle to dramatic affect. Yet, the correlation between these modes of aesthetic production and consumption continues to be largely overlooked. That is not to say that significant scholarship regarding the relationship between fashion and film or spatial design and film does not exist. However, there is to date, no existing comprehensive academic volume that is solely dedicated to surveying the relationship between fashion, interior design and architecture as mediated through film that takes into account developments from the silent era to the present moment, as is the focus of this book.

Cinematic Style proposes fashion, spatial design and cinema as a triumvirate system of symbolic narrative production that enables the translation of glamorous lifestyles from the screen to real-life consumer culture. Specifically, I argue that two central concerns can be discerned from this triangulation. Firstly, the representation of gender and sexuality on screen is closely related to the aesthetic alignment of silhouettes, styles, and spaces to visually convey complex identity performances based in concepts of masquerade and interiority. Secondly, cinematic style is calibrated to the fantasies of consumer desire, where self-actualization is represented as realized through alluring surfaces and spaces. This results in a mutually reinforcing dialogue between fashion, spatial design and film, which privileges narratives of transformation as the answer to self-fulfilment and is articulated through fashion spaces beyond the screen.

Recognizing that there is an intersection between fashion, interior design and architecture is not new. As I have previously outlined in *House of Fashion: Haute Couture and the Modern Interior* these seemingly disparate areas of design share much in common.[7] Since haute couture's inception, luxury fashion has sought to leverage architecture and interior spaces as a way of enhancing value. It is worth restating some of these confluences here to make clear my premise that fashion and spatial design can be understood in tandem with each other. This approach underpins the structure of the book. By considering body and space together rather than as separate entities, a holistic understanding of how mise-en-scène functions to produce narrative meaning is elucidated.

Fashion, interior design and architecture operate as both material and conceptual manifestation. That is, they act as physical space inhabited by bodies, but also appear as images and in the cultural imaginary aided by their representation in illustrations, photographs and significantly to this book – on film. It is my contention that film mediates the representation of interior design and architecture in ways that are fashionable, aligning them with the purposes of the fashion system. That is, the symbolic production of value that shifts clothing to fashion relies on the representation of fashion as image and cultural object associated with the social construction of identity, status and aesthetic tastes. These apparatuses of myth making can equally be applied to the consumption of the interior and architecture.

The aforementioned integration of fashion and spatial design through aesthetic form in the case of Art Nouveau is just one example of this relationship throughout the history of design that was reiterated in cinematic contexts. For instance, Art Deco saw confluences between the slick polished surfaces of steam liners and sumptuous hotels and the glamorous, silhouettes of streamlined evening gowns. Hollywood art directors and costumers including Cedric Gibbons and Adrian, as well as Van Nest Polglase and Bernard Newman, worked together on complementary interiors and fashions, orchestrating a cogent approach to shades of white styling in films such as *Grand Hotel* (1932) and *Top Hat* (1932).[8] In the post-Second World War era, Christian Dior's New Look (1947) and Tulip-Line (1953) silhouettes dominated fashion. This exaggeration of form was also carried out in mid-century modern home furnishings such as Arne Jacobsen's *Series 7 chair* (1955) and Eero Saarien's *Tulip Chair* (1956) heralding a shift in modernism towards organic forms.[9] This type of correlation can be seen in costumer Edith Head and set decorator Sam Comer's approach in films such as Alfred Hitchcock's *Rear Window* (1954) and *Vertigo* (1958).[10] Similarly, Pop materializations manifest in futuristic fashion looks by Paco Rabanne coupled with Op Art and Verner Panton style interiors such as those in *Who Are You Polly Maggoo?* (1966), and *Barbarella* (1968), demonstrate stylistic synergies across design modes. This set of examples, while by no means exhaustive, gives weight to John Potvin's claim that 'both fashion and furniture might be conceptualised as two dialects emerging from the language of design'.[11] Here, I extend this idea to interiors more broadly, along with architecture, to elaborate on how these dialects converge in film to convey narrative meaning.

Significantly, fashion and interior design not only share a common aesthetic history, they also play an important role in modern identity formation – their significance is underlined by their ability to act as sociocultural form linked with human individuality and self-hood.[12] The concept of architectural 'interiority' – the emergence of individual persona and its relationship to the decorated room as a marker of the inhabitant's personality or state of mind – also resonates with the way we understand fashion as an extension of one's distinctiveness, status, and taste linked to the performance of gender and sexuality.[13] In this way both fashion and the interior can be understood as a visible surface that conveys the 'interiority' of wearer or inhabitant. This position is somewhat complicated by the concept of masquerade. First identified by the psychoanalyst Joan Riviere, in 'Womanliness as a Masquerade', she proposes femininity as a surface or mask to conceal traits that go against the grain of the cultural requirements of being a woman.[14] Through this concept, with the help of Mary Ann Doane and Judith Butler, we can assume that the accoutrements that aid women's performance of femininity – such as the fashion and the interior – might not represent the 'interiority' of a character on screen, but instead a mask assisting in the performativity of gender.[15] As such, masquerade can be held in tension with interiority – an outside in relation to an inside, surface to depth, performance to authenticity. The playing out of these complexities is not just pertinent to representations of femininity, but also masculinity, as well as gender and sexually diverse identities.

Fashion and the interior also come together in the physical spaces of consumer culture, such as department stores, boutiques and flagship stores. They are similarly conjoined in the representational spaces of fashion and design – in magazines, new media forms and cinema. Significantly, glamorous architecture has increasingly come to operate with this system also – where spectacular buildings by celebrity architects are a further manifestation of fashion's cultural capital. In the early twentieth century this commercial context contributed to circumstances where couturiers and *ensembliers* were professionally aligned. Fashion designers recognized how the interior might contribute to fashion's spectacular reception. They also used these sites to enhance their own branded identities as entrepreneurs of lifestyle. Similarly, interior designers emulated the commercial strategies and workings of the fashion system in developing their own branded identities and by promoting change in redecorating the home to suit inhabitants' evolving tastes. The design historian Penny Sparke draws our attention to these developments and outlines how theatre also played a significant mediating role in this relationship, where couturiers and interior designers both recognized the stage as an important commercial strategy to display their wares.[16] As this book will show, this relationship also carried over to the screen, where the integration of luxury fashion and the interior reached new mass audiences throughout the twentieth century. These alliances continue in the current millennium.

Designer fashions have often played a starring role in film. For instance, Paul Poiret's exotic confections appeared in eighteen silent films between 1912 and 1932; Gabrielle Chanel's elegant gowns featured in a number of films including *La Règle du Jeu* (*The Rules of the Game*, 1939) and *Tonight or Never* (1931); and Yves Saint Laurent designed wardrobes for Catherine Deneuve in *Belle de Jour* (1967) and *La Sirène du Mississippi* (1969).[17] In these examples couture fashion creates visual spectacle, while complimenting film narrative and conveying character traits. Within the contemporary mediascape, as fashion and film scholar Pamela Church Gibson claims: 'Fashion has become omnipotent, moving now from walk-on parts of the past to claim not only its own narrative strand, but its complete mastery over *mise-en-scène*.'[18] Her book *Fashion and Celebrity Culture* provides convincing arguments regarding the ways that film intersects with the fashion system. Celebrities on and off screen have been integral to the promotion of designer fashions, fashion designers have appeared as stars in fashion films, and the glamour attributed to the stylish wardrobes of cinematic fantasies have fuelled consumer desire.[19] Fashion as it relates to cinema then, can be understood as a complex set of representations, embodiments, social relations and consumer culture products and images. It is for this reason I use the term 'fashion' throughout this book, rather than costume – as it implies the ways that dress circulates beyond the screen.

My interpretation of the 'fashion film' is similarly broad. Here, designated as films in which fashion is a significant component of the mise-en-scène, that also operates within commercial contexts either through magazine editorial, advertising, branding or retail strategies. This definition differs to how the term is primarily understood in the fashion industry, where the production of digital content by designer labels has laid claim to the format as an integral branded media strategy in the new millennium. Nick Rees-Roberts' insightful book *Fashion Film: Art and Advertising in the Digital Age,* provides a thorough analysis of the fashion film in relation to these new media forms of branded entertainment, as well as recent interest in the lives of designers in documentaries and dramatized biopics.[20] These contemporary forms of fashion film also have their place in the context of this book. However, in taking a broader view to primarily focus on narrative cinema, I consider the long history of the fashion film – from the silent era to the contemporary moment – as a representational system that intersects with architecture and interior design, both on screen and in everyday consumer culture. It is worth noting here, that I also use the terms interior design, architecture and spatial design to describe what would be termed as set design or production design in film studies.[21] This not only allows for an engagement with rich interdisciplinary discourses, to further situate the significance of these cinematic examples within broader design histories; it also recognizes that audiences often associate the manifestation of space on screen in terms of these familiar, everyday designations.

Cinematic Style builds on perspectives that have focused on the role of fashion in film, as well as the appreciation of architecture and the interior as components of film production. The relationship between fashion and film has been examined by a range of scholars whose perspectives have foregrounded the symbolic role of costume in narrative construction and the ways that fashion on screen has intersected with consumer culture.[22] Edited collections such as Adrienne Munich's *Fashion in Film,* Rachel Moseley's *Fashioning Film Stars* and Jane Gains' and Charlotte Herzog's *Fabrications: Costume and the Female Body* contain many excellent essays that elucidate the relationship between fashion, gender, identity, and film.[23] This rich and diverse scholarship has spanned a range of genres, eras and styles, from the elaborate costumes of period films such as *Marie Antoinette* (2006) to the influence of designer Italian suiting in *American Gigolo* (1980), and much in between. Stella Bruzzi's important book *Undressing Cinema,* regarding the representation of dress and gendered and sexual identities on screen is fundamental to my approach here; where I am keen to extend the analysis of dress and unpick some of the complications that arise when fashioned identities also come into contact with architecture and the interior.[24]

Some of this analysis has been previously undertaken by Merrill Schleier in her book *Skyscraper Cinema: Architecture and Gender in American Film.*[25] Presenting the case for tall buildings as characters in films such as *The Fountainhead* (1949), and the ways that these structures mediate representations of masculinity and femininity, Schleier's approach augments other texts that focus on cities in cinema.[26] Edited books such as David Clarke's *The Cinematic City* and Mark Lamster's *Architecture and Film* look to celebrated examples such as the buildings of *Metropolis* (1923), *Blade Runner* (1982) and Jacques Tati's *Playtime* (1967) to examine utopian and dystopian dichotomies of architectural modernism.[27] Particularly instructive to my purposes here is Pamela Robertson Wojcik's *The Apartment Plot* which offers an insightful model for the analysis of gender and sexual identity in relation to domestic spaces on film.[28]

Just as haute couturiers-cum-costumers have made their mark on cinema, interior designers and architects have also contributed to film narrative and character development. For example, the Art Deco *ensemblier* Francis Jourdain designed simple pared back furniture for Louis Delluc's *La Femme de Nulle* (1922) and Jean Vigo's *L'Atalante* (1934) in his role as production designer; Charles and Ray Eames were consultants on *The Moon is Blue* (1953) which featured design classics such as the Vitra wire chair; and interior designer Violante Visconti di Modrone created a 'lived in quality' through a selection of eclectic furnishings for the Perlman family in *Call Me by Your Name* (2017).[29] These contributions to cinematic style can be understood more broadly in relation to the profession of set design, production design and art direction, where there has been significant scholarship on individual practitioners such as Cedric Gibbons and Ken Adam.[30]

Within this context, interior design histories have found an emerging scholarship that has sought to understand intersections with screen style. For example, Donald Albrecht's *Designing Dreams,* and Lucy Fischer's *Cinema by Design* and *Designing Women* are amongst the few monographs that recognize the multifaceted nature of design on film. Focusing primarily on interiors of the early twentieth century – the International Style, Art Nouveau and Art Deco – these important studies provide period-focused histories of design in cinema.[31] These design styles are significant to this book also. However, in thematically examining a broad range of films, I am interested in the reoccurrence of modes of representation across time, and their continuing influence on consumer cultures. Pat Kirkham and Sarah A. Lichtman's edited book *Screen Interiors* provides much needed further insight as to how interior décor conveys aspects of class, gender and sexuality.[32] Its broad reach across diverse genres spanning sci-fi, horror and romantic comedy amongst others speaks to the increasing scholarly interest in design's intersections with film. Importantly, its scope focuses beyond the golden years of Hollywood, with a range of contemporary examples used to explore the psychological element of the interior on screen, an approach which this book also shares in common.

This book relies on methods of analysis familiar to fashion and interior studies adopted from the fields of design history, gender studies and sociology. They are combined with the visual analysis of film to provide an understanding of the various ways that fashion, spatial design and film enrich each other's surfaces and embedded meanings. The approach throughout privileges discourses of fashion, interior design and architecture as they are represented in film examples, rather than the intricacies of critically reading cinematic histories and techniques. The selection of case study examples ranges from silent film, European art house, Hollywood cinema, break-through independent film and advertising short-film – deemed pertinent for their aesthetic circulation within the fashion system. Alongside the films themselves, images of fashion and spatial design provide important evidence of the ways that these modes of surface and style are conceptually and aesthetically aligned. This scope is intentionally broad, and undoubtedly significant examples are omitted. My aim is to demonstrate the reoccurrence of particular modes of intersection between fashion and spatial design across a range of cinematic and consumer contexts, in the hope that this survey will encourage further scholarship.

The book is structured in two parts. *Part 1: Fashion and the Interior as Filmic Device* thematically explores representations of gender and sexuality through fashion and interior design and architecture. Each of the chapters here contribute to the overarching argument that the interrelationship between fashion and spatial design is central to character and narrative development, while simultaneously aligning film with consumer culture and the fashion system. Recognizing the dynamic combination of sex, sets and costumes as an ostentatious showcase for the desires of consumer culture, the chapters in this section are underpinned by the argument that gendered and sexual representations of characters on screen are indebted to the culmination of fashion, the interior and architecture to provide audiences with an understanding of character's interior motivations and identities. I consider the ways that gender and sexual identity have been positioned in relation to sites of domesticity and kinship, and the ways that fashioned bodies both reinforce and contest traditional roles and representations.

Chapter 1 argues that bedrooms, boudoirs and bathrooms, as intimate domestic spaces, coupled with form-fitting sensuous silhouettes, have been inherently tied to women's gender and sexual identities. Drawing on a range of films spanning classical Hollywood cinema such as *Dinner at Eight* (1933) and *The Women* (1939), along with romances *In the Mood for Love* (2000) and *Une Parisienne* (1957) amongst others, this chapter examines the figure of the modern woman across time and how her identity has been linked to luxurious surfaces on the body and in the home. Here, I draw on the feminist film discourses of Laura Mulvey and Mary Ann Doane to articulate some of the contradictory positions of visual pleasure that are tied to these representations.[33] The intersection between female protagonist as spectacle and object of consumption is well-worn within cinematic discourse. However, it is relevant to revisit these debates in order to understand the complex ways that female characters seek to fulfil their own desires and visible autonomy within the context of the sensory pleasures of fashion and the interior. The regulation between maternal, marital, moral and material obligation that is played out in the cinematic examples discussed in this chapter is testament to the complex ways received concepts of femininity have been constituted through fashion and the interior on screen and interpellated within consumer culture.

The perceived overvaluation of surface and appearance that is associated with feminine identities is called into question in Chapter 2. The unconventional correlation between heroic masculinity, fashion, stylish interiors and glamorous architecture is brought to bear on Alfred Hitchcock's *North by Northwest* (1959) and the James Bond film franchise. While much film scholarship would have us believe that women have been unduly influenced by the consumer cultures of cinema, in fact it is clear that men have also sought to engage with the pleasures of fashion and spatial design. Here, I rely on the architect Adolf Loos' cultural theories of modernism to draw out some of the contradictions that have emerged regarding the relationship between masculinity, the modern body and the modern home. I argue that the protagonists of spy films can be understood as playboy dandies who engage with the consumerist desires of heteronormativity. This chapter considers the sexualization of space and bodies that have been promoted to male consumers in ways not dissimilar to the representation of feminine and queer identities. As such, Chapter 2 reinforces the argument that intersections between fashion and spatial design reveal the unstable relations of conventional assumptions regarding how gender identities are constituted through these surfaces.

Questions of gender and sexuality as they relate to fashion and spatial design culminate in Chapter 3. Focusing on queer film and representations of surface and space, this chapter moves towards a more complex theoretical position regarding the relationship between pleasure, spectacle and spectatorship. I argue that recent queer nostalgia films, *Carol* (2015), *A Single Man* (2009) and *Laurence Anyways* (2012) develop a queer sensibility through highly stylized dress and décor that operate in ways similar to Michel Foucault's 'heterotopias'.[34] That is, fashion and the interior have the potential to operate as spaces where individuals are free to perform their gender and sexual identities in ways that challenge normative positions. The aesthetic excesses and artifice of queer cinema are situated here to challenge long-standing views that fashion and the interior, surface and style, lack substance and are instead revealed to convey emotional depth. With reference to Judith Butler, these examples further complicate relationships between bodies, clothes and space and reiterate the performative capacity of bodies and space to convey the fluidities of gender and sexual identities outside of cinema.

These three chapters, while covering a broad array of examples and theoretical perspectives, are underpinned by intersections that reveal synergies between fashion and spatial design, that both challenge and reinforce debates concerning the representation of gender and sexual identities on screen. These arguments are posed alongside consideration of these surfaces as constituting a form of visual pleasure that is at times contradictory. By drawing on examples from fashion and design media that promote screen lifestyles as a social performance that can be adopted by consumers in everyday life, I position the intersection of fashion, spatial design and cinema within the fashion system of representation, mediation and consumption.

The role of architecture and interior design as the mise-en-scène of fashion retail and its connection to cinematic discourses has gone largely unconsidered. The exception being Jean Whitehead's *Creating Interior Atmospheres*, which proposes mise-en-scène as a mode for interpreting interiors on screen, as well as domestic, exhibition and retail environments.[35] *Part 2- Film Interiors as Fashion Spaces* redresses this paucity in scholarship and examines the multiple ways that the fictional fantasies of film have been translated into commercial contexts. Focusing on spaces of fashion consumption, each of the chapters in part two demonstrate how film characters and narratives have been converted into fashionable products. As such the structure of the book highlights the confluence between fashion, spatial design and film, whereby part one demonstrates how film promotes luxury fashion styles and glamorous spaces to consumers; and part two demonstrates how fashion adopts film narratives and applies these to architecture and the interior so that consumers might experience these silver-screen fantasies in real life.

Chapter 4 provides historical understanding of the confluence between fashion and film mediated through the motif of the staircase. As a staging device, staircases have positioned bodies as spectacles for viewing pleasure, both on the catwalk and on screen. Arguing for the fashionable iconicity of these spatial affordances, I consider the staircase in fashion photography, film and retail environments as sites for transformation, social arrival and acceptance through examples including Dior and Chanel, *Ziegfield Girl* (1941) and *Funny Face* (1957). With reference to the sociologist Pierre Bourdieu I examine the metaphoric potency of the fashion staircase as symbol that apparently traverses class boundaries, altering states of social status and cultural capital.[36] In this way, the relationship between fashion, spatial design and film is examined in this chapter as operating within both dream and cultural imaginaries, as well as the real spaces of commodity transaction.

The relationship between film and consumer culture is further elucidated in Chapter 5, which takes as its focus the analogy between window shopping and film spectatorship as mechanisms of the fashion image. This chapter traces the passage from arcade to cinema through examples from familiar department stores, and film tie-ins, as well as lesser known intersections between French avant-garde cinema, couture fashion and architecture, pioneered by collaborations between Sonia Delaunay and Robert Mallet-Stevens. Developing from Mike Featherstone's argument that the glamorous surfaces of screens and windows mediate fashion as an aesthetic and pleasurable experience, this chapter also considers how fashion, space and cinema are mobilized to translate the illusionary world of film to tangible real-world desires on display.[37] Here again, the commodification of bodies and spaces through the mechanisms of spectacle comes into tension with the sociocultural affordances of these dynamics.

The final chapter is further concerned with the sensory, emotional and aesthetic experiences that fashion and interior design produce, enhanced through the mise-en-scène and narrative associations of film. Examining the fashion flagship store and other experiential retail environments through the lens of Gilles Lipovetsky's concepts of 'artification' and aesthetic capitalism, Chapter 6 examines how fashion brands have adopted scenographic interiors as core components of their marketable identities.[38] Here, I develop the concept of 'brand heterotopias' to examine how luxury fashion brands such as Gucci, Prada, Fendi and Ralph Lauren develop an inter-spatial layering of narrative associations, that merge past and present through heritage indicators and the evocation of screen styles. Specifically, I argue that luxury brands commodify history and nostalgia through the borrowing of film sets and narrative contexts to leverage and enhance designer mythologies.

My aim in this book is to provide an overview of the relationship between fashion and spatial design mediated by cinema from the silent era to the contemporary digital age. In doing so, I highlight the important role that this previously overlooked triangulation produces in the representation of gendered identities and appeal to the lifestyle aspirations of consumers. It does not claim to be exhaustive, but rather acts as a foundation to elucidate the significance of surface and style to cinematic spectacle. As such, this book aims to further embed the intersections between fashion, interior design and architecture within histories of cinema and discourses of design. The importance of recognizing these confluences is to challenge why these different dialects of design have often been kept apart despite similar aesthetic styles, modes of representation and sociocultural contexts. It speaks to the power of design and cinema studies sometimes exclusionary discourses that disregard surface and style as frivolous and feminine. Saying this, I am aware that this book also in some ways reproduces exclusion. While I have attempted to incorporate cinema and fashion media examples that represent people of colour and non-western perspectives where relevant, there should be more. This is a problem of the Western fashion and film industries, as well as a problem of their repeated histories, and a subject to which I will return in the conclusion of this book.

1

Bedrooms, boudoirs and bathrooms: Modern women, seductive spaces and spectacular silhouettes

The aesthetic limitations of black and white film required tactile and reflective surfaces of fashionable luxury that included silk, satin, velvet, fur and feathers. The sensual nature of these fabrics implied a link between sexuality and consumption and were synonymous with the spaces occupied by the female protagonists of the 'woman's film'. Here, I broadly identify this genre as focusing on the lives of women characters engaged with themes of love, marriage, sex, career, fashion and glamour.[1] Bedrooms, boudoirs and bathrooms have been historically gendered as feminine spaces associated with intimacy, romance and sex. On film, they provide equally seductive surfaces to imagine fantasy lifestyles and performative roles. From the era of early silent film onwards, fashion and the domestic interior provided audiences with an appreciation of female characters' identities, motivations and desires that were aligned with consumer culture. This understanding stemmed from a broader cultural milieu in which domestic interiors and fashion were perceived as an extension of a woman's inner-being and part of her decorative role in the home. Through a series of examples including *The Single Standard* (1929), *Dinner at Eight* (1933) and *The Women* (1939), this chapter will consider intimate spaces associated with women and their corresponding silhouettes to argue that surface and style have been inextricably linked to women's sexuality in ways that suggest agency and emancipation, yet are also ultimately tied up with consumption and questionable morality.

In comparing early woman's films and their representation of fashion and intimate interiors to later examples from the romantic comedy genre of the 1950s such as *Pillow Talk* (1959), and more recently, post-feminist 'chick flick' *Pretty Woman* (1990) as well as art house romance *In the Mood for Love* (2000), this chapter will draw on film theories of consumption to examine the pleasure of surface and style and their relationship to changing sexual mores for women. It is not my intention here to suggest a linear and continuous trajectory of representation but rather to identify the recurrence of particular modes of intersection between fashion and the interior in a number of cinematic contexts. Throughout this chapter particular attention will be paid to the history of women's intimate domestic spaces to provide narrative understanding of the interior motivations of female characters on film, and how these are reinforced through fashion. The translation of these cinematic styles through fashion and interior design magazines such as *Vogue*, *Harper's Bazaar*, *Good Housekeeping* and *House Beautiful* will be examined to consider the ways in which fantasy representations on film are promoted to modern women consumers beyond the cinema.

Marketing the modern woman

Film historian Charles Eckert's influential 1978 essay 'The Carol Lombard in Macy's Window' recognized the role of Hollywood film in mass marketing fashion, furnishings and cosmetics to American audiences – particularly women – during the 1920s and 1930s.[2] Eckert surmises that Hollywood's role in consumer culture was due to a number of conditions: the dominant role of women as consumers, the film industry's commitment to schemes of product display and a star-system dominated by women who were 'merchandising assets' – which in turn influenced the types of films that were made. So-called 'woman's films' provided the perfect settings for fashion and furnishings to be displayed. With their focus on bedrooms, bathrooms and boudoirs, it is not surprising, as Eckert notes, that by 1929 'foreign sales of bedroom and bathroom furnishing had increased 100 percent because of movies'.[3]

The figure of the 'modern woman' – at this point, also known as the flapper or new woman – was particularly important to early woman's films. As both cultural figure and sociological phenomenon the modern woman was characterized by her non-traditional approach to sexual relationships, employment outside the home, education and economic independence, as well as visibility in the public sphere. As historian Mary Louise Roberts states, 'the modern woman became associated with the aesthetic of a modern consumerism … [and] became the means by which women expressed a more liberated self'.[4] Cinema, along with fashion, literature and advertising, was one of the central mediums to promote the image of the modern woman in her various forms to audiences.

Understanding the role of the modern woman in cinema and her relationship to consumer culture is confounded by her position as both subject and object. For example, within the context of Laura Mulvey's seminal essay 'Visual Pleasure and Narrative Cinema', the modern woman, indeed any woman, on film is the object of the 'male gaze', susceptible to objectification and fetishization for the pleasure of the spectator.[5] This idea complies with broader psychoanalytic feminist understandings regarding the status of women in patriarchal society where: 'the use, consumption and circulation of [women's] sexualised bodies underwrite the organisation and reproduction of the social order'.[6] Further, cinema not only represents women as objects of desire, they are also desiring subjects – through the positioning of women as consumers, both on screen and in the audience. The feminist film theorist Mary Ann Doane elucidates how:

> The female spectator is invited to witness her own commodification, and ... to buy an image of herself ... this level involves not only the currency of a body but of a space in which to display that body.[7]

In other words, through the medium of film, the female spectator is encouraged to participate in her own objectification and commodification by identifying narcissistically with the woman on screen. Further, she performs the role of consumer by not only desiring to be like the woman on display, but to also consume her fashions, and the interior spaces she inhabits.

The double-bind of this condition is further complicated by the ways in which both fashion and the interior operate as markers of identity formation – especially for women – and the forms of agency and pleasure that these modes of adornment offer. As Elizabeth Wilson outlines in *Adorned in Dreams*, fashion can be understood as both an object of oppression, but also a cultural, social and aesthetic form that can express the ambiguities of identity, relating the self to body and the world.[8] With this in mind, I contend that the modern woman character on film, as associated with fashion and the interior, can be seen to both limit and reinforce gender roles and objectified positions, while simultaneously articulating agency. As Liz Conor deftly explains, 'modern women saw self-display to be part of the quest for mobility, self-determination and sexual identity'.[9]

The modern woman character was established as a particular type in films, beginning with the new woman and flapper of the 1920s, and the femme fatale of the 1930s and 1940s. However, echoes of her type can be seen in future decades, up until the present moment – if we understand her as a reoccurring figure of women's emancipation, be it social, sexual, economic or political.

Undoubtedly these are complex characters. The modern woman, in many of her film guises, is bound to a mode of femininity that much feminist thinking would define as oppressive. That is, bodily adornment through clothing or setting, contributes to women being defined by their sexuality in relation to men.[10] Yet, these women also destabilize the patriarchal order by offering performances of female identities that are morally ambiguous and outside of the constraints of traditional femininity. Many of the female characters outlined here are understood as 'fallen women', however, the disjuncture between this image and their association with pleasurable lifestyles and fashionable forms makes them desirable to many female audiences. As such, it is worth considering that female spectatorship of bedrooms, boudoirs and bathrooms and their corresponding silhouettes is not only framed within the context of voyeuristic, narcissistic, sexual desire but also a pleasure in looking at the surfaces and spaces of fashion and the interior that are tied to their embodied experience. Instructive here is art historian Susan Best's position, that Mulvey's analysis of ways of looking at cinema 'leaves us much better informed about the sexual dynamics of looking, but also impoverished when it comes to discussing visual pleasure … [for it excludes] other modes of looking or other sources of pleasure'.[11] Perhaps some of the pleasure that female audiences derive from these films is the triangulation that occurs between an embodied understanding of the sensuality of slinky fabrics and shiny surfaces, identification with female characters that primarily seek to fulfil their own desires beyond traditional patriarchal restraints, and the latent possibility of how this fantasy might be enacted beyond the screen.

Bedrooms

When MGM art director Cedric Gibbons introduced 'modern' bedrooms to American silent-film audiences in the late 1920s, low beds, gold and black ziggurat wall panels, and geometric light fixtures became immediately associated with the freedoms of the modern woman and her lifestyle.[12] *Our Dancing Daughters* (1928) is one of the first Hollywood films to be dominated by Art Deco interiors, which was coupled with the exotic short skirts of the flapper. The opening sequence, in which the film's heroine Diana Medford (Joan Crawford) dances to jazz music in her bedroom highlights how shimmering surfaces and sequined streamlined silhouettes became associated with modern women's increasing social, sexual and physical mobility. Such luxurious surfaces both on the body and in the home were suggestive of decadence and seduction.

The women who inhabited these spaces on screen were generally engaged in some form of impropriety, be it Crawford's lascivious half-naked dancing as Diana, Greta Garbo's juggling of numerous suitors as Arden Stuart in *The Single Standard* (1929) (Figure 1.1), or as the adulteress Irene in *The Kiss* (1929).

In this way 'modern' design was synonymous with questionable morals. For example, Arden's Deco bedroom in *The Single Standard* represents her free-thinking and free-spirited approach to romantic liaisons. Similarly, her costumes in various scenes remind us of her progressive approach to womanhood. Consisting of stripped pyjamas, black and silver zig-zag embellished top, and lame coat dress,

Figure 1.1 Greta Garbo as Arden in *The Single Standard* (1929). Credits: John S. Robertson (Director), Metro-Goldwyn-Mayer (MGM) (Film Production). Photo: ullstein bild via Getty Images.

the use of geometric patterns and at times masculine attire, reinforced her modern woman character. Living alone in her stylish apartment wearing an Adrian-designed wardrobe, Arden pursues sexual equality by engaging in relationships with a number of men, yet ultimately ends up as wife and mother in a traditionally styled abode, underscoring the polarity between modern and maternal woman.[13] Women's morality was equated with dress, and taste in interior accoutrement, so encapsulating broader sociocultural anxieties of the era. Populist commentators, religious groups and conservative politicians were concerned by modern women's seemingly loose morals and competition with men in working environments, which they perceived resulted in the erosion of home and family life.[14]

In these examples, fashion and the interior in tandem represent the interiority of modern women characters on film and are an extension of her inner being. Women's fashions and interiors were often designed in correlation with each other, operating to position women as decorative augmentation in the domestic sphere. This close affiliation served the role of aligning women's identities to consumer products. Film, magazines and advertising artfully suggested that the desirable attributes of the modern woman's lifestyle – social mobility, economic independence and sexual freedom – might be achieved through surrounding oneself with the style. While Art Deco has frequently been denigrated in design history due to its relationship with the feminine and consumerism, I argue that these spaces and fashionable forms of modernity also allowed women to imagine new social, cultural and professional identities.[15]

Art Deco schemes, inspired by the furniture and interiors on display at the 1925 *Exposition des Arts Decoratifs et Industriels Moderns* in Paris, became the hallmark of Gibbons' sets, influencing American design aesthetics until the 1940s. Whether Gibbons attended the fair in person or not has been debated.[16] However, it is clear that photographs and reports, along with examples of this bold new style reached the art director.[17] The 1925 Paris Exposition's emphasis on fashion, opulent home décor and women's luxury goods was represented across multiple pavilions. Modern French bedrooms, boudoirs and bathroom settings coupled with mannequins wearing the latest in haute couture in the Galeries Lafayette Pavilion and the Pavilion de l'Elégance showcased how female consumers might adopt both fashion and interior looks to enhance their lifestyles. As a 1925 review of the Pavilion de l'Elegance proclaimed: 'this is not a fantasy to seduce the eye: rather instruction for those who wish to realise it in their own home, where the relationship between personal style and beautiful home is never in conflict.'[18]

Many of the features that made Gibbons' sets notable can be found in photographs of *ensembles* at the 1925 Exposition by Maurice Dufrêne,

Émile-Jacques Ruhlmann and Pierre Block, including low set beds, metallic printed geometric wallpapers, pyramid-shaped light fixtures, graphic rugs and angular furnishings. As will be explored further in Chapter 5, while these styles were new to the American audiences of Gibbons' films in 1928, French avant-garde silent cinema was already employing new modern set designs through the innovations of architect Robert Mallet-Stevens in 1924. Jean Epstein's *Le Double Amour* (1925) is another example of the confluence between modern fashions and interiors prior to Hollywood's championing of the style (Figure 1.2). The melodrama is the story of a countess who partakes in a love affair with a gambler, resulting in her financial ruin and single motherhood, before she becomes a successful cabaret singer. Here, Pierre Kèfer's geometric set designs, and furniture featuring Francis Jourdain style floral textile prints, are coupled with floaty handkerchief hem dresses by fashion designers Drecoll and Paul Poiret to convey Laure Maresco's (Nathalie Lissenko) interiority. The contrast between Art Deco geometric gridded windows, abstract patterned covered cushions, and floral-patterned furniture creates an uneasy tension, suggestive of Laure's inner turmoil in choosing love over honesty. While cinema often represented modern design as the backdrop to moral failings, its glamour provided a unique promotional opportunity for fashion and décor designers. As Francis Jourdain said of lending set decorations to Louis Delluc, Germain Dulac and others: 'My

Figure 1.2 Laure Maresco as Nathalie Lissenko in *Le Double Amour* (1925). Credits: Jean Epstein (Director), Films Albatros (Film Production). Screen still.

sponsors saw these loans as advertising interest, as long as the name of the store appeared in the credits.'[19]

The visual effectiveness of what would come to be known as Art Deco on screen and in the home was also being relayed to French consumers through feature articles in the interior magazine *Art et Decoration* from 1925 onwards.[20] Similarly, French *Vogue* reported on the relationship between interior design ensembles at the 1925 Exposition and fashions of the time, encouraging women to 'live as they dress', with both architecture and fashion turned towards simple, clean, harmonized forms.[21] This formula, uniting modern women, modern fashion and modern interiors on the page, and on screen, would become remarkably successful in the Hollywood context.

Initially promoters were unsure of how American audiences might receive Gibbons' new screen style, noting that: 'Weird beds, almost to the floor, have little woodwork frame, [apart from] foot-high boards which conceal the springs and do away with the conventional legs of a bed' – a surprising feature of modern furniture.[22] The novelty of the sets in *Our Dancing Daughters* was similarly reported in newspapers, noting that:

> It is the first time that the screen has shown such a faithful picture of the great revolution the French mode in home furnishings is about to effect. The moderniste motif is carried out even to architectural details, and it will afford no end of keen amusement to see square, solid, severe lines and the quixotism of strange lighting arrangements.[23]

Despite these misgivings, readers of women's fashion and interior magazines were keen to apply this new style to their own homes. In an interview with *Ladies Home Journal* from 1933 Gibbons enthusiastically recounts how his set furnishings were copied in homes throughout America. His reflections on how rooms should reflect the personality of their inhabitant are commensurate with his ideas about how sets should be decorated in accordance with a character, noting that:

> Norma Shearer is a feminine, responsive, vibrant sort of person. Hence, I have decorated her home so that the backgrounds are very simple ... Joan Crawford is more vivid, more restless personality. She can have a bolder background in her settings.[24]

Significantly, Gibbons also identifies the importance of fashion for women's home decorating advising that: 'Instead of wondering if a rug should fit into her room, she should visualise herself against it in her new blue or pink dress and ask, 'Would it be becoming to me?'[25] Women readers of fashion, style and film magazines were given further cues by Hollywood stars as to how she might envision herself in such a way, through photographic editorials depicting the stars at home, or in modern interior settings wearing the latest fashions. Joan Crawford often appeared in this manner, for example, wearing Schiaparelli posed next to a 'modern glass chair, a new idea in decoration' for *Vogue*, or photographed in her New York apartment wearing a dark mink coat for *Town and Country*.[26]

One of the most memorable of classic Hollywood bedrooms is that of Kitty Packard (Jean Harlow) in George Cukor's *Dinner at Eight* (1933). The all-white quilted headboard framing a double-bed covered in taffeta linen, strewn with huge pillows and surrounded by diaphanous curtains is almost absurdly decadent nouveau-riche luxury. This excessive spectacle of pleasurable surfaces suggests that we should understand Kitty as a hedonistic, shallow woman, consumed by appearances. Designed by interior decorator Hobe Erwin and MGM designer Frederic Hope, the room incorporated ten different shades of white. As Erwin said of the design:

> The idea was to present a setting which would give the observer insight into the occupant, namely the pretty but common Kitty Packard ... the audience will take one look at this room and would have little difficulty in recognising the character of the person who would live in it.[27]

Rich in textural qualities, the bedroom and boudoir to which I will return – are perfectly matched to Adrian-designed loungewear and gowns. Dressed in a slinky halter-necked satin nightgown and plush fur shrug, Kitty entertains her doctor lover, eats chocolates, admires herself in the mirror and talks on the phone to make social engagements, all while lounging in bed. An evening gown version of this garment is revisited later in the film at the dinner of the title. Here, Kitty wears a long, form-fitting white satin gown with gold halter-neck, its exposed back framed by a fur stole, recalls the earlier bedroom scene. The implied relationship between nightgown and evening gown would not be missed by astute fashion readers. Magazines such as *Vogue* often promoted their similarities, recognizing that negligees were a more affordable form of wearable luxury for middle-class women than an extravagant dress. Fashion advertorials also referred to cinema, inviting women to imagine themselves 'cast in new roles' by wearing a 'gay, mad Lillian Russell' nightdress, for example.[28] *Dinner at Eight* makes the connection between nightwear and evening wear, not to suggest an economy of clothing, but to enhance our understanding of Kitty's attire as sexually provocative. Gold-digging behaviour, social climbing and sexual indiscretion are equated with showy glamour. However, while Kitty's character is presented as morally flawed, fashion and the interior as they relate to her body represent an image of highly desirable, easy to come by wealth, sexuality and pleasure at a time when American society was beholden to the impacts of the Great Depression and Protestant values pertaining to work and sex. Despite Kitty's shortcomings, her character is ultimately redeemed due to these very character traits, as will be discussed further in relation to the boudoir.

Dinner at Eight creates a complex understanding of the relationship between the modern woman's sexual liberation, the modern bedroom and streamlined fashions. Modern design is coded as glamorous and desirable, yet also threatens to destabilize women's traditional role as submissive wife and mother, and instead encourages morally ambiguous behaviour. Surface style, it seems, allows for women to perform in ways that would otherwise be frowned upon. As Joan Crawford described of her fans' reaction to her role as a prostitute in *Rain* (1932): 'They would accept me as Letty Lynton who was just as vulgar, but she had style.'[29] With this in mind, we can understand sexually promiscuous characters in the bedrooms of 1920s and 1930s Hollywood cinema to be perceived as heroines if they artfully used fashion in their quest for self-determination, making them likable and desirable.

By 1934, with the introduction of the Production Code and the censorship of sexual references in Hollywood film, fashions of silk, satin, velvet, feathers and fur became even more laden with sexual connotations. While these luxurious materials were still associated with characters of dubious morality, respectable women wore high-necked blouses coupled with trim suits. In the bedroom, house-coats and dressing gowns kept erotic effect under wraps. Not long after this, the luxuriously appointed bedroom of the sexually liberated heroine almost entirely disappeared, to be replaced by the twin beds of sexually repressed relationships. Interior design historian Hilary Hinds explains: 'a double bed was too explicit in its sexual associations ... Only twins had the necessary cultural delicacy ... to [imply] marital sexual intimacy' without the possibility of facilitating it.'[30] In her exhaustive cultural study, Hinds draws attention to readings of twin beds that allowed for women to forge a separate space within marriage, suggestive of positions of equality and autonomy. On film, such a reading might apply to *Adam's Rib* (1949), in which Katherine Hepburn as Amanda is more than a match for her husband Adam (Spencer Tracey). The plot involves a case in which Amanda and Adam are pitted against each other as opposing lawyers, which Amanda wins based on an argument regarding equality of the sexes. However, this results in the pair filing for divorce. The twin beds of Amanda and Adam's household imply a marriage based on a companionable meeting of the minds rather than a passionate love affair. As with other films such as

Twin Beds (1942), the subtext is that marriages in which the wife works, or seeks equality, subsequently lack sexual intimacy. It is not until women submit to their husband's wishes or ideas that the dysfunctional aspects of a relationship can be overcome. Ultimately, while twin beds may have represented equality for modern women in some contexts, they were overwhelmingly associated with sexual repression and unsuccessful unions.

By the late 1950s and early 1960s, with the waning of the Production Code a new bedroom emerged for the modern woman on film. Now an economically autonomous career girl, living in a designer apartment, the bedroom of the single girl was functional rather than a place of indulgent pleasure. For example, in *Pillow Talk* (1959) (Figure 1.3) in which Doris Day plays successful interior designer, Jan Morrow, her bedroom is seen as a 'problem'. In the opening scenes of the film the audience is introduced to Jan as a career-focused woman to the detriment of her love life. Wanting to make a business call in her bedroom, the plot problem emerges as she is caught in a three-way telephone call between her neighbour Brad (Rock Hudson) and his lover Eileen. The

Figure 1.3 Doris Day as Jan Morrow and Thelma Ritter as Alma in *Pillow Talk* (1959). Credits: Michael Gordon (Director). Photo: Silver Screen Collection/Getty Images.

split-screen technique used here draws attention to the differences between the women's characters. Jan's bedroom decorated in lemon and white appears almost virginal compared with Eileen's seductive boudoir with its pale pink satin décor. When Jan complains about the romantic nature of the phone call she is privy to, Brad intimates that her 'bedroom problem' is due to her single woman, career girl status – resulting in her uptight demeanour and lack of sex.

As the plot develops, Brad concocts an alter ego, Rex to seduce Jan in revenge for her complaints about his phone-manner to the telephone company. The pair's budding romance is conducted primarily over a series of split-screen telephone conversations occurring in their respective bathrooms and bedrooms. With each call, the split screen spatially evolves to bring the couple closer, until their beds appear fused together. We understand this as Jan's increasing willingness to sleep with Rex/Brad. *Pillow Talk* generally follows a stereotypical representation of a womanizing bachelor who does not want to get married, and an uptight single woman who does not want to have sex until she is in a relationship. Interestingly, Jan's sexual desires are finally asserted through the symbolic reconfiguration of Brad's bedroom.

After learning of Brad's deception, Jan is given the opportunity to decorate his apartment in the hope that he can win her back. A comical scene ensues in which the bachelor pad's technological functions of seduction are exposed. In particular, a hidden bed which springs from the couch highlights how the designer décor is a ruse that conceals Brad's playboy personality. Through her professional knowledge, Jan seeks her revenge by making Brad's womanizing ways visible through her choice of refurbishments. She converts his stylish bachelor pad into a harem – complete with silk draperies, red walls and velvet-covered bed strewn with pillows. The result is garish and tasteless but reveals that Jan has an understanding of the relationship between the bedroom and sexual persona, which until this point, she seems to repress. In one of the final scenes, Brad kidnaps Jan from her bed and delivers her into his apartment wrapped in her pyjamas and bed sheet in order to remonstrate with her over the decoration. However, she flips the switch on the situation both literally and figuratively, using the bachelor pad's technologies of seduction to lock him in, and we assume consummate their relationship.

In this way, the final bedroom scene of *Pillow Talk* suggests a subversion of the character's interiority and associated sexual desires. As will be discussed further in Chapter 3, the modernist bachelor pad, as seen on screen and in magazines such as *Playboy*, represented masculine virility and a refusal of suburban married life. This is true to Brad's character until he falls in love. Jan's redecoration of his bedroom, however, does not follow the mid-century modern aesthetic of her own apartment which is understood as a representation of her career-minded, no-nonsense, modern-woman persona. Nor does she convert it into traditional homely domesticity which would be associated with marriage. Instead the bordello decorating schema suggests a wildly, passionate persona. This does not conform with our understanding of Jan as a sexually repressed woman, rather, her desire is displayed through the configuration of the bedroom in an overtly sexualized schema.[31] The bedroom in this instance allows for the modern woman to act outside familiar gendered roles of seduction and assert her own desires, where premarital sex occurs on Jan's terms.

While the redecoration of Brad's bedroom to convey Jan's sexual desires occurs at the end of the film, this aspect of her character is not completely out of context as it is alluded to through her Jean Louis designed costumes. While her attire at times complies with the idea of sexual inexperience – for example, a series of demure pyjamas and house coats – she also wears the dress code of a sexually assured woman. This takes some familiar forms in the case of a figure-hugging deep-red velvet strapless gown and white evening dress complete with fur stole, deigned in the same mode as femme fatale characters of the 1930s. Perhaps the most telling ensemble however is a fire engine red-coat worn with leopard print hat and muff which she wears immediately after learning of Brad's deception. Conveying a wild and passionate side of Jan's character, sparked by both her anger and sexual frustration, this look has its counterpart in the final bedroom scene. Through the combination of fashion and the interior, the audience becomes privy to Jan's increasing sexual assuredness even at times when the dialogue or narrative implies otherwise.

The bedrooms and associated glamorous fashions of Hollywood films from the 1920s onwards established a syntax through which to understand the interior lives and motivations of modern women characters on screen. While the meanings of women's bedrooms and fashions changed according to social mores, gender norms and evolving consumer cultures, the symbolic association between these spaces was formative in developing a correspondence between fashion and the interior and their relationship to a character's interiority. These correspondences continue to be developed in a range of Hollywood and art-house cinema contexts, where the cultural connotations between women's sexual identities and bedroom settings exploit or subvert these associations.

For example, Wong Kar-Wai's much celebrated *In the Mood for Love* (2000) (Figure 1.4) offers an alternative image of the bedroom, in which, despite the sensuous setting, sexuality is repressed. Set in Hong Kong during the 1960s, this

Figure 1.4 Maggie Cheung as Su Lizhen *In the Mood for Love* (2000). Credits: Wong Kar-Wai (Director), Jet Tone Productions and Paradise Films (Film Production). Screen still.

visually arresting romantic melodrama tells the story of two married neighbours, whose spouses are conducting an extramarital affair. As the central protagonists, Su Lizhen (Maggie Cheung) and Chow Mo-Wan (Tony Leung Chiu-wai) attempt to come to terms with their spouse's betrayal, they imagine and enact encounters from the affair and in turn gradually become attracted to each other. Despite their feelings of loneliness, yearning, desire and love, they are determined not to behave like their spouses and never sexually consummate their feelings.

The film relies heavily on the lustrous and expressive surfaces of cramped apartment rooms to cast the protagonists' emotional composure in sharp relief. Wong Kar-Wai has said, 'I sometimes treat space as a main character in my films', and in the case of *In the Mood for Love,* bedrooms play a prominent role.[32] These spaces are cast as highly sensuous and are heavy with emotional longing. As architectural historian Anne Troutman describes, the erotic dimension of architecture: 'is the unconscious, instinctual side of our experience of form and space […] eschewing the overtly sexual, the erotic is a state of phenomenal ambiguity, indirection, tension and suspension'.[33] I suggest that the bedrooms of *In the Mood for Love* fulfil this spatial erotic dimension through the excesses of the interior in combination with Su Lizhen's highly decorative and fashionable cheongsam.

The confluence of dress and décor conveys Su Lizhen's interiority. Her cheongsam is in constant conversation with the walls that surround her. Sometimes they blend in almost completely – where the distinction between an olive-green dress with yellow daffodil print and the floral curtains she stands next to blur together like a Monet painting. In this particular instance, we understand her melancholy mood as her body is enveloped by soft muted tones. In the bedroom scenes, the relationship between fashion and the interior appears indicative of her emotions, which fail to be communicated through facial expression or words. Discord and contrast between dress and wallpaper are apparent in the bedroom she shares with her husband, as opposed to the harmonious effect achieved when she visits her neighbour, alerting us to their easy companionability. The most evocative bedroom of the film is a hotel room. Chow Mo-Wan hires this secret space, symbolically hidden behind a fluttering red curtain, in order to write a martial arts serial story that he hopes Su Lizhen will help him with, and we intuit, also consummate their love. This bedroom appears heavy with erotic tension, the wall paper is a deep fuchsia, patterned with striking blue flowers, and lit romantically by exotic light fittings. In a montage scene depicting the growing closeness of their relationship, Su Lizhen wears a number of cheongsams that echo the colours and floral decorations of the bedroom. While this bedroom in not witness to any kind of sexual passion between the pair, it seems to conspire with Su Lizhen's clothed body to convey the depth of emotion, sensuality and desire that the audience senses is underneath the couple's reserved demeanour. Erotic tension also comes to bear on Su Lizhen's body, as we understand the fabric to convey a hidden syntax of sexual desire, and the silhouette, to represent traditional ideas of womanhood as respectability, restraint and repression.

While Wong Kar-Wai's nostalgic representation of women's repressed sexual identities in 1960s Hong Kong is out of step with contemporary understandings, *In the Mood for Love* proved to be highly influential to contemporary branded-fashion. The visual excesses and sensory mood of the film echo the aesthetic and atmosphere of short fashion films and long-form perfume and cosmetic commercials that have been a significant part of the fashion mediascape since the early 2000s. As will be discussed further in Chapter 3, the use of auteur directors to couple art house film with luxury fashion branding has been a concerted campaign for asserting cultural capital. Wong Kar-Wai has directed advertisements and fashion films for Saint Laurent (2019), Shu Uemura (2011), Dior Midnight Poison (2015), Lancôme Hypnose (2005) and Lacoste (2002). This branded content draws on familiar leitmotifs from *In the Mood for Love*, including fluttering curtains, melancholic music score, vivid colours and highly textured wall surfaces to create the appearance of embodied and olfactory experiences of fashion and cosmetics. The seamless merging of the director's cinematic lexicon with commercial luxury branding can be understood as yet another way that cinema has marketed fashion to female spectators, which has its roots in film tie-ins established in the boudoir.

Boudoirs

The boudoir has been recognized as an inherently female space since its appearance in the early 1700s within aristocratic households. Its French linguistic origins indicate it was a place for women to 'sulk', suggesting the need of a private location for women to withdraw from the masquerade of feminine duties within the household.[34] While its initial purpose may well have been pejoratively termed as a site for female moodiness, over time the boudoir came to represent a space where women might undertake a range of activities; reading, daydreaming, bathing, dressing, intimate conversation and erotic seduction. The boudoirs of literature and art in the eighteenth-century were elaborate sensuous spaces, furnished with chaise-longue, mirrors, patterned wallpapers and plush soft furnishings. French libertine erotic literature of the period provided detailed description of the architecture and interior decoration of the boudoir for the purposes of seduction and pleasure. In many instances, the boudoir itself was metaphoric of the female body. Opulent, soft and inviting materials, diaphanous curtains, hidden alcoves and secret enclosures were portrayed in such a way as to provoke imaginative reverie in broaching such spaces to arousing affect.[35] While the encroachment of these feminine spaces by men in literature was an allegorical allusion to sexual encounter, in reality it was also one of the few spaces in the home set aside for individual female retreat, where women might have control of this private sphere. As Troutman outlines, the boudoir came to represent the locus of female sexual, political and intellectual power in the home, where she might obtain:

> some measure of freedom from the social and sexual conventions of the time ... [providing] the physical and psychological space for subversion of a fixed and rigid social system from within.[36]

The boudoirs of early twentieth-century cinema play a similar role in the portrayal of female agency. The soft lighting and sensuous surfaces of satin sofas, silky curtains and plush velvet cushions provided the perfect setting for sexually liberated modern women to stage their seductions and power plays in scenes where they might partake in intimate tête-à-tête or gossipy telephone conversations. For example, Kitty Packard's boudoir in *Dinner at Eight* (Figure 1.5) is the setting for a coup d'ètat in which she gets the upper hand over her brutish husband Dan (Wallace Beery). An elaborate, white-fringed dressing table, supporting numerous glass bottles of perfumes and creams, framed by brightly lit mirrors and gauzy curtains is integral to the mise-en-scène. As Kitty puts on her make-up and prepares to go out for dinner she argues with her husband about his numerous short comings. Dressed in a chemise and sparkling sequined robe accented by plumes of ostrich feathers, the allure of this garment is tied to obvious connections between

Figure 1.5 Jean Harlow as Kitty Packard in *Dinner at Eight* (1933). Credits: George Cukor (Director) Metro-Goldwyn-Mayer (MGM) (Film Production). Photo Credit: John Springer Collection/CORBIS via Getty Images.

glitter and wealth, but also the ostentatious seductive associations of feathers. Fashion historian Emmanuelle Dirix provides clues to the sexual connotation of feathers where they are tied to Vaudeville costume and the associated glamorous vulgarity of the demi-monde. Feathered gowns in Hollywood were linked to the 'easy but exciting' sexuality of gold-digger characters or courtesans as evidenced in *Shanghai Express* (1932), *Red-Headed Woman* (1932) and *Gold Diggers of 1933* (1933).[37]

Kitty's sexually provocative attire coupled with the overwhelmingly hyper-feminine space of the boudoir provides a sharp contrast to the lumbering physic of her husband. We sense that he is out of place in this soft, alluring setting. Despite his forceful, and at times physical attacks on Kitty, she is able to manipulate him to her will – both in relation to the affair she is having with her doctor, and in coercing him not to take over the business of their socially respectable dinner host. The boudoir here not only represents Kitty's opportunistic use of her sexuality to gain wealth, social capital and pleasure on her own terms, but is also the seat of her power, as she manages to obscure her own moral failings by correcting those of her husband through her fast-talking social intelligence.

Film noir of the 1940s similarly positioned the boudoir as a space of power and seduction for femme fatale characters in examples such as *The Big Sleep* (1946) and *Gilda* (1946). For instance, the first time we meet the title role character in *Gilda* (Rita Hayworth) we are given insight into her captivating and sexually empowered interiority through her well-appointed boudoir (Figure 1.6). The sheen of a long satin skirted dressing table with matching ottoman, and large mirror framed by heavy drapes appear as coded references to her social climbing, 'gold-digger' character. This is reinforced through her gauzy nightdress which slips from her shoulder. At this moment, and with a flick of her hair, her answer to her husband's question 'are you decent?' merges the meaning of her dress and moral character. Her state of undress and indecent behaviour are spectacularly brought to the audience's attention. As with the example of Kitty in *Dinner at Eight*, the negligees and nightdresses Gilda wears throughout the film have their double in a series of form-fitting white evening gowns. These are in contrast to a striking black satin sleeveless gown with long black opera gloves she wears while singing 'Put the Blame on Mame' at the height of the film, which is suggestive of her deadly sexuality. Through these shifts in costume, designer Jean Louis reveals Gilda's complex character, as a woman who uses her sexual power to achieve her goals but who also has a 'good' side. Ultimately fashion and the interior come together to represent the femme fatale figure as a decadent body. The sartorially sensuous and sumptuous surfaces of décor allude to the femme

Figure 1.6 Rita Hayworth as Gilda and George Macredy as Ballian Mudson in *Gilda* (1946). Credits: Charles Vidor (Director), Columbia Pictures (Film Production). Photo Credits: Columbia/Getty Images.

fatale's pleasure in her sexuality, which while represented as darkly dangerous, also suggests freedom from the constraints of traditional femininity.

In addition to providing a backdrop of luxurious decadence, the boudoir also offered the opportunity for film tie-ins. In these scenes audiences were educated that even the most attractive film stars required beauty routines to enhance their looks. The careful application of cosmetics while seated at a luxuriously appointed dressing table – à la Greta Garbo in *The Kiss*, or Marilyn Monroe, Betty Grable and Lauren Bacall in *How to Marry a Millionaire* (1953) – offered consumers an achievable image of modern glamour which they might replicate in their own life. Like fashion and the interior, cosmetics were a key component of the performance of modern woman identities. Magazines similarly promoted the relationship between boudoir beauty routines and movie star glamour. Max Factor advertisements featuring the likes of Joan Crawford, Norma Shearer and Rita Hayworth sat comfortably alongside articles on beauty advice and tips for a well-appointed dressing-table. The ongoing column 'The Cosmetic Urge' which featured in *Harper's Bazaar* magazine in the 1930s and 1940s often made reference to perfume atomizers, make-up boxes and even tissues as the constituents of boudoir luxury and glamour, where displaying these products seemed almost as important as using them to adorn the body.[38]

Similarly, the designs of cinema art directors and set designers in the 1920s and 1930s were often pictured on the pages of fashion and design magazines as inspirations for home styling. These were not the overly ornate romantic spaces associated with Madame de Pompadour and the French aristocracy of the past, but rather modern and glamorous retreats. For example, the illustrator and designer Paul Iribe who worked in Hollywood on Cecil B. DeMille films, wrote an article for *Vogue* in 1919 imploring women to deploy 'The Audacious Note of Modernism in the Boudoir', promoting his gold and red-lacquer deco style dressing table as the answer to a modern woman's decorating dilemmas.[39] Iribe's approach to the seductive setting of the boudoir would be later seen on screen in *The Affairs of Anatol* (1921), all be it a vamped-up version. Joseph Urban's black glass and black ebony 'Repose' boudoir (1929) recalling his work for *The Young Diana* (1922) was similarly presented to extoll the virtues of modernism to fashion readers.[40] It seems likely that these magazines also provided inspiration for set designers. While Kitty's all-white boudoir was innovative in the cinematic context, it was a style already promoted to female consumers, where 'The Rising Tide of White Decors' in boudoirs was recognized by *Harper's Bazaar* in 1931.[41]

As the gender-specific function and inhabitation of rooms declined in the twentieth century, the physical space of the boudoir became less common in modern houses and by mid-century boudoirs were all but extinct in cinematic space. However, the dressing table came to encapsulate some of its purposes. With its mirrors, secret drawers and decorative embellishments, the dressing table is a feminine piece of furnishing that operates as a private space where women take control of their appearance for performing in public. Functioning in a similar way to the boudoir, dressing tables in films are spaces where female characters reflect on love and engage in conversation around their desires. For example, the dressing table is a leitmotif in Douglas Sirk melodramas *Written on the Wind* (1956) and *All That Heaven Allows* (1955) playing the role of confident to expose relationship problems and character flaws. Mirrors in particular highlight the artifice and illusions that the women of Sirkian melodramas are subject to, not least of all their own feminine masquerade of performing idealized images as wives and mothers who are destined to forgo their own desires.

In contemporary cinema, the boudoir is most likely to appear in heritage films and costume dramas. As with previous representations, these spaces are the domain of characters who portray unconventional or promiscuous sexual identities. Recent representations of boudoirs in *Dangerous Liaisons* (1989), *Marie Antoinette* (2006) and *The Favourite* (2018) convey their historic function as spaces that enabled women's intimacy, pleasure and erotic seduction. Coupled with period costume, boudoirs offer audiences insights into the lavish world of royalty and the aristocracy. They serve as a site of déshabillé, where protagonists are literally undressed – albeit merely down to complicated undergarments – and figuratively exposed to reveal character flaws and wanton secret desires. Often period boudoir scenes disclose the stakes of female power. They are spaces where politics and sexuality can be performed with some degree of autonomy, yet, also allude to the risks to reputation and social position that are tied to the discursive forces of female pleasure. While the boudoirs of contemporary costume dramas are often represented as spaces where women's ambitions are at odds with their romantic desires, the bathrooms of cinema provide yet further moral tensions in the portrayal of female protagonists.

Bathrooms

The relationship between boudoirs and bathrooms likely has its origins in nineteenth-century Paris, when Baron Haussman's development of the French capital enabled water to be piped to domestic residences and bathing became a regular occurrence. As the social historian Michael Adcock argues:

> The bathroom began to change from being the site of rather awkward ablutions to being a place of stylishness and comfort … companies began to advertise baths as luxurious pieces of furniture. The bathroom was now a place to tarry and relax, and has taken on some of the romantic connotations of the boudoir.[42]

Paintings of the period, such as Alfred Stevens *The Bath* (1873–1874), reinforced the association between sexual enjoyment and bathing, as courtesans and prostitutes were sometimes models for these intimate nude scenes.[43] Arguably, this association continued well into the twentieth century, whereby women bathers were often portrayed as characters who were sexually promiscuous and morally corrupt in cinema.

Despite the seemingly scandalous behaviour of women bathers, elevation of bathrooms to stylish and luxurious spaces in the home was in part due to the influence of Hollywood. Cecil B. DeMille's silent film *Male and Female* (1919) features one of many risqué bath scenes that would be a hallmark of his career. Characterized by striking tiles, mirrored walls and large bathtubs, DeMille films glamorized bathing as an art form, and instructed viewers in styling and accessorizing the bathroom. For example, in *Male and Female*, the actress Gloria Swanson is introduced to the audience as she is helped to disrobe by two maids and then steps into a sunken bath. Later, an intertitle educates audiences by asking: 'Why shouldn't the Bath Room express as much Art and Beauty as the Drawing Room?' Other films such as *Dynamite* (1929), with its dazzling marble spa presented the pleasures of the bathroom to American consumers, with DeMille taking credit for his 'pictures [having] something to do with [the] wholesome development of bathrooms as a comfortable part of the American home'.[44] The 'wholesome' idea of promoting cleanliness was perhaps outweighed by the fact that DeMille bathroom scenes primarily provided an appropriate setting for female protagonists to disrobe to titillating effect. This was particularly true of the biblical epic *Sign of the Cross* (1932), which controversially portrayed Claudette Colbert as Poppaea in a sensuous milk-bath scene, purportedly contributing to the enforcement of the Hollywood Production Code and its subsequent censorship of nudity and allusions to sex.[45]

While films made after 1934 could no longer use bathrooms to overt erotic effect, they could be useful in providing characters with the sheen of sexual impropriety. For example, Joan Crawford as Crystal Allen in George Cukor's *The Women* (1939) (Figure 1.7) portrays her immorality to audiences in a memorable scene in which she lounges in a clear glass bathtub whilst talking on the telephone to her lover. The bath – with its satin backed cushioning – appears to act almost as a chaise lounge within a boudoir. The room itself is decorated with diaphanous curtains hanging across the ceiling, a richly appointed dressing table and enclave of back-lit shelves dedicated to perfumes and cosmetics, with glimpses through to the bedroom. The bathtub and boudoir's glamorous styling is suggestive of Crystal Allen's sexual prowess, decadent lifestyle and pursuit of material luxury. This representation of the bath reflects art historical allegorical understandings of women bathing where, as Anthea Callen contends:

> Bathing was directly associated with lascivious sexual activity, in particular with prostitution ... Writers both for and against intimate hygiene for women recognised the sensuality of water. They likened immersion in it and its intimate contact with every bodily crevice to the sexual act itself; water was perceived as a surrogate lover.[46]

As the film's villain – the shop-girl mistress of heroine Mary Haines' (Norma Shearer) husband – Crystal's brazen bathing rituals are presented as indicative of a woman willing to use her sexual appeal to obtain her avaricious aspirations.

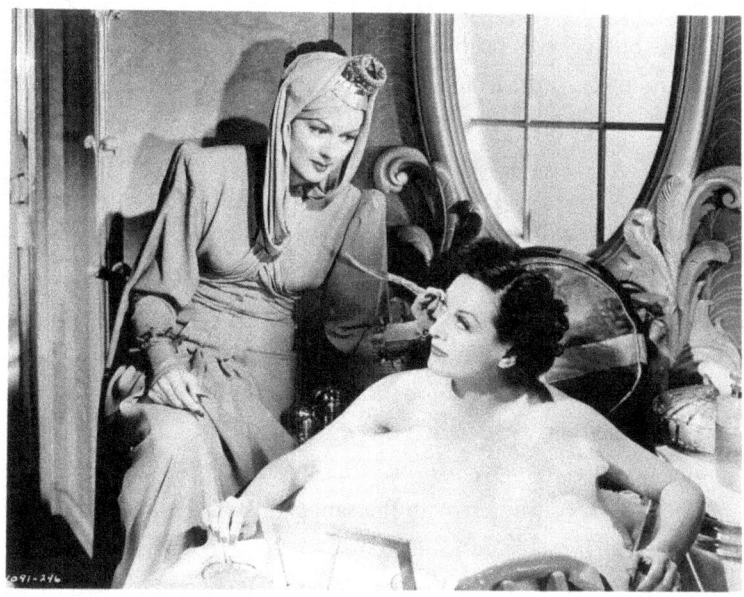

Figure 1.7 Joan Crawford as Crystal Allen in the bath and Rosalind Rusell as Sylvia in *The Women* (1939). Credits: George Cukor (Director), Metro-Goldwyn-Mayer (MGM) (Film Production). Photo Credits: Metro-Goldwyn-Mayer/Getty Images.

While morally the film suggests that Crawford's character and lifestyle should be reproached, her fashions and interior décor are presented as highly desirable. The costumer Adrian carefully contrasted Crawford's and Shearer's looks. Where Shearer's Mary wears prim suits to suggest her traditional values and 'good-girl' attitude, Crawford's shop-girl uniform of basic black, accessorized with pearls is no-nonsense chic, in accordance with her forthright character. Later, when Mary confronts Crystal about the affair with her husband, Crystal wears an ostentatious gold lame dress with large bows at the throat and waist, coupled with a matching turban, which is again contrasted with Mary's understated, black full-skirted evening gown. As bold and brash as Crawford's dress is in this scene, it is upstaged in the finale. In a bitingly bitchy exit, Crawford wears a glittering two-piece gold-sequinned evening gown with exposed midriff. As she delivers her final cutting remark, 'there's a name for you ladies, but it isn't used in high society – outside of a kennel' the shimmering sequins underscore Crystal's words as she departs in glamorous glory.

The synergy between Adrian's costuming and Cedric Gibbons' art direction has the effect of casting the bathtub as a further fashion ensemble for Crawford's character. The bubbles that frame her face and caress her body as she luxuriates in the bath and talks on the telephone are reminiscent of Adrian costumes from earlier films. The striking white organdie dress with ruffled shoulders Crawford wears in *Letty Lynton* (1932) and the feathery white dressing-gown worn by Jean Harlow as Kitty Packard in *Dinner at Eight* can be read as extra-textual fashion narrative moments that further reinforce Crystal's unscrupulous character through visual reference to the conniving Letty and socially ambitious Kitty. Costume historian Christian Esquevin observes that Adrian often used luscious white materials for costumes, not only for the reflective properties that white held on the silver screen, but also as a powerful symbolic contradiction between the colour's association with purity and innocence and a character's persona of scheming sexual allure.[47] While the gleaming foam of Crystal's bubble bath could not be sold to consumers with the same effect as the Letty Lynton white dress – a replica of which sold 50,000 copies at Macy's department store – the glamorous appeal of Gibbons' bathroom designs were indicative of how movie sets had the ability to set trends and inspire home decorators.

The relationship between bathrooms, fashionable silhouettes and sexually alluring characters was further developed in films of the 1950s and 1960s. The demise of the Hollywood studio system and concurrent rise of European art-house cinema saw the decline of censorship laws and more frequent portrayal of overt female sexuality. For example, bathroom scenes became a leitmotif of numerous Brigitte Bardot films, an opportunity to voyeuristically view the actress' erotically voluptuous body while wrapped in a towel. *Une Parisienne* (1957) in which Bardot plays the sexually assured daughter of the French prime minister features a typically seductive bath routine, in which her character, Brigitte, washes her legs with a sponge for her watching husband (Henri Vidal) to admire. The subsequent towel drying and playful chase escapade between the couple results in Brigitte's towel being stripped away to reveal a glimpse of her naked bottom before she hides behind a plant. Here, titillated audiences are provided with a sense of gratification after having seen Bardot wear a series of form fitting Balmain day dresses and gowns. In particular, a siren-red satin dress which amplifies her hourglass figure is worn while she seduces a prince (Charles Boyer). This striking silhouette emphasizes her vampish qualities, as she attempts to have an affair in order to seek revenge on her husband. Bardot's sexuality was considered quintessential to her modern woman persona. Having appeared as a model for *Elle* magazine, her fashionable, youthful image was amplified in film, and was in contrast to the middle-aged bourgeois aesthetic of haute couture, epitomized by Dior's 'New Look'. Bardot occupied a complex position of female sexuality on film, both an object of the male gaze but also, as Simone de Beauvoir described, an image of progressive female sexuality, who is concerned with her own desires and pleasures, initiates sex and is 'as much hunter as she is prey'.[48]

Aside from providing audiences with the opportunity to ogle Bardot's body, the bathroom scene in *Une Parisienne* is designed to make us aware of the actress' 'naturalness'. While the fashion scenes of the film allude to the idea of constructed femininity as masquerade, the bathing which occurs in the film, both in the bathroom, and at a beach in Nice, are reminders of her 'wild' irrepressible sexuality. The perceived naturalness of Bardot's sexuality was seen as a symbol of liberated womanhood in the 1960s. Yet, this representation is deeply paradoxical. Bardot's image is at once the epitome of the 'to-be-looked-at-ness' described by Mulvey, yet also opened the door for women to perceive the possibility of female agency in her own pleasure and desire.[49] As film studies scholar, Ginette Vincendeau argues this discrepancy is indicative of women's position in French society at the time, where:

> patriarchal power was inscribed in law and the regime of the double standard which gave male sexuality a free reign, while containing female sexuality – a deeply oppressive situation … [where Bardot] flaunted an image of a largely unapproachable freedom.[50]

The combination of naturalness, child-like naivety and sexual liberation that Bardot epitomized in the *Une Parisienne* bathroom scene might be understood as a precursor to the character of Vivian Ward, played by Julia Roberts in *Pretty Woman* (1990) (Figure 1.8). The bathroom at the Beverly Wiltshire Hotel, in which Vivian performs her off-key rendition of Prince's 'Kiss', is the setting for one of the more enchanting scenes of the film. Surrounded by bubbles, with eyes closed, Vivian listens to her Walkman and sings with abandon, oblivious as love interest Edward (Richard Gere) watches on. This comic scene occurs as part of the transformation that Vivian undergoes over the course of the film. Reinforcing her goofy charm, it also reveals her true character as a 'natural' beauty compared to her heavily made-up masquerade as prostitute. The bathroom with pink and white marble, Art Deco style lights, and gilt framed mirrors is typical of Hollywood luxury bathrooms. A large back-lit glass etching depicting a roman vase on a pedestal provides reference to classical ideals of beauty, and suggests that this scene might be a modern equivalent to an ancient Greek or Roman

Figure 1.8 Julia Roberts as Vivian Ward and Richard Gere as Edward Lewis in *Pretty Woman* (1990). Credits: Garry Marshall (Director), Touchstone Pictures (Film Production). Screen still.

goddess bathing. As film theorist Mari Ruti argues, the morning sequences after Vivian and Edward spend the night together, are important to the interpretation of the other transformative fashion makeovers in the film. Her authentic 'noble' persona represented by her natural, classical beauty is 'closer to a lady than a hooker' so the new clothes that follow are then understood to 'make her a more sparkly version of who she *already* is'.[51]

While the bubble bath scene reminds audiences of Vivian's 'natural' and noble character it also reinforces that Vivian operates on her own terms. As she negotiates to be Edward's 'beck and call girl' for the week, her excitement at bargaining to her benefit is celebrated with an underwater dance. It is a reminder of Vivian's occupation as sex worker, yet as film theorist Hilary Radner contends, the film does not condemn prostitution on moral terms but rather because 'it fails to provide self-fulfilment'.[52] Linking the bathtub in *Pretty Woman* to a situation in which sex is traded for material rewards is indicative of broader associations perpetuated in Hollywood film in which women's sexual desires are represented as mercenary. The conflict in Vivian's character as both noble and avaricious established in this scene is ultimately resolved through consumer culture, and fashion transformation. The subsequent Rodeo drive shopping montage in which Vivian parades a series of glamorous ensembles to the Roy Orbison title song, provides audiences with a fantasy of pleasurable fashion metamorphosis which negates her character's previous sexual impropriety. While Vivian appears to be transformed from prostitute to lady through tasteful consumption of fashion, ultimately self-commodification merely takes a different form.

By and large, the bedrooms, boudoirs and bathrooms of cinema in conjunction with spectacular slinky silhouettes have been associated with the modern women's sexuality. As I have outlined here, this relationship is a complex one. The modern woman's social, economic and sexual emancipation in cinema has been closely tied to objectification and consumption. Women's access to power, wealth and prestige is regulated by her ability to use her body. Gold-diggers, femme fatales, adulteresses and prostitutes have been associated with intimate spaces, states of undress, and form-fitting silhouettes to make this clear. Yet, many of these characters are immensely likeable. Self-assured sexuality and an unwillingness to compromise her own pleasure or personal desires are characteristics that make protagonists played by Joan Crawford, Rita Hayworth and Jean Harlow appealing to women audiences. While these figures might be understood as objects of the male gaze, and the rooms and spaces they inhabit as indicative of confining domesticity, they are also women who don't appear to be regulated by maternal or marital obligation. While material obligation, in the form of fashion and interior accoutrements are integral to the modern woman's persona and in particular her morally ambiguous sexual proclivities, it is disingenuous to think of this relationship as only pertaining to female consumer cultures. As the following chapter will show, representations of heroic masculinity on film are just as open to desire for glamorous fashion and stylish abodes.

2

Evil lairs and bachelor dandies: Modernist architecture, spies and the suit

The French architect Robert Mallet-Stevens was amongst the first to formulate a theory of set design. He saw the cinema as the ideal mode of representation to portray the virtues of modern design to the public, stating in 1928, that:

> Cinema educates and will continue to educate the mass public in artistic matters … Art will be communicated to all classes in society; French art will travel across boarders; and décor in the cinema will become even more ambitious.[1]

His set designs for Marcel L'Herbier's *L'Inhumaine* (1924) (discussed further in Chapter 5) saw his architecture of clean lines, geometric forms and plain surfaces translated to the screen, predicting a style that would dominate both architecture and cinema for the next twenty years. Versions of modernist domestic architecture – be it Art Deco luxury, or the International Style model of glass, concrete and steel – normalized the aesthetics of modernism for general consumption by audiences and spread beyond French avant-garde films to Hollywood cinema.

In the post-Second World War period, mid-century modern style became associated with glamorous architecture. Intriguingly, while buildings by the likes of Richard Neutra, Eero Saarinen and John Lautner served as fashionable abodes for Hollywood film-makers, on-screen these spaces were viewed with suspicion.[2] The destructive power of modernism, science and technology associated with war saw the integration of traditional domesticity in the form of both gender roles and living environments in the aesthetics of 1950s cinema. At this point, the mid-century modern home becomes immoral. As curator Joseph Rosa observes, while modern architecture was considered appropriate for the workplace, Hollywood positioned the modern home as lairs for characters who 'are evil, unstable, selfish, obsessive and driven by pleasures of the flesh'.[3]

Focusing on Alfred Hitchcock's *North by Northwest* (1959) and the Bond movie franchise (1962–2015), this chapter examines the prevalence of

Machiavellian modernism as a cinematic trope in Hollywood spy films. Yet, despite Hollywood's misgivings for mid-century architecture's claim to devious world domination, another modern icon prevails in these films in the form of the suit. The hero protagonists of spy movies are svelte and sharply dressed. Sean Connery in Anthony Sinclair's Conduit Cut and Cary Grant wearing impeccable Savile Row tailoring are indicative of a secret agent style of reliable rationalism that continues to be perpetuated in contemporary cinema. Specifically, I argue that Hollywood spy films have established a rivalry between the modern home and the modern body that reflects long-standing tensions around gender, sexuality and fashion. Drawing on Adolf Loos' writings on modernist architecture and its equation with the gentleman's suit as a foil to the criminality of ornament, coupled with an analysis of *Playboy* magazine, this chapter proposes that the ultimate victor of the spy film is in fact modernism's stylish surfaces and forms as objects of desire.

The glamour of masculinity and modernism

The glamorization of male bodies as erotic objects in cinema has been far less frequently examined than that of women. Yet, as numerous film scholars have identified, there is pleasure in viewing male bodies on screen in action.[4] According to film theorist Steve Neale, part of the tension of the eroticized male body in cinema stems from heterosexist and patriarchal positions that the male body cannot be marked as erotic by another man's gaze, so sadism and violence must occur to that body in order to repress erotic contemplation and desire.[5] This persuasive argument applies particularly to action films – such as the spy movie – in which the protagonist's body is under constant threat. However, as Stella Bruzzi argues, this position fails to take into account the ways that style and mise-en-scène, contribute to the eroticization and aestheticization of masculinity. Further, by foregrounding accounts of style in understanding the way that masculinity is portrayed in cinema, more nuanced interpretations of male identities can be revealed, in much the same way that we have come to understand women through these surfaces.[6] In other words, fantasies of consumerism, hedonism and pleasure can be attributed to representations of masculinity that are glamorous and desirable, further complicating the representation of the male spectacle on screen.

As I have outlined in Chapter 1, the Art Deco styling of bedrooms, bathrooms and boudoirs in combination with the sartorial syntax of slinky silhouettes, established a visual discourse that associated these intimate domestic domains with modern women and contentious sexual morality. The relationship between glamorous women, overt sexuality and Art Deco design decadence cast this mode of modernism as sensuous, frivolous and distinctively feminine. The style was at odds with the principles of influential high-modernist architects such as Adolf Loos and Le Corbusier, who sought a utopian and radical program of rationalization and functionality. Their mode of modernity, consisting of geometric white walls, glass, concrete and steel was underpinned by the ideal of a classless society, and the realities of everyday urban living – as opposed to the glamorous, and luxurious surfaces of consumer oriented Art Deco. As I have argued elsewhere, Loos manipulated understandings of fashion, femininity and the interior to radically recast the aesthetics of modernist design as a masculine mode that had long-lasting consequences.[7]

The American mid-century modern architecture I discuss here might be considered somewhat removed from Loosian ideals. As proponents of organic architecture, Frank Lloyd Wright and John Lautner were concerned with integrating their buildings into the surrounding landscape. By incorporating natural materials such as wood and stone, they sought to develop a more 'human' approach to architecture than the machine-like efficiency of the European modernists. Yet, the modernist aesthetic of concrete, glass, steel and geometric forms still dominated the spatial paradigm of their buildings. Loos was likely inspired by Wright's Robie House when he visited Chicago, and there are also similarities in the way that Lautner and Loos approached architectures of masculinity in the interior.[8] What is perhaps more relevant for my purposes here is the idea that Loos developed a theatrical approach to the interior. As architectural historian, Beatriz Colomina argues, Loos' interiors are designed like a theatre set to frame the occupant. Highlighting the photographic representation of Loos' architecture – which poses the interior as a stage for the performance of domestic life – Colomina draws attention to the way the architect saw his role in creating an 'effect that he wishes to impose on the spectator'.[9]

In recognizing the photogenic qualities of Loos' interior architecture that was disseminated through design magazines of the period, and the later glamour images of American mid-century modernism that would be similarly staged, it is possible to see how both forms promote an alluring image. Much like fashion, architecture and the interior are presented as a product of the mass media and consumption. Alice Friedman astutely recognizes that buildings by the likes of Wright and Lautner share a self-conscious approach to the styling of architecture that appealed to American consumers accustomed to seeing such images in the mass media, where: 'these buildings were intended to be looked at and photographed, and they were styled to appear camera ready and "glamourized" [...] like fashion models.'[10] These representations functioned to create desire and to perpetuate a fantasy of control. Making the link between masculine heterosexist fantasies and architecture, George Wagner affirms that, 'the idea of control becomes the spectacle of a project, [...] through the manipulations of geometry, contrivances of the visual field and the subject's view [...] It is no secret that architecture is a medium of domination.'[11] Just as much of the literature on modern architecture has sought to associate ornament with the feminine, so obscuring the ways in which style and the white walls of modernism were also an artificial surface; the literature regarding fashion, film and consumption would have us believe that it largely exploits female audiences.[12] As I argue here, the relationship between spy films and mid-century modern design tells a different story, one in which overt concern for style is integral to the performance of heterosexual masculinity.

Machiavellian modernism: architecture of evil

Machiavellian modernism in the cold war climate is a central theme of Alfred Hitchcock's *North by Northwest* (1959). The film tells the wrong man story of an advertising executive, Roger Thornhill (Cary Grant), who is mistakenly confused for a spy by the villain Philip Vandamm (James Mason). The 'catch me if you can' action that ensues across a succession of spectacular locations climaxes in a life-and-death struggle on the face of Mount Rushmore, before the hero wins the girl, Eve Kendall (Eva Marie Saint). Throughout the film, icons of modernity, including the towers of the United Nations Headquarters, Henry Dreyfuss' luxury twentieth-century train, aeroplanes and automobiles provide perilous moments for the lead protagonist to overcome. Perhaps the most memorable of these is an architectural adversary in the form of Vandamm House, the first evil lair of its kind in Hollywood cinema.

Based on the architecture of Frank Lloyd Wright's cantilevered Fallingwater (1936–1939) and the interiors of Usonian houses (1937–1958), the Vandamm House was imagined by production designer Robert Boyle as a series of stage sets and matt-painted backdrops (Figure 2.1). The house appears towards the end of the film, providing the setting for a series of suspenseful scenes. Situated in a seemingly remote location, with a panoptic mountain top position near Mount Rushmore, the house represents Vandamm's inhumanity and formidable power.

Figure 2.1 Vandamm House in *North by Northwest* (1959). Credits: Alfred Hitchcock (Director), Metro-Goldwyn-Mayer (MGM) (Film Production). Screen still.

As a metaphor for its wealthy mastermind owner and his dangerous vision for the future, Hitchcock casts modernism as the dastardly dream of designers who wanted their brutalism to take over the world. The house's panoramic glass facade suggestive of surveillance, combined with its cantilevered steel structure, which teeters perilously over a precipice, proves to be a worthy antagonist.

Thornhill's first physical encounter with the house involves grappling with the steel-structure's slippery surfaces whilst dangling over a cliff-face. Boyle describes his set-design decisions here as integral to the action, and important to the film's themes where he states:

> If it's just an ordinary porch, or something it couldn't be. So he has to be in a position where if he is dislodged, he will fall to his death. There has to be some suspense there. And then, cantilevered meant modern, so it just fell into place.[13]

The house's interior proves similarly problematic once Thornhill makes his way inside. The exposed interior of open-plan living room surrounded by a mezzanine balcony, and floor-to-ceiling windows, requires Thornhill to perform ingenuity and stealth to navigate the space undetected, as he attempts to save love interest Eve from the clutches of his nemesis. In this way, Thornhill's ability to overcome the maleficent modernist home is a metaphor for his ongoing struggle with Vandamm.

The audience is given further insight into Vandamm's villainous character through interior décor (Figure 2.2). The living room is furnished with geometric textiles, Edward Wormley inspired furniture and Scandinavian design accents. A prominent Sunburst clock mounted on the horizontally striated stone wall and numerous Kaiser Leuchten-like floor lamps are recognizable to alert design aficionado audiences. These interior accoutrements underscore Vandamm's wealth and connoisseur identity, the art collector as criminal being a recognizable cinematic convention for a psychopathy of control, where collecting the world is contiguous with ruling it. Cold, cruel and calculating, modern design is cast as criminal.

Yet, this positioning is at odds with modernism's utopian goals, and in particular the architect Adolf Loos' assertion that 'Ornament is Crime'. In his polemic essay of 1910, Loos sets out the virtues of modernism by arguing that ornamentation is a symptom of degeneracy, the domain of so-called 'primitive-man' and women.[14] Loos' aim is to condemn architecture that applies stylistic facades to clothe its surfaces, and adopts the analogy of women and their

Figure 2.2 Interior of Vandamm House, *North by Northwest* (1959). Credits: Alfred Hitchcock (Director), Metro-Goldwyn-Mayer (MGM) (Film Production). Screen still.

seductive and erotic use of decorative fashions to entice men as an example of the immorality of ornamentation. In this way, Loos contributes to the gendering of modernism as masculine, and is at odds with what he discerns as feminine tastes for decorative domesticity. Loos sees both women's fashion and ornament in architecture as equally deceptive in their purpose of attracting attention through frivolous display and in their shared interest in representing social distinction through surface design. For Loos, modernism's simplicity, rationality and lack of ornamentation represents masculine authority, intelligence and moral integrity, ideas that would underpin the thinking of a range of architects and designers from Le Corbusier to the Bauhaus. In fact, the characteristics that underpin Loos' architecture are found in his penchant for fashion, in the form of the English gentlemen's suit. Loos wrote a series of essays that proceed 'Ornament and Crime' outlining his ideas about the importance of austerity in dress including 'Men's Fashion' (1898) and 'In Praise of the Present' (1908). As numerous architectural historians have identified, it is clear that Loos' thinking about the suit as a form of simple, functional, attire was the basis to his innovations in architectural style.[15] For Loos the modern man is masked by the uniform nature of his clothing, allowing him to protect his interiority, and function in the social sphere, the suit represents 'a desire for the disguise of difference'.[16] Loos explicitly connects his architectural purpose and men's austere attire when he states:

> When I was given the task of building a house, I said to myself: in its external appearance, a house can only have changed as much as a dinner jacket. Not a lot therefore ... It had to become significantly simpler. I had to substitute gold buttons with black ones. The house has to look inconspicuous.[17]

In drawing attention to the relationship between modernist architecture and the suit, Loos essentially equates modernism with heroic masculinity, and in particular the style of the English dandy. Exemplified by Beau Brummell, the dandy reformed male dress from its previous ostentatious form to a more retrained style of dark sobriety and understated, carefully constructed, elegance.[18] The dandy's rational, tailored attire came to represent modern urban masculinity – uniform dress that made it possible to merge with the crowd. This approach to dressing compliments Loos' views that both architecture and the suit should produce a masquerade – a facade that obscures the personal aspects of character associated with the interior. For Loos, the masculine mode of modernist architecture was rational, controlled, surface. However, a number of tensions emerge from this alignment. Loos equation of architectural surface and male suit as a mask fails to recognize that the masquerade of austerity is just as artificial as female fashions and decorations. The concept of masquerade on film has primarily been associated with the excesses of femininity, as Doane outlines, the feminine masquerade is 'constituted by a hyperbolisation of the accoutrements of femininity'.[19] However, as Butler reminds us, the acts, gestures and accoutrements of gender are performative, they are manufactured fabrications that can equally apply to the men's performance of the traits of masculinity.[20] With this in mind, I argue that the relationship between modern architecture and the suit underpins gendered understandings of modernism and its relationship to seemingly 'natural' rationality, authority and control, which in turn reveals a further set of tensions that arise in the rivalry between modern home and modern man in spy films.

Bachelor dandies

In her book *Sex and Suits,* Ann Hollander establishes the male suit as inherently modern, from its initial manifestation in the form of Neo-classical dandy attire. The suit represented a shift from decorative dress for men toward utility and rationality, embedding gender divisions and challenging visible class differentiation. She argues that from its beginnings the suit held an erotic charge in its shaping of the male body to highlight classical heroic masculinity:

> The male figure was recut and the ideal man recast … Now the noble proportions of his manly form, created only by the rigorous use of natural materials, seemed to give him an individual moral strength founded on natural virtue, an integrity that flowers in aesthetic purity without artifice, and made him an appropriate vessel for forthright modern opinion.[21]

Roger Thornhill's suit in *North by Northwest* is fitting attire for a classic hero (Figure 2.3). The grey-flannel Savile Row bespoke tailoring by Klingour, French & Stanbury is perfectly moulded to Grant's physique. Reinforcing the actor's panache on and off screen, the suit is a stylish metaphor for machismo. Grant's well-known acute personal interest in clothing is associated with a type of masculine, bachelor dandyism that the audience also associates with Thornhill's character – a lady's man who also has homosexual appeal. Yet, this is not just any well-cut suit, it has gained iconic status in the minds of movie goers. As Jonathan Faiers suggests, Grant's suits have an almost magical power, where:

Figure 2.3 Cary Grant as Roger Thornhill in *North by Northwest* (1959). Credits: Alfred Hitchcock (Director), Metro-Goldwyn-Mayer (MGM) (Film Production). Photo Credit: Sunset Boulevard/Corbis via Getty Images.

> The majority of suits on screen function fairly simply, connoting respectability, authority and conservatism, but there are certain sets of clothing that transcend this expected function and assume a super-functional existence as 'armour-plated' suits which bestow a mythical status on their wearers.[22]

This certainly applies to Thornhill's grey suit, which adapts admirably to his character's every challenge. As fashion theorist Ulrich Lehmann contends, throughout the film the suit shows remarkable endurance in its ability to recover from pursuit and assault. Even after the memorable crop-dusting sequence in which Thornhill narrowly escapes a swooping aeroplane, the crease in the trousers remains sharp and the crisp of the collar perfectly in place.²³ The suit is invulnerable to adversity and its consistency and functionality suggests the dependability of its wearer. Thornhill's English tailoring conveys self-restraint and the ability to act in a time of crisis while maintaining a stiff upper-lip. The suit also adapts to each aspect of Thornhill's character as it emerges. Whether erroneous or actual – advertising executive, government spy, suspected criminal and sophisticated lover are shifting personas that Thornhill adopts throughout the film. In Loosian terms then, the suit comes to represent a mask or disguise that adjusts to each new identity. Writer Todd McEwan for *Granata* magazine astutely recognizes that *North by Northwest* 'isn't a film about what happens to Cary Grant, it's about what happens to his suit'.²⁴ In his sartorial satire, McEwan notes that Grant '*grows into his suit* over the course of the adventure and finds a life (and a wife) to suit him'.²⁵ The suit transforms him from a lad-about-town to responsible and reliable suitor, Thornhill's character must live up to the suit's admirable qualities.

Similarly, to Cary Grant's Thornhill, the various Bond actors of the 007 movie franchise use the suit as a metaphor of the character's reliability in times of crisis. However, James Bond's suits never attained the quality of transforming its wearer into a committed companion. Its suave silhouette continues to signify the spy as sex symbol. As film historian Andrew Spicer explains of Sean Connery wearing an Anthony Sinclair Conduit Cut suit in the first Bond film *Dr. No* (1962):

> He incarnated [...] the international playboy who embodied the Swinging Sixties. Bond became [...] a hero of consumption, refined, hedonistic and liberated[...] the projection of audiences' aspirational fantasy of stylish and successful living.²⁶

As with Thornhill's character, Connery's Bond adopts bachelor dandy styling (Figure 2.4). British tailoring offers understated simplicity that also mirrored Beau Brummell's blatant eroticism of skin-tight breeches and cut-away jackets designed to emphasize a sculpted male body. Connery's sharp suits similarly heightened the contours of his figure and his sexual allure and were fetishized in men's magazines of the period. For example, a 1966 article in *GQ: Gentleman's Quarterly* provides rich details regarding Bond's suit proportions: 'natural shoulders ... two buttons ... flapped pockets ... 10 [inch] side vents' are presumably outlined as an education in style that readers might copy.²⁷ The Bond image complies with spy style more broadly in fashion editorial and advertisements of the 1960s – where trench coats, trilby hats and debonair smoking jackets were frequently portrayed to convey their elegant, distinctive, 'racy' and sophisticated attributes.²⁸

Figure 2.4 Sean Connery as James Bond and Jack Lord as Felix Leiter in *Dr. No* (1962). Credits: Terrance Young (Director), Eon Productions (Film Production). Photo Credit: United Artist/Getty Images.

While Bond's suit has changed according to the times and the physics of his various actors, for the most part it represents these same fantasy ideals to its consuming audience. For example, Pamela Church Gibson observes that Roger Moore's 1970s flared trousers seem to reflect his characterization of Bond as a bawdy humourist, while Timothy Dalton and Pierce Brosnan adopted the double-breasted, light-weight, silhouette of Italian tailoring – a suave realignment to Britain's position within the EU.[29] Daniel Craig's Bond is perhaps the most eroticized of all, switching from casual, linen Brioni tailoring in *Casino Royale* to the tightly fitting, short narrow cut jackets that his body all but bursts out of in *Spectre* (Figure 2.5). Church Gibson wittily identifies that audiences fear for the Tom Ford clad Bond, 'but it is a sartorial mishap, a split seam, that they worry about, rather than a properly-aimed bullet from one of his adversaries'.[30] The form-fitting look is designed to heighten Craig's physical strength and masculinity, perhaps at the expense of soignée. Though expense does seem to be part of the equation, as designer Tom Ford claims, 'James Bond epitomises the

Figure 2.5 Daniel Craig as James Bond wearing Tom Ford in *Spectre* (2015). Credits: Sam Mendes (Director), Eon Productions (Film Production). Screen still.

Tom Ford man in his elegance, style, and love of luxury.'[31] Undeniably, whatever the cut of his cloth, Bond's sartorial slickness in the series of films aligns male consumption with sexuality. In this way, the suit becomes a sign of what Loos would consider immorality, the eroticism of the suit degenerates its decency and lack of distinction. Bond's suits are not a disguise of difference – rather, his eroticized body is overtly on display. In much the same way, as the Bond girl is interchangeable, the various Bonds are in some ways reduced to their bodies, or at least the stylishness of their suits.

Playboy styling

North by Northwest's Thornhill and the various Bonds are represented as playboys – sleek, sophisticated, urbane men whose adventurous exploits are equalled by their womanizing heterosexuality. As Viki Karaminas and Adam Geczy argue, playboys as Hollywood types were role models to young urban bachelors who sought hedonism and indulgence through 'fashion, style and spending … [they] fetishized the sophisticated world of the connoisseur' as a means of obtaining a multitude of women.[32] Men's style magazines in the 1960s were keen to exploit Bond's connoisseur tastes as a way to convince their readership to partake in luxurious consumer lifestyles. Articles such as 'The Impassioned Palate of James Bond' and advertisements for Jim Beam, Rolex and Aramis cologne provided insights into the fictional character's pronounced preferences.[33] Bond's sophisticated style and that of playboy dandies in general were a particularly rich subject for producing consumerist heteronormativity.

The suit as a symbol of sexual prowess and a wardrobe staple for the Hollywood dandy bachelor, was advocated by *Playboy* magazine, in keeping with its founder Hugh Hefner's attitudes towards masculine fashionability. As fashion historian Becky Conekin observes, *Playboy* promoted 'an elegance of uniformity' achieved through a well-tailored suit in a neutral colour.[34] The sharp and slim-fit suits that Thornhill and Bond wear are emblematic of the playboy lifestyle of conspicuous consumption. *Playboy* took fashion seriously, describing in detail the essential elements of distinguished dressing. For example, editorial copy outlining the exploits of a playboy at a party in the January 1965 issue reads: 'Host is impeccable in Italian olive-colour nubby-silk dinner jacket with black satin lapels and sleeve cuffs, black mohair-worsted trousers with satin extension waistband and side stripes.'[35] Presumably the playboy's knowledge of sartorial sophistication was just as significant to his persona as the ability to apply effective seduction techniques.

In fact, from its beginnings in 1953, *Playboy* magazine forged an association with the James Bond character of Fleming's novels, a relationship reinforced through the film adaptations. In the 1960s *Octopussy* was serialized in its pages and the magazine featured 'Bond girls' from the movies as covers, beginning with a special 'James Bond' issue published in November 1965, which featured thirteen actresses from the first four Bond films. These pictorial features continued throughout the 1960s and 1970s along with interviews with each of the Bond actors.[36] Intriguingly, these features often ran alongside stories that profiled architects including Frank Lloyd Wright and Mies van der Rohe, as well as articles aimed at educating bachelors in the latest tastes for home decorating. As architectural historian Reyner Banham confessed of his illicit readership of the magazine: '*Playboy* has over the years discussed and illustrated quite a lot of furniture … plans and perspectives.'[37] The bachelor dandy in Bond's vein was not just a well-heeled, immaculately suited, cad – he was also a sophisticated design aficionado.

The playboy's penchant for home decoration occurs within the context of deeply gendered heterosexist expectations of family life in post-war America. As identified in Chapter 1, with the example of Rock Hudson's bachelor character in *Pillow Talk,* at this time, opposing domesticities were pitted as rivals. The bachelor pad as sexual lair versus the white-picket fence, and family-life of the suburban home encapsulated the gender binaries and sexual politics that emerged in the 1950s. This designation follows from the development of nineteenth-century separate spheres which defined men's public function in the urban space of work and situated women as tastemakers in the private space of the home. In addition, gendered spaces within the home also reinforced these separate spheres with the parlour, bedroom or boudoir marked as feminine and the dining room, smoking room and study as masculine. These spaces were decorated according to traditional gender distinctions – masculine spaces were dark with heavy furniture, while feminine spaces were designed with lighter colours and decorative objects. As Sparke outlines, codification of décor in this way served to reinforce gendered self-identities. As women entered public life in the late nineteenth and early twentieth centuries these distinctions slowly eroded; however, decorative considerations in the domestic sphere were still considered the domain of women.[38] Modern design ideals such as open plan living and rationalist approaches to the interior also meant that the gendered division between these spheres became less evident, where social and intimate spaces redefined the home's functions.[39]

The relationship between women's sexuality and bedrooms, bathrooms and boudoirs examined in Chapter 1 highlights that the boundaries between these separate spheres are unstable, and that gender identities and power relations are negotiated in both public and private space in complex ways. I argue that the bachelor pad is another example indicative of this tension, emerging as a space where men might occupy domesticity in ways that were traditionally associated with women. Design historian John Potvin suggests that, 'men progressively turned to alternate spaces and sought out venues in which homosociability was welcomed ... [allowing men] to escape the constraints of domestic servitude.'[40] This observation is remarkably close to the way that *Playboy* marketed the bachelor pad to it readers:

> A man dreams of his own domain, a place that is exclusively his own ... Playboy has designed, planned and decorated, from the floor up, a penthouse apartment for the urban bachelor – a man who enjoys good living, a sophisticated connoisseur of the lively arts, food and drink and congenial companions of both sexes.[41]

Hedonistic consumption, marketed by men's magazines, became a prevalent mode of male desire in ways that had been traditionally associated with the feminine, and was closely aligned to heterosexual ideals of masculine conquest. Features such as the latest electronic entertainment equipment, a built-in bar, light dimmers and luxurious bed linen were discussed alongside erotic photo spreads and lengthy narratives on the art of seduction. In her influential study of domestic space on film, *The Apartment Plot*, Pamela Robertson Wojcik proposes that the bachelor pad is linked to urban sophistication and seduction, in contrast with the suburban, and its association with marriage and emasculation. She associates this with the way that *Playboy* magazine marketed a lifestyle to its readership where the 'apartment functions as the exciting expression of the person he is and the lifestyle he leads', with the bachelor pad demanding men's participation in a consumerist design culture.[42] Modernist decorating tastes in particular are aligned with the bachelor pad aesthetic, where:

> clean lines, smooth surfaces ... designer furniture made of steel, leather and wood such as an Eames Lounge chair, a Florence Knoll desk or a Noguchi coffee table" defines the playboy "in opposition to both feminine and queer tastes.[43]

In essence, *Playboy* modernism at home was shorthand for hyper-masculine virility on display and facilitated a program of sexual coercion. Text accompanying bachelor pad plans often outlined how designer furnishings might be used by *Playboy* predators. For example:

> Knoll cabinets ... hold a built-in bar. This permits the canny bachelor to remain in the room while mixing a cool one for his intended quarry ... no chance of leaving ... and returning to find her mind changed, purse in hand, and the young lady ready to go home.[44]

In this way, the architecture and furnishings of the bachelor pad lair were presented as modern technologies that assisted in the control and domination of the playboy's guests. These scenarios are not so far removed from the Bond villains' use of technological gadgets to keep their victims captive.

Playboy sexualized the modern bachelor pad as a commercial strategy, and as such might be seen as a corruption of Loos' moral ideas for modern architecture. Yet, Loos also sought a world of bachelorhood through his work. His 'reverence for male society in the military, men's clubs and the board-room' was reflected in his architecture for bars, cafes and the gentleman outfitters Knize (Figure 2.6).[45] Through these homosocial spaces he sought to reinstate masculine culture and aesthetics in the context of a world that he thought had become overtly feminized through the styles of Art Nouveau and the Weiner Werkstätte. For Loos, these overtly sensual styles had allowed women to penetrate the public sphere with effeminacy and eroticism. Rather she should stay solely in the private sphere of the domestic, and even then, the bedroom should be the place for her ornamental occupation.

Figure 2.6 Adolf Loos interior design for the gentleman's outfitters Knize, Vienna (1910–1913). Photography by Photo Studio Gerlach. Photo Credit: Imagno/Getty Images.

This demarcation between masculine and feminine space was realized in the apartment he designed for his first wife Lina, in 1908. The salon and living rooms furnished with wooden, sturdy and geometric forms were representative of the bachelor masculine realm, 'more akin to a hunting lodge than the domestic sphere'.[46] His wife's bedroom appears to be the only place she might inhabit – sheathed in gauzy fabrics, flowing white curtains and sheep-skin floor-coverings. It is worth noting the conflict here between Loos' assertion that modernist masculine architecture was morally forthright in opposition to the erotic, feminine and decorative, and Loos' own sexual morality. As Colomina outlines, Loos was accused of paedophilia and had a succession of child-like wives and affairs with very young women, suggesting that: 'Loos' public moralism denouncing ornament as a savage perversion is perhaps a pathological symptom of what it attacks, a disguise, a displacement.'[47] Certainly Loos personal behaviour casts him in the realm of the playboy in a similar mould to Bond.

Given the link between the modern suit, modern architecture and the playboy lifestyle I have outlined here, it is somewhat antithetical that Bond seems to hold such disdain for the modern home. The Regency style, Georgian home he inhabits in *Dr. No* and the barely furnished apartment of *Spectre* are curiously at odds with Bond's otherwise fashionable, luxurious and technologically advanced consumer desires. Bond is presented as a modern man on the go, racing cars and commandeering speedboats, he is travelled and experienced. It is clear he lives a life of hedonism and pleasure as well as pursuit. His lack of interest in the interior suggests a lack of 'interiority', that is, a lack of inner life. As theorized by Walter Benjamin, regarding the emergence of individual persona and its relationship to the decorated room as a marker of the inhabitant's personality – the concept of interiority is concerned with both the psychological effects a space might have on its inhabitant, and how the space might be configured by the inhabitant to reflect individual subjectivity.[48] Bond's house, with its blank walls and banal furnishings that provide little insight into his personal tastes, acts as the mask rather than the suit. Indeed, the suit in *Spectre* gives us clues to Bond's inner turmoil, its visibly restricting tightness is metaphoric of his desire to break free from the constraints of his role as spy. This is not so true of Bond's adversaries who are just as much playboy dandies as the franchise hero, all of whom seem to revel in modern interior decoration.

The formula of master-criminal inhabiting ultra-modern and remote lair became a leitmotif for set-designer Ken Adam in *Dr. No*, *Goldfinger* (1964), and *Diamonds Are Forever* (1971). This style has been further perpetuated in the recent films *Quantum of Solace* (2008) and *Spectre* designed by Dennis Gassner, who draws on Adam's original aesthetics. According to architectural critic Steve Rose, Bond's desire to destroy modern architecture was based in his creator, Ian Fleming's scorn for the style, after his neighbour, Italian architect Erno Goldfinger demolished Victorian houses to build modern villas on Willow Road in Hampstead. The act provided Fleming with the name for one of his most notorious villains and a recurring finale where Bond demolishes modernism in his victory over schemes of world domination.[49] For Adam, a trained architect, and set designer for seven of the early James Bond movies, modernism represented power and material wealth. Parallels between architectural order and Cold War villains' desires for a 'new world order' were epitomized in sets for Dr. No's Command centre, Goldfinger's Rumpus room and Ernst Blofeld's Lair in *You Only Live Twice* (1967). Despite Bond's eye for style in the form of the suit, his seeming dislike for modernism at home represents conservative and traditional values in conflict with his playboy image.

One of the most memorable of Bond's modernist architectural nemeses is Elrod House, in *Diamonds Are Forever* (1971). Designed by John Lautner for interior designer Arthur Elrod in 1968, like his mentor Frank Lloyd Wright's Fallingwater, it incorporates natural formations with modernist materials of concrete and glass. Built on the side of a mountain, with sweeping desert vistas, the cinematic references to the Vandamm House of *North by Northwest* and its panoptic view, along with remote location on a precipice, reinforces the relationship between modernist architecture, domination of the landscape and devious desires. While both Lautner and Wright sought to incorporate rock formations, water features and wooden surfaces in their architecture as a way of softening and humanizing the cold, stark surfaces of modernism, on film these types of spaces instead suggest a villainous control over nature. Lautner's architecture has frequently featured in similar roles, including the Sheats-Goldstein House as a pornographer's den in *The Big Lebowski* (1998), the Malin House as home to a sexual voyeur in *Body Double* (1984) and the Garcia house as drug smuggler's hide out in *Lethal Weapon II* (1989). The circular architectural forms and wide-reaching views of Lautner's Elrod House appealed to Adam as set designer for their ability to symbolically convey the Bond villain's lair as a command centre to enable world domination. He described it as a 'fantastic house made of reinforced concrete. It was very futuristic, and I thought, 'I couldn't have designed it better myself'.[50]

In *Diamonds Are Forever*, Elrod House plays a fortress designed to hide a kidnapped Hugh Hefner type billionaire, guarded by two 'playmate'-like swimsuit-clad adversaries, Bambi (Lola Larson) and Thumper (Trina Parks). The sequence begins with a cream linen-suited Connory navigating the circular concrete structure of the house and a series of glass doors, to be confronted by Bambi – who cartwheels out of the womanly shaped Gaetano Pesce UP5 armchair, and Thumper – who lounges seductively on the building's internal rock formation (Figure 2.7). The titillating fight scene that ensues involves unnecessary acrobatic prowess, the destruction of a glass coffee table, a thigh clenching headlock and Bond's catapult out of an open window into the swimming pool below. A playboy's dream, Bond appears almost at home, or at least to enjoy the erotic wrestling.

The link between Bond films and playboy style is further reinforced in the photo-story depicting Elrod House, 'A Playboy Pad: Pleasure on the Rocks' in the November 1971 issue of the magazine.[51] Like Bond movies, particular

Figure 2.7 Lola Larson as Bambi, Elrod House interior, *Diamonds Are Forever* (1971). Credits: Guy Hamilton (Director), Eon Productions (Film Production). Screen still.

attention is paid to the technological gadgets that operate the home, as well as spatial arrangements which would presumably help in the bachelor's seductive performance – including a king-sized shower, tiled mirrored sauna, mini-bar and bed with lighting control panel. It is worth noting here the way in which Lautner's architecture at Elrod House positioned the bedroom so that it would extend directly onto the living space. This configuration suggests a social exhibitionism of sexual performativity. Not unlike the portrayal of bedrooms in women's films, the bedrooms of playboy architecture are associated with sexual promiscuity – though a much more socially sanctioned form. In the same way that *Playboy* turned sex and women's bodies into representational visual consumption, modern architecture and design are presented as an erotic and elicit fetish. The real-world Elrod House, like the many modernist 'Playboy Pads' that featured in the magazine, is described as an architecture of seduction, where the fantasy of hosting some acrobatic swimsuit models, doesn't seem entirely out of the question. *Playboy* magazine essentially equates Bond's character as suave, sophisticated sex symbol with the suit he owns and a modernist home that fits with his image as a bachelor.

Cinema and consumer magazines were not alone in conflating American mid-century architecture such as Lautner's Elrod House with playboy imagery. As the prominent architectural historian Sigfried Giedion wrote in the introduction to the fifth edition of *Space, Time and Architecture*, fashionable architecture of the 1960s is 'a kind of playboy-architecture ... an architecture treated as playboy's treat life, jumping from one sensation to another'.[52] While Giedion was critical of this style of fashionable modern architecture, American consumer society was much more receptive. The glamour of playboy architecture appealed to the aspirational ideals of middle-class male consumers who sought social mobility, economic prosperity and sexual fantasy. The triangulation of Bond's fashionable persona, playboy identities and modernist design produced the body, interiors and architecture as sites for men to seduce women. In this way, architectural modernism, design and the suit are in fact not in conflict at all. While modernism was connected to the Machiavellian in the movies, pitted against stylishly suited sex symbol spies, together they represented a lifestyle of hedonistic pleasure and luxurious consumer culture. While Loos argued for the suppression of fashion in both clothing and architecture as a sociopolitical critique of distinction through taste, where lack of ornamentation opposed the conspicuous display of wealth, instead modernist architecture and the suit appealed to middle-class consumerist bachelor dandy identities for their ability to convey these very attributes.

Interestingly, and in contradiction with the heterosexist fantasies perpetuated by *Playboy*, an alternative version of the relationship between modernist architecture and the suit is also present in spy films, where queer characters also tend to inhabit these spaces. For example, *North by Northwest*'s Leonard (Martin Landau) is stereotypically represented in the realm of Production Code gay, concealing his homoerotic and 'immoral' desires for his partner in crime, Vandamm. The cut of his suit is tight and slim, as Lehmann argues, suggestive of a feminine silhouette.[53] Leonard and Vandamm's shared interest in objet d'art and unclear living arrangements inside the Fallingwater styled lair are further suggestive of stereotypical Hollywood representations of queer characters. Similar to the characters in Hitchcock's *Rope* (1948), *North by Northwest* equates overt concern for wardrobe and interior décor with moral depravity and homosexuality. Wojcik pinpoints that the bachelor pad in Alfred Hitchcock's *Rope*, 'participates in the discourse of the closet ... in which one can try on, secrete or disclose one's identity'.[54] Apprehension surrounding men's domestic behaviour becomes code for homosexuality. The representation of gay protagonists and modernist interiors will be explored further in Chapter 3, through the case study of Tom Ford's *A Single Man* (2009). Here, however, it is worth drawing attention to the social conditions that contributed to these cinematic associations. As Potvin outlines in

Bachelors of a Different Sort, queer bachelors were often perceived as a threat to heteronormative ideals. Bachelor homemaking activities were equally conceived as aberrant in their propensity for extravagance, decoration and artifice where:

> Gayness, in patriarchal ideology, is the repository of whatever is symbolically expelled from hegemonic masculinity, the items ranging from fastidious taste in home decoration to receptive anal pleasure. Hence from the point of view of hegemonic masculinity, gayness is easily assimilated to femininity.[55]

In the case of *North by Northwest,* homosexuality is portrayed as a literal threat to heteronormativity, where presumably if Leonard was able to kill Eve as he had intended, the way would be open for him to pursue a relationship with Vandamm. The relationship between homosexual identities, modernist styling and threats to heterosexuality has often been suggested within the Bond franchise, where villains including Le Chiffre in *Casino Royale,* and Raoul Silva in *Skyfall* have been coded queer. The 'deviant' behaviour of these characters is problematically associated with their sexual orientation. The Bond villain's taste for glamorous modern architecture is just another stereotype of queer deviancy perpetuated by Hollywood, where a love of surface style, much as Loos suggested, is seen as a crime against heteronormative convention. The relationship between queer identities and modernist aesthetics might appear at odds with Loos homophobic views on anti-ornamentalism – an idea alluded to when he claims 'the person who runs around in a velvet suit is no artist but a buffoon or merely a decorator.'[56] However, modernism – if regarded as a style – can be understood as a strategy of survival to avoid surveillance for those performing queer identities.[57] As we will see in the following chapter, the gender-based assumptions that are associated with fashion and the interior on film are more complex than simple readings of modernism as a heroic, heterosexual masculine pursuit might have us believe.

3

Luxurious longings: Queer heterotopias in décor and dress

The concept of 'camp' has been a useful mechanism within queer discourse as a means of interpreting and encoding the visual and stylistic excesses of cinema to expose gender and sexuality as performative constructs.[1] During the Production Code era of classic Hollywood cinema, performances by Greta Garbo, Bette Davis and Joan Crawford, along with the extravagant dances of Busby Berkeley, or the lavish costumes of Adrian, might be understood by queer audiences as operating within the camp paradigm. Film historians Harry Benshoff and Sean Griffin explain that, 'shared appreciation of certain films and stars was a way for queer communities to coalesce and feel a sense of connection.'[2] Camp – as a practice of reception and representation – is understood as both performative mode and aesthetic sensibility.

Consensus on the constituents of camp and its affiliation with queer aesthetics is much contested, with debates surrounding its association to specific genders, cultures, tastes and styles. Here, I am interested in camp as a self-conscious stylistic construction relevant to the interpretation of fashion and the interior on film.[3] Susan Sontag's 'Notes on Camp', while obscuring much of camp's queer sensibility, identifies artifice and stylization as central components to camp aesthetics. For Sontag:

> Clothes, furniture, all the elements of visual décor for instance make up a large part of Camp. For Camp art is often decorative art, emphasizing texture, sensuous surface and style at the expense of content.[4]

This is not to suggest that all fashion or interior design on film can be read through the lens of camp, but rather acknowledges the significance of appearances, surfaces and style to certain queer audiences. Jack Babuscio, who focuses on film in 'Camp and the Gay Sensibility', draws attention to these same stylistic devices. However, he argues that camp's emphasis on sensuous surfaces is not devoid of politics, nor empty of meaning as Sontag suggests; rather it is an expression of emotion, a means of asserting identity and performing a role.[5] Within this discourse of aesthetic excess and artifice, I propose the aesthetics of nostalgia as another element in this lexicon of queer cinematic style.

Queer nostalgia in cinema can be understood as a mode of camp; where, as Mark Booth contends, camp recreates retrograde, outmoded versions of the past, redefined in ways that are ironic.[6] However, more melancholy and romantic forms of nostalgia are also relevant to the aesthetic pleasures of queer cinema. The films primarily under discussion here, *Carol* (2015), *A Single Man* (2009) and *Laurence Anyways* (2012), are indicative of a queer sensibility where highly stylized dress and dècor are fundamental forms of dramatic storytelling. It is important here to note, that following Janet Jacobsen, I use the term queer throughout this chapter as a noun – for example, to describe space, as an identity that is not heteronormative and as a verb – a way of doing that that challenges or resists expectations or norms.[7] Through an examination of queer nostalgia on screen, I argue that these films develop the aesthetics of 'camp' to produce a new type of queer heterotopic space. These 'other spaces' challenge the order of things by subverting the ordinary to reveal contradictions and disrupt time and space, allowing for queer histories to emerge as sites of pleasure, desire, longing and kinship.

Queer nostalgia as a cinematic style

Literary theorist, Svetlana Boym describes nostalgia as reflective, embracing longing, loss and the imperfect process of remembrance, it is 'a romance of one's own fantasy'.[8] However, queer nostalgia is in some ways contradictory, as the past is not idealized, nor necessarily fondly remembered. The lived experience of queer people is often a history of stigma, shame and suffering – something to be overcome. In this way queer nostalgia is a reminder of what the present lacks and hints at what a utopian future might look like. It suggests fluidity between past, present and future to arrive at other ways of being in the world.

Much queer nostalgia in cinema, imagines a melancholy view of the closeted past in order to view the present as progressive, but often fails to critique current conditions.[9] Certainly, the representation of queer romances in cinema is predominantly a history of tragedy, loneliness, depression and oppression. It is only more recently – in the wake of the Stonewall riots in 1973, the effects of gay liberation, the influence of avant-garde cinema and the development of New Queer Cinema in the 1990s – that narratives challenging heteronormative stereotypes, celebrating a variety of queer identities and diverse sexualities emerged on screen.[10]

Heritage cinema, as Richard Dyer argues, has also been 'notably hospitable to the homosexual subject' affirming 'the place of queers in cultural patrimony' where dress and décor are the 'defining pleasures of heritage spectacle'.[11] Many historical biopics and period fictions of queer experience, while not designated as heritage films, similarly rely on developing an aesthetics of nostalgia that signals a reimagining of past familiar styles. For example, Todd Haynes' *Carol*, Tom Ford's *A Single Man* and Xavier Dolan's *Laurence Anyways* follow histories of queer tragic romance that highlight past oppression. Yet, they also complicate the problems of the past in that they produce an aesthetic form of viewing pleasure. The longing and loss associated with the past is not a fantasy of returning to that time, but rather an attempt at recuperating a history of queer desire. Queer nostalgia involves a retelling of the past in order to create a LGBTQI heritage with its own imaginaries, symbols and stories.[12] I argue that queer nostalgia is constituted through the aesthetic tone of sensuous surface to depict queer desire as pleasurable in order to produce a past that is not just fraught with difficulty, but also luxuriates in longing.[13]

The aesthetics of nostalgia, especially in décor and dress are often coded queer. Interior design historian Christopher Reed observes that queer spaces often reclaim and exaggerate past historical styles, such as Victorian ornamentation or Art Deco, where: 'extravagant interior décor signifies gay space in Hollywood'.[14] Devotion to beauty has often been positioned as pejorative, and to suggest a relationship between queer ways of seeing and aestheticism might easily fall prey to essentialist stereotypes in how to account for the overt presence of style in these films. Indeed, numerous film critics have suggested that all three of these films privilege style over substance, and surface over emotional depth.[15] However, to dismiss the emotional content contained in surface details would be to overlook a history of queer coding that was affirming in certain cinematic contexts, and fails to see that the aesthetics of sumptuous surface are a transgression against patriarchal norms of aesthetic austerity.

Queering surface and space

Based on Patricia Highsmith's novel *The Price of Salt* (1952), Todd Haynes' *Carol* tells the story of a burgeoning lesbian relationship between a department store shopgirl Therese (Rooney Mara), and a wealthy housewife Carol (Cate Blanchett). The narrative is problematized by the sexually repressive culture of 1950s America, and the heterosexual relationships that both women are involved in. From the outset Haynes uses overt stylization as a mode of 'queering' the audience's perspective – that is challenging normative viewpoints – where he notes that:

There are a lot of films with gay subjects ... that are formally very straight and don't challenge the dominant ways of representing the world. And films like some of Hitchcock's or Sirk's that have these weird, perverse, complex perspectives that can be far more gay than most movies about gay themes – because they're coming from an outsider's perspective and change how you see things.[16]

In the case of *Carol*, Judy Becker's production design and Sandy Powell's costume design are responsible for the deeply sensuous surfaces and styles that punctuate the film's mise-en-scène. The pleasures of surface are central to the audience's understanding of Carol and Therese's desire for each other. It is a love story based in looking, but also in small gestures and touch, where studied attentiveness to textural details reveals the character's deeper desires. From their initial meeting at the department store, tactile surface and the longings of touch are conveyed through Carol's luxurious, plush fur coat, emphasized by its juxtaposition with the ratty appearance of the fake fur trimming of Therese's Santa Claus hat (Figure 3.1). In the transaction that follows Carol leaves her smooth, grey kid-leather gloves as an invitation to Therese's touch. This sartorial catalyst to their relationship conveys the significance of clothing to our understanding of both characters. Here we see concepts of the masquerade and interiority at play, where Carol's restrictive tailored silhouette reminds us of her confinement to rigid heteronormative societal expectations, while Therese's transformation

Figure 3.1 Contrasting textures. Rooney Mara as Therese and Cate Blanchett as Carol in *Carol* (2015). Credits: Todd Haynes (Director), Number 9 Films, Film 4, Killer Films (Film Production). Screen still.

from childlike Peter Pan collars to sophisticated plaid suits tells of her growing confidence and self-awareness.

Clothing also comes to represent the intimate space between their bodies. For example, a sequence where Therese smells Carol's teal-blue sweater and gently caresses her peach-coloured camisole neatly folded in a suitcase subtly implies the disrobing of Carol's cool demeanour to find the softness beneath, and creates a sense of sexual frisson. Erotic effect is similarly implied in two moments where Carol places her hand on Therese's shoulder that bookend the couple's romance. These instances are tightly shot, making us pay close attention to the textures and tones that the protagonist wear in a way that slows down time, so that we might also linger in the languid moments of their longing for each other (Figure 3.2). A squeeze of a shoulder, a touch of a cuff or a smoothing of a skirt presents audiences with a highly pleasurable surface experience of the sensuality of textiles, creating spectatorial identification and desire. These cherished moments captured in cloth are a metaphor for Carol's and Therese's love materialized through the desire to touch the body beneath, the space held in fabric is this anticipated moment unfolded. Haynes' obsession with surface here is reminiscent of his earlier film, *Far from Heaven,* which similarly deals with forbidden love, both gay and interracial. He described the approach of this earlier film – which equally applies to Carol – as: 'an embodiment of dissident

Figure 3.2 Attention to fabric. Rooney Mara as Therese and Cate Blanchett as Carol in *Carol* (2015). Credits: Todd Haynes (Director). Number 9 Films, Film 4, Killer Films (Film Production). Screen still.

desire that is too overwhelming for its characters and thus spills out into the world, of things, objects and costumes'.[17]

Fine details depicting heightened emotional content are similarly present in Tom Ford's adaptation of Christopher Isherwood's 1964 novel, *A Single Man*. The film follows a day in the life of George Falconer (Colin Firth) as he grieves the death of his partner of sixteen years, Jim (Matthew Goode) and contemplates suicide. Engaging with a nostalgic interpretation of 1960s design, inherent artifice is again a mode of mise-en-scène that constitutes a visual language associated with queer desire. As the film progresses, pleasure in surface becomes increasingly palpable as George begins to see beauty in all that surrounds him through an intensification of colour. Similar to Haynes approach in *Carol*, colour, surface and style are presented as a queer way of seeing – asserting the protagonist's vision at a time of queer invisibility. As established in Chapter 2, this perspective differs from the patriarchal restraints of modernism that historically positioned colour, decoration and ornamentation as deviant, overtly feminine and queer.[18] In this way, as film theorist Kirsten Moana Thompson suggests, *A Single Man* represents colour and attention to surface as embodied sexual passion, and presents the central character George, as 'an artfully constructed series of beautiful surfaces'.[19] However, as I delineate here, these surfaces are not without meaning or emotion.

Arianne Phillips' costume design portrays George's character as a carefully composed perfectionist through his impeccably tailored, slim-fit suits. His ritual of dressing – one of the opening scenes of the film – is, as George describes, 'a layer of polish' that helps him to perform a role. George's suit is understood as a fabrication, an impersonation of conservatism and rigidity that masks his sexual identity, while his female friend, Charley (Julianne Moore) is also presented as overly concerned with appearances through her chic 1960s geometric fashions and lush, Moroccan inspired interiors (Figure 3.3).

Rich colour and attention to fashioned surfaces, coupled with the presence of Moore, creates intertextual dialogue with Haynes' *Far from Heaven* (2002), and in turn, the Sirkian melodrama *All That Heaven Allows* (1955). As queer film theorist Brett Farmer explains, 'with its scenarios of sexual and social transgression and its highly stylised *mise-en-scène*, the melodrama opens a space for queer ... meaning and desire.'[20] A queer sensibility is common to all of these films, where the aesthetics of fashion, interiors and objects stand in for emotional content and the inner lives of characters. Yet, *A Single Man* plays with the possibilities of queer nostalgia beyond reference to previous camp cinematic styles and 1960s design fetishism. The diegesis of the film revolves around the fluidity between past,

Figure 3.3 Surface style. Colin Firth as George and Julianne Moore as Charlie in *A Single Man* (2009). Credits: Tom Ford (Director), Artina Films, Depth of Field and Fade to Black (Film Production). Screen still.

present and future. George is constantly reminded of his lover Jim and revisits past moments of their life together. These scenes are imbued with lush tonal qualities that are replicated in his present as he becomes aware of the beauty, love and desire that appear in his daily life, so hinting at the possibilities of the future.

Perhaps even more than his clothes, George's mid-century modern house provides insight into his character. Architect John Lautner's Schaffer Residence, designed in 1949, is here cast against type. Modernism in this film is not presented as evil or menacing, though Ford may well be playing with the conventions of Hollywood cinema that also attributed the modernist home to the deviant sexuality of 'bachelors of a different sort'. In his study of the queer aesthetics and the lived experiences of notable homosexual men in Britain in the early twentieth century, Potvin investigates how these men who lived together, 'sought to redefine the parameters of domestic life and fashion a new cultural order' through the design of their domestic interiors.[21] We might then understand *A Single Man*'s George and his Lautner designed home through the aesthetics of queer sensibility, representing modern domesticity as a space where interiority, shared tastes, emotional bonds, comfort, pleasure, intimacy, kinship and love are present. This is vastly different to the playboy pad representation of Lautner's Elrod House in the Bond classic *Diamonds Are Forever*, discussed in Chapter 2.

The house's mood mimics George's interiority. Its red-wood walls, vast glass surfaces and beige and grey décor are at times melancholy, cold and lonely. Conversely, in a number of scenes in which George looks through the house's windows and glimpses back to his previous life with Jim, the interiors are warmly lit, but also cluttered with books, objects and soft furnishings that reflect the fullness of these moments (Figure 3.4). Nostalgia bleeds through the mise-en-scène as sensual encounters with the past, but also connects to imminent possibilities of the future. In the final scenes of the film, when George brings potential love interest Kenny (Nicolas Hoult) home, the house vibrates with emotion (Figure 3.5). Its wooden surfaces reflect orange and red tones suggestive of intimacy and passion that George and Kenny might yet share, provoking George to rethink his suicide and instead live in the present.

In this way, nostalgia is represented in its conventional form – through George's longing for his relationship with his dead lover. Yet, the house also provides insight to queer nostalgia for contemporary audiences. The glass exterior walls of the Schaffer house prompt a dialogue between the protagonists about the visibility of George and Jim's relationship, and remind viewers that at the time of the film's setting, homosexuality was culturally in the closet. As Potvin's study highlights, homosexuality was often perceived as a threat to the stability of domesticity and heteronormativity: 'not only were homosexual, gay or queer men meant to perform closeted identities in the public domain, but

Figure 3.4 John Lautner Schaffer Residence. Colin Firth as George in *A Single Man* (2009). Credits: Tom Ford (Director), Artina Films, Depth of Field and Fade to Black (Film Production). Screen still.

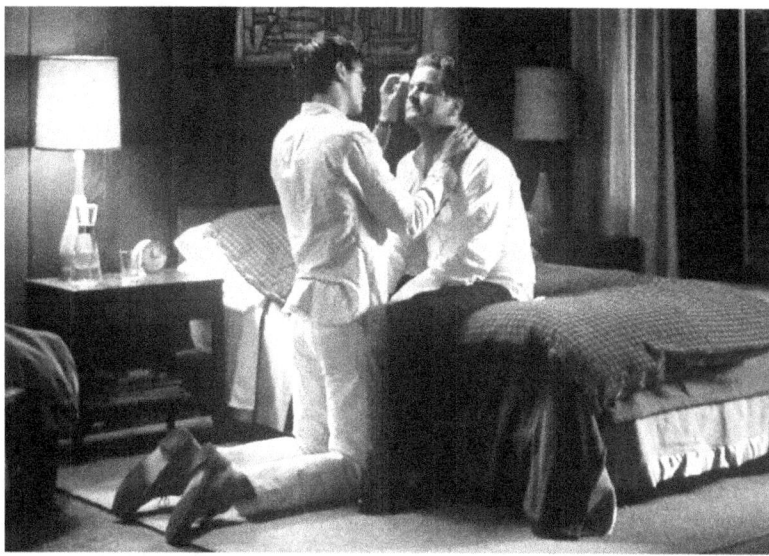

Figure 3.5 The intimate interior. Colin Firth as George and Nicolas Hoult as Kenny in *A Single Man* (2009). Credits: Tom Ford (Director), Artina Films, Depth of Field and Fade to Black (Film Production). Screen still.

they were also meant to be invisible within the supposed safety of their home.'[22] The closet as the 'defining structure of gay oppression', as described by Eve Kosofsky Sedgwick, denies, conceals, erases and makes invisible queer sexual identities.[23] For George and Jim to co-exist in their glass house made their homosexual relationship visible to their neighbours, so inviting the possibility of persecution. Yet, their cohabitation also plays with understandings of the closet, which is not only seen as a space of shameful secrecy, but can also be a site of nurturing, pleasure and becoming. Their relationship is presented as decidedly domestic, caring and intimate. In his influential book, *Queer Space*, Aaron Betsky argues for the complexities of 'the closet' as a psychologically nuanced space of interiority and a physical space that:

> Contains the building blocks for your social constructions, such as your clothes … a place to hide, to create worlds for yourself out of the past and for the future in a secure environment … the closet contains both the secret recesses of the soul and the masks that you wear.[24]

A Single Man overtly connects the relationship between fashion and the interior to George's interiority and anxieties around the visibility of his sexual identity. His carefully constructed, fashioned exterior, conveyed through his clothes is an integral part of his disguise. The mask that he shows to the world is similarly created inside the sanctuary of his home which conveys an equally polished surface interior of glamorous modernism. Yet, we also understand this space as the locus for George's nostalgic, emotional yearnings for his past life of domestic pleasure with his partner, Jim. As such, I suggest that George's house is closer to a queer heterotopia than a closet, its glass walls at times act like a mirror, producing a space in between past, present and future. A space that simultaneously reveals and conceals, where he can reconstitute his identity according to context and desire for visibility or invisibility as he crosses thresholds between public and private.

Queer heterotopias: Motels and mirrors

For Michel Foucault, heterotopias are 'other' spaces that deviate from the ordinary spaces we inhabit through a disruption of time and space. He includes examples such as cemeteries, cinemas, brothels, museums and libraries; spaces which replicate normalcy while simultaneously calling it into question through ways that merge past and present are both isolated yet penetrable, or juxtapose illusion with the real. The motel, for example, is a site where illicit sex might take place, sheltered and hidden, it is a space that anyone can enter but is also a space of exclusion.[25] Extending this concept, 'queer heterotopias' are 'places where individuals are "free" to perform their gender and sexuality without fear of being qualified, marginalised or punished' outside of the norms of heterocentrist space.[26]

The concept of queer heterotopias is complicated in *Carol*, where we are constantly reminded that the protagonists are confined by the society that they live in and the tragic choices that must be made, here true freedom is not possible. Yet, within the diegesis queer heterotopias emerge as reminders of the possibilities that may be available in the future. For example, the road trip Carol and Therese take to explore their relationship is punctuated by a series of hotel rooms in which their desire can take its expression. They are other worlds within the other world of nostalgic 1950s America. Motel and hotel rooms are familiar domestic spaces that, for these women, lie outside the traditional heteronormative households that entrap them, giving them permission to act otherwise to their confining heterosexual roles.

The first of these spaces is the Presidential Suite at a motel in Ohio (Figure 3.6). The tones of the room are olive greens, beige and brown, with Victorian replica furniture, Americana wallpaper and printed curtains. The contrast of textures in the scene – velveteen upholstery, an angora throw, satin cushions, Carol's silk pyjamas and tweed dressing gown – while incongruous, creates a

Figure 3.6 The Presidential Suite. Rooney Mara as Therese and Cate Blanchett as Carol in *Carol* (2015). Credits: Todd Haynes (Director), Number 9 Films, Film 4, Killer Films (Film Production). Screen still.

sense of intimacy and comfort as the women flirtatiously play with make-up. Here, they are able to be relaxed in their attraction to one another as they perform the masquerades of gender. The next hotel in their travels, The Drake in Chicago, is traditionally luxurious. Chintz floral curtains and pink striped upholstery are sentimentally romantic. Therese's excited exclamation: 'This furniture, this fabric' draws our attention to how physical space reflects the interiority of the character's emotions as they enter into another realm of feeling for each other.

Their final motel stay is the most dire, reflecting the situation of their relationship exposed, and the consequences for Carol's custody battle. The room's vivid chartreuse green is a visual climax to the persistence of the colour throughout the film's sets in various shades. Scriptwriter Phyllis Nagy has described how it was important that the hotel where the physical consummation of Carol and Therese's desire takes place should be mundane: 'an ordinary place, ordinary women in an extraordinary situation'.[27] As a queer heterotopia it is far from a glamorous space, though the intensity of surface colour is suggestive of other worldliness far from the aesthetics of traditional domesticity. The indication of this being a queer heterotopic space is further reinforced through a seduction scene that begins as a reflection in a mirror (Figure 3.7).[28]

Figure 3.7 Mirror as queer heterotopia. Rooney Mara as Therese and Cate Blanchett as Carol in *Carol* (2015). Credits: Todd Haynes (Director), Number 9 Films, Film 4, Killer Films (Film Production). Screen still.

For Foucault, the mirror is a heterotopia, a virtual space that opens up on the other side of the glass, both real and unreal. As he explains:

> In the mirror, I see myself there where I am not … I am over there where I am not … From the standpoint of the mirror I discover my absence from the place where I am since I see myself over there … The mirror functions as a heterotopia in this respect: it makes this place that I occupy at the moment that I look at myself in the glass absolutely real, connected with all that surrounds it, and absolutely unreal, since in order to be perceived it has to pass through this virtual point which is over there.[29]

As a queer heterotopic space the mirror opens up another world for Carol and Therese in which their love is possible, a place beyond where they currently stand where they can speak openly of their desire for each other. At once we see where they are not, but also where they could be, reminding viewers of the constraints of history and the possibilities of the future. Just as the mirrored qualities of George's modernist glass house allowed him to revisit his past love with Jim in *A Single Man*, queer heterotopias elucidate the dynamics of nostalgia as a space of loss and longing, a temporality that is in the past, of the moment, and not here yet. In this way audiences are positioned to view both these films as if they were Hollywood melodramas from the 1950s and 1960s, inserting queer experiences retrospectively to open up these unrecognized histories in the present. Importantly, the surfaces of queer heterotopias not only allow for movement between multiple temporalities, they also function to create transition spaces where fluid identities and sexualities are made possible.

Betsky's architectural treatise on queer space also draws attention to the symbolic significance of the mirror to queer identity, a space of appearance, 'free and open, shifting and ephemeral'.[30] The mirror represents something of queer experience, an alternative space where the world is reordered allowing for gender and sexual fluidity. Queer theorist, Fabio Cleto provides some insight as to the role of mirrors in the performance of gender and sexuality as masquerade:

> The history and theory of camp is a theory and history of gazes ... apparatuses of display ... and Mirrors ... the made-up camp eye [sees] a lot ... it tells the truth of masks ... That is what camp *re-cognition* displays, reimagining ordinariness as it reacknowledges it, appreciating the limits and excesses of perception ... is the overstylized, self-fashioning gesture of reinvention.[31]

This aspect of the mirror, as a queer heterotopic space of self-recognition and transformation, is further examined in Xavier Dolan's *Laurence Anyways* (2012). Similar to Haynes and Ford, Dolan's cinematic style challenges traditional cinematic conventions of surface, with an emphasis on fashion and the interior in order to represent themes of gender and sexual identity.

Spanning a ten-year period that begins in the late 1980s, the narrative follows Laurence Alia's (Melvin Poupaud) transition from man to woman and her shifting relationship with girlfriend Fred (Suzanne Clement).[32] After establishing the passionate and performative nature of their romance, the film shifts to examine Laurence's process of transition and Fred's ambivalence towards her partner's gender self-actualization that ultimately leads to the couple's separation. A pivotal moment, signalling Fred's acceptance of Laurence's identity as a woman, occurs in the intimate space of their bathroom, in which Fred watches Laurence apply make-up in a small handheld mirror. Laurence's carefully made-up eye, reflected back to her in the mirror, sees herself as herself, reinvented and reimagined. The dialogue is telling, when Fred encourages Laurence to use the large mirror, she replies 'I know what I look like', implying that the larger mirror would break the illusion of Laurence's carefully composed vision of herself – that her overall appearance does not completely comply with her identity. This scene represents a queer way of seeing that challenges heteronormative and patriarchal attitudes towards pleasure in appearance, and opens up the possibility for understanding queer heterotopias as sites for transformation.

Fashioning queer heterotopic space

As with *Carol* and *A Single Man*, *Laurence Anyways* – through Dolan's costume design and art direction – positions pleasure in surface and style as a central mediator between queer relationships. The opening sequence in which Laurence showers Fred with laundry while she lies asleep in their richly hued azure blue bedroom is accompanied by dialogue that is revisited throughout the film regarding the nature of what minimizes their pleasure – a discussion that often centres around colour, sound and sensuality. Suffusion of colour bleeds across scenes to suggest mood, affect and emotion; a throbbing purple discotheque full of latent possibility and a red-light that highlights the erotic sentiment behind an inviting smile, are just some of the visual reminders in this film that surfaces are important to queer identities in the ways that they are enacted, encountered and encoded in everyday life. The contrast between this queer sensibility and normative ways of seeing is brought into sharp relief when Fred decides to leave Laurence to pursue a suburban life with a new partner. This shift is symbolically represented by the blinding white modernist house Fred inhabits, its blandness conveys the emotional emptiness her new life entails.

The concept of queer heterotopic space is revisited in one of the most evocative scenes of the film, in which the couple are reunited after years of living apart. Laurence and Fred decide to visit the fictitious Black Island to see if they might return to life together. As they walk down its deserted, peaceful, white streets blanketed in snow, they are showered with brightly coloured clothes falling from the sky. This rain of fashion represents their shared exuberance at being together in a space where they can be themselves, visible as a couple, outside of social restraints. For Laurence, fashion as a primary signifier of gender identity in society, is both liberating and repressive. Presenting as a man, wearing men's clothes she was unable to express her true identity, in this moment living as a woman, she is liberated by the pleasurable and expressive qualities of fashion, and so is surrounded by the possibilities of queer heterotopic space as sites of transformation and self-realization.

This scene is one of many that emphasize how surface appearances and style operate as a queer space to express fluid and diverse gender and sexual identities. Two scenes that engage nostalgic 1980s music video sequences highlight how fashion acts as a transformative self-expression. For example, Laurence's first experience at work dressed as a woman is marked by her choice to wear a forest green pencil-skirt and jacket coupled with a gold blouse, yellow heels and one long earring. Determinedly embodying her gender identity, her new look is met with a range of gazes that are bemused, embarrassed, admiring and intrigued. Set to upbeat music, in a sequence that implies a catwalk, Laurence's fearless and triumphant embrace of her identity, is a transformative fashion moment. Another scene, again set to a music video score, highlights the artificial staging of femininity. Fred, dressed in a sequined evening dress with large shoulder pads, attends a ball. Understood through the lens of Judith Butler's concept of gender performativity, Fred exaggerates her appearance of femininity to the point of impersonating a drag queen.[33] As she dramatically reasserts her heterosexual identity, sparking her return to a heteronormative lifestyle, interior and exterior qualities of gender experience are further questioned as the underlying theme of the film.

Fred's performance of womanliness as masquerade in the ball scene is just one example of how drag and camp fashions are used by Dolan as recurring leitmotifs that emphasize the negotiation of gender identity. However, as Nick Rees-Roberts suggests, Laurence's costuming also 'problematically boarders on drag ... compounded by the casting of a cisgender actor in the title role ... [it] potentially reifies and renaturalises binary difference through the narrative vehicle of transgender'.[34] In this way, the drag and camp styling of Laurence's appearance might be interpreted as misrepresenting and misgendering trans lives, with audiences possibly viewing this character as simply a man in a dress (Figure 3.8). While drag styling might be understood

Figure 3.8 Melvin Poupaud as Laurence Alia in *Laurence Anyways* (2012). Credits: Xavier Dolan (Director), Layla Films and MK2 (Film Production). Screen still.

as highlighting the performative nature of gender roles in the case of Fred's character, in the case of Laurence, it fails to adequately represent trans lived experience.

A further nuance to the deployment of drag and camp fashions in this film occurs with the introduction of the Five Roses. Following a scene in which Laurence is beaten up in a bar, she stumbles upon the home of the Five Roses, a performing family of queer characters and drag queens who inhabit a church, decorated in flamboyantly kitsch op-shop thrift (Figure 3.9). Stained-glass windows shrouded with glittery beaded curtains, leopard print sofas, gold cherub statues, candles and an abundance of 1950s lamps produce an eclectic effect which is further exaggerated by the Five Roses personal styles, consisting of kimono, plastic ponchos and 1970s brightly coloured prints. In this queer heterotopia, Laurence finds acceptance and a place of belonging for the first time. Drag and camp fashion and the interior in this instance convey the emancipatory possibilities of living outside of the societal constraints of gender normativity. This scene is also representative of subversive models of kinship, recalling the 'houses', 'mothers' and 'children' of the drag scene. As Butler outlines regarding the ballroom subculture represented in the documentary *Paris in Burning* (1990) these people:

Figure 3.9 The Five Roses in *Laurence Anyways* (2012). Credits: Xavier Dolan (Director), Layla Films and MK2 (Film Production). Screen still.

'mother' one another, 'house' one another, 'rear' one another, and the resignification of the family through these terms is not a vain or useless imitation, but the social and discursive building of community, a community that binds, cares and teaches, that shelters and enables.[35]

In both the ballroom scene, to which Butler refers, and the queer family of Five Roses into which Laurence is initiated, fashion plays a crucial role in providing a queer heterotopic space where everyday life is reordered through self-defined ways of being in the world creating a sense of community and kinship.

While it is not my intention to compare the representation of drag in *Laurence Anyways* to *Paris Is Burning*, directed by Jennie Livingston, it is appropriate to digress here from the central argument and make reference to the film due to its status as New Queer Cinema classic and influential fashion film which demonstrates how fashion, camp and drag operate as queer heterotopic space.[36] The film has sparked important debates based on issues of cross-cultural representation, voyeurism, power relations and the artifice of gender identity.[37]

Paris Is Burning documents the underground ballroom culture of New York in the late 1980s. Attended by a spectrum of gender-diverse identities primarily of African American and Hispanic descent, the ballrooms of *Paris Is Burning* are a catwalk where contestants perform their fashioned identity based on categories of dress that relate to class, race and gender. The importance of fashion to ball participants identities and the building of community relations is embedded in the organizational structure of the scene, where ball 'houses' are named in the tradition of fashion houses, such as the House of Saint Laurent, the House of Miyake-Mugler and the House of Balenciaga. This naming is a symbolic association. Rather than a reflection of a member's economic capital, it signals towards subcultural capital of identifying with a particular fashionable ethos within the scene, and importantly, helps to galvanize kinship codes of care and support. Within these 'houses' gay men and trans men and women become part of a family. Basing their looks on fashion models, performing the poses of magazine covers through 'voguing' dance moves, the constructs of fashion provide ball participants with a shared lexicon of style and a space where fashioned queer identities can be explored to transcend the systems and spaces that exclude them. For Foucault, heterotopias are real places that act as a kind of utopia, and are sites within culture that 'are simultaneously represented, contested and inverted'.[38] The queer heterotopic space of ballroom culture mediated through fashion, as represented in *Paris Is Burning*, highlights the ways that appearance, surface and style coalesce as a site that queer communities might identify with, and build a sense of connection through social inclusion and create a 'safe space' in solidarity against sexual and racial oppression.[39]

Paris Is Burning also makes visible the relationship between queer identity, fashion, celebrity and branding that is perpetuated through film media. The film's release coincided with a number of other cultural moments that brought the ballroom scene to mainstream fashion attention – including Madonna's *Vogue* video clip in 1990 – raising important questions regarding how cultural forms are appropriated and commodified within the fashion system.[40] Arguably, due to its reception as a 'fashion film' *Paris Is Burning* could not avoid this form of commodified exploitation. It is a reflection of how the fashion and film system operates within a mutually reinforcing relationship of celebrity branding, advertising and publicity in their contribution to consumer culture.[41] Certainly, *Carol*, *A Single Man* and *Laurence Anyways* engage with this system to varying degrees as well, due to their emphasis on surface as style. The way these films represent queer fashionability as integral to self-actualization is central to their circulation within consumer culture.

Luxury and surface style

The sensorial appeal of surface and style in *Carol*, *A Single Man* and *Laurence Anyways*, with their heightened attention to costuming that equates being queer with high-fashion 'looks', situates them within in the broader commercial realm of fashion editorial and branded advertising. The 'look' of each of these films is reliant on an aesthetic expressiveness of surface that is far from the 'normality' of everyday experience. Fashion and the interior are treated with heightened attention to detail in order to reconfigure the clichés of romantic love from a queer perspective. Visceral colour representations of emotion, decorative sensibility and vintage styling all contribute to an understanding that self-fashioning equates with the interior lives of characters. This approach is not dissimilar to the way in which fashion photography, branding and advertising seeks to imbue clothing with narrative appeal within consumer culture, and is also indicative of the way that the relationship between queer style, emotion and expressiveness is marketed as a cultural form.

Tom Ford's *A Single Man* has been widely criticized as a highly stylized fashion shoot and vehicle for promoting the designer's brand. Certainly, the presence of Tom Ford menswear worn by Colin Firth as George, throughout the film can be seen as an exercise in product placement. As Pamela Church Gibson suggests, the 'film rather resembles a series of commercials; it contains a number of vignettes, each with a particular visual feel.'[42] This reading highlights how the melodramatic fashion film draws on the photographic magazine editorial style to imbue both fashion and the interior with glamour, and the way that fashion and film employ intertextual branding elements. In this case, Nicholas Hoult who plays Kenny featured in the Tom Ford 2010 eyewear campaign and Tom Ford Menswear model, Jon Kortajerena played the role of Carlos in the film. Ford's claim that he identified particularly with George's character and adapted the original novel's narrative to convey autobiographical details from his own life further reinforces that this film can be closely aligned with the Tom Ford brand. As Lee Wallace observes, 'Ford's mood film relaunches homosexual style, once a coterie fashion as an aspirant brand [... and ...] retools homosexual feeling as an on-trend sensation.' Ford's foray into fashion film, as designer turned director, is indicative of the changing mediascape of fashion, where online fashion films of branded entertainment are commissioned by luxury labels for promotional purposes. Regarded as a long-form perfume commercial, *A Single Man* follows the logic of advertisement turned art cinema.[43] Ford's film can be understood as an extension of a range of branded content where auteur directors create short films for fashion houses. Lynch's *Lady Blue Shanghai* (2009) for Christian Dior, Yang Fudong's *First Spring* (2010) for Prada and Jean-Pierre Jeunet *Train de Nuit* (2009) for Chanel are just a few examples of how the cultural capital associated with acclaimed avant-garde cinema is transposed onto luxury fashion objects. This alliance is part of a broader cultural strategy adopted by fashion conglomerates that use film along with art, architecture and design to create a system of consumption that is increasingly based on immaterial value – a subject to which I will return in the second part of this book. Each of these cultural forms provides fashion with a layer of artistic longevity beyond the possibilities of a typical seasonal collection. Fashion films offer brands like Tom Ford a set of qualities that seemingly justify luxury status. In the case of *A Single Man*, the aura of a 'genius' queer designer/director, aesthetic beauty, connoisseurship and heritage are luxury values that are transposed onto Tom Ford the brand. Interestingly, these qualities appear to be a continuation of themes that are also important values to queer heritage film, a comparison that is useful in elucidating how fashionable homosexuality has been portrayed within consumer culture.

A Single Man presents audiences with a number of elements that, as Dyer argues of queer heritage cinema, envisions homosexuality 'among the attractions of pastness', affirming a history that has often been denied or ignored.[44] These elements include: the source material of queer literary heritage – in this case Isherwood's novel, queer creative direction and emphasis on aesthetic beauty and connoisseurship that 'savours the qualities and presence of dwellings, costumes, artworks, objects'.[45] *A Single Man* continues a trajectory established by films such Merchant-Ivory's *Maurice* (1987), which finds pleasure in homosexual desire in a period of oppression and self-repression. Based on E. M. Forster's semi-autobiographical novel, *Maurice* shares many of the same qualities as Ford's film, including queer authorship, creative direction and attention to surface – in particular, fashion – to convey queer identity. For example, the film's central protagonists, Maurice (James Wiley) and Clive (Hugh Grant) wear the restraints of their social condition through elegant tuxedos of stiff white collars and conservative English tailoring. As Dyer astutely observes, the well turned out gentleman is a significant element of queer heritage cinema, 'a declaration that gay men too could form part of graceful, decorous masculinity … [rather than] something abnormal … [also facilitating] the exploration of what men may find attractive in each other'.[46] Similarly, *A Single Man* represents homosexual identity as a stylish endeavour that continues a history of pleasure in dressing and being looked at. The social legitimization of dressing well is equated with an ideal of mainstream social integration. This contradiction – the pleasure of dressing in order to conform to heteronormative ideals – is also present in the way cinematic fashion is represented as aspirational to both queer and mass audiences. For example, a *British Vogue* article from November 1987 titled 'Actor's Tweeds' features Wiley, Grant and Rupert Graves to promote *Maurice* through a six-page spread of English country gentry fashions. While the article is careful to note the heterosexual identities of the actors, it highlights that 'a more emotional, feminine side' and 'depth of feeling' are desirable homosexual character traits and are overtly tied to dressing well in herringbone jackets and cashmere coats.[47] This coupling of queer fashionability with emotional expressiveness or melodrama becomes a commercial trope shared across film and magazine advertorial, creating an image of queer consumer lifestyle that is inherently tied to luxury aesthetics. In the case of the *Maurice* fashion spread for *Vogue* emotional sensitivity is equated with the subtleties of minimalist luxury styling courtesy of Armani. For Tom Ford the brand as envisaged in *A Single Man,* luxury consumerism becomes an integral component of aspirational queer lifestyle.

Xavier Dolan also engages with luxury queer lifestyle branding. As an ambassador for Louis Vuitton menswear, his promotional work for the fashion label inflects his films with another layer of stylish veneer and positions Dolan within the league of other celebrity auteur directors, including Francis Ford

Coppola, Sofia Coppola and Wes Anderson who have similarly collaborated with the brand. Since 2015, Dolan has featured in five menswear campaigns that sartorially shift between what Rees-Roberts describes as 'normative (straight) masculinity ... [in contrast] with the more seductively subversive (queer) editorial shots of Dolan in style magazines'.[48] For example, Dolan seemingly flaunts his queer sensibility in a December 2014 *L'Uomo Vogue* cover story.[49] Dressed in a series of extravagant coats and jackets, including a leopard print by Saint Laurent, along with boldly patterned styles by Burberry and Valentino, Dolan appears as bare-chested, bohemian, enfant terrible as he smokes his way through a ten-page photographic spread to promote the film *Mommy* (2014). A more polished and sophisticated version of this 'queer' image of Dolan is presented in the Louis Vuitton Men's Summer 2016 campaign. Beginning with a Dolan quote, 'aesthetics are nothing if there is no connection with meaning', the one-minute short film consists of a series of dissolving images of Dolan wearing an embroidered bomber jacket and floral printed bowling shirt.[50] The retro clothes, quiff hairstyle and tropical leafy backdrop are a nod to Dolan's vintage and camp aesthetic as seen in *Heartbeats* (*Les Amours Imaginaires*) (2010) and *Laurence Anyways*. The advertisement's voice-over espouses Dolan's views on the building of characters through costume, the designer as storyteller and the relationship between style and identity. Through this narrative, consumers are led to make the connection between Dolan's queer cinema and Louis Vuitton style. Dolan's masquerade of fashionable costumes suggests clothing as the conduit to a range of possible identities, where a wardrobe of different selves is part of a lexicon of queer aspirational lifestyle.

Interestingly, the circulating fashion imagery associated with *Carol* does not operate within the same paradigm as the queer creative director/designer discourse associated with Ford and Dolan. Rather, the potential for mass-market appeal obscures the lesbian content of the film and associated queer lifestyle branding codes and instead focuses on the trend-setting styles that might be translated into women's wardrobes. For example, a 'What's Now' advertorial for *Instyle* magazine (2015) suggests cat's eye sunglasses, lady-like gloves and a top-handle satchel, as essential purchases in capturing the Carol 'look'.[51] Similarly, *Vogue* magazine connects the style of *Carol* to contemporary fashion to inform consumers about how they might be inspired by catwalk shows at New York fashion week, asking costume designer Sandy Powell and director Todd Haynes to share their views on collections by Anna Sui, Marchesa and Thom Browne.[52] In these examples, the ways in which fashion advertising content often serves to reinforce traditional gender roles relating women to consumptive practice is clear. As Diane Waldman outlines in her analysis of 1940s Hollywood publicity campaigns, although a film might encourage oppositional readings, overwhelmingly the related publicity directed at women 'channelled their interests towards romance, marriage and consumption'.[53]

Shifting the codes of fashions associated with lesbian characters in heritage films towards consumer culture's focus on heterosexual ideals has its precedence in *Queen Christina* (1933). The film, starring Greta Garbo as a bisexual, cross-dressing seventeenth-century Swedish monarch is considered a lesbian classic for the kiss shared between Christina and her lady in waiting. The costumes, designed by Adrian, blur gender distinctions and include, stiff black-velvet smocks with white collars reminiscent of Calvinist clerical garments, a cavalier outfit of velvet tunic and trousers, and a regal bejewelled gown of Marie-Antoinette proportions. As film theorist Jane Gaines argues, the costumes in *Queen Christina* make connections between clothes and gender roles, whereby dressing in different styles, Christina is seen to perform a 'homosexual/heterosexual flip-flop'.[54] This sexual ambiguity, when translated into commercial contexts, was presented as concretely heterosexual. As Gaines outlines, 'tie-ups and co-operative advertising [such as a] window display connecting *Queen Christina* with a half price flatware sale secured the meanings of the film and resolved its fluctuations for heterosexuality'.[55] Similarly, *Queen Christina*-inspired fashion displays at department stores presented the consumption of Hollywood style within reach of everyday women, where their appeal lies in their association to Garbo and designer Adrian, rather than Christina's queer aesthetic. In this case, as with *Carol* commodity tie-ins, the film's queer meanings conveyed through costume are deflected by the fashion system as they are recontextualized in fashion advertisements, magazines and shop window dressings. Surfaces and styles that were heavily imbued with queer love and longing become emptied of these meanings and are instead flattened projections of consumer pleasure and desire. Section two of this book 'Film Interiors as Fashion Spaces', will examine the multiple ways that the fictional fashion fantasies on film have been translated into the commercial spaces of fashion, to provide further insight into the ways narrative and identity become aligned with consumer culture and the fashion system.

4

Grand entrances: Staircases, stages and fashion parades

Fashion has long been associated with theatrical excess. As sociologist Gilles Lipovetsky argues, since the fourteenth century, when rapid change in clothing and differentiated dress styles first occurred in Western Europe, fashion shifted 'overall appearance into the order of theatricality, seduction and enchanted spectacle'.[1] Lipovetsky is referring here to the fantastical fripperies of style – think the pointed tippets of medieval dress, or the baroque embellished robes of Louis XIV. Yet, he is also speaking generally of the power of fashion to create a desirable fantasy image, a dreamworld that continues to entice audiences well into the new millennium. In this way fashion cannot be separated from aesthetic seduction, where 'fashion goes hand in glove with the pleasure of seeing, but also with the pleasure of being seen, of exhibiting oneself to the gaze of others'.[2] The fashion show is in many ways the apogee of fashion's spectacular form, enticing audiences with surfaces that hold meanings and mythologies well beyond the realities of woven cloth. The spectacle of fashion, as many have argued, is deeply problematic; it can be understood to conceal the workings of patriarchy and the male gaze, as well as the mechanisms of capitalism and the real nature of commodity transactions that obscure human labour.[3] Yet, these aesthetic excesses also open new possibilities for individual creative expression and complex social negotiations of identity. The performance of fashion in the fashion show, while a commercial endeavour, is also a form of visual pleasure that at its heart is a transformation story, predicated on the radical changes of appearance and symbolically, social situation.

While the relationship between the fashion show and cinema has been examined by fashion and film historians including Sarah Berry, Caroline Evans and Charlotte Herzog, the spatial affordances that enable this spectacle to operate so effectively across modes of representation are rarely examined.[4] This chapter contends that staircases and stages are visual cues that support narratives of character transformation and transcendence while simultaneously spectacularizing a fashion moment. Here, I make the case for the staircase as fashion icon across cinema, photography, fashion parades and retail environments.[5]

Staging the salon: When the lights are lowered to a rosy glow

The British couturière Lucile, also known as Lady Duff Gordon, has been widely credited for introducing a theatrical element to the staging of fashion shows in 1900.[6] She recounts in her memoir that, based on her experience designing for the West End, she was the first to install a stage at one end of the couture salon – complete with footlights and framed by an olive chiffon curtain.[7] In addition, she hired a number of beautiful working-class women as mannequins, and alluded to the relationship between fashion and narrative with her 'Gowns of Emotion'.[8] Duff Gordon described the transformational and enchanting effect of her clothes displayed in this manner:

> When the lights are lowered to a rosy glow, and soft music is played, and the mannequins parade, there is not a woman in the audience, though she may be fat and middle-aged, who is not seeing herself looking at those slim, beautiful girls … And that is the inevitable prelude to buying.[9]

Here, the couturière might as well be referring to the effects of the cinema spectacle on female audiences. The theatrical staging of fashion shows was no doubt a prelude to later developments in film where drama, star quality and the performance of fashion collide to instigate consumptive desire. Film historian Sarah Berry elucidates these origins further: 'Hollywood's use of fashion as spectacle has its roots in entertainment forms like the theatrical tableau, night club revue … and fashion show.'[10]

Lucile's salon innovations were soon adopted by a number of French couturiers including Paul Poiret, Jeanne Paquin and Maison Beer, all of whom installed stages to striking effect. The stage, slightly raised, with two or three steps leading down to the salon floor, offered couture customers an opportunity to view fashion within the frame of atmospheric fantasy, but also alluded to how one might 'appear' to admiring onlookers. Articles in magazines such as *Vogue* frequently reported on the elaborate staging of fashion shows to their readers. For example, an article on 'The House of Nicole Grout' from 1927 explains the setting where:

The deep doorway leading from the mannequin's quarters is really a tiny stage with a glass floor and lighted from four directions. A girl comes through, stands for an instant in startling illumination, and then steps down into the salon. A Groult gown, you observe instantly, is as distinctively Groult as a Picasso painting is a Picasso.[11]

Similar reports on the House of Lucien Lelong in 1925, The House of Bechoff and The House of Jean Magnin in 1927, draw attention to stages and staircases as important features of the décor that enhanced the reception of the couture show. By alluding to relationships between theatre, art and design, these spaces further sanctified fashion in the eyes of the consumer.[12]

The relationship between early haute couture fashion and the theatre has been thoroughly investigated by art historian, Nancy Troy. *Couture Culture: A Study in Modern Art and Fashion* is one of the few monographs that examine the interrelationship between fashion and the interior.[13] This study, which focuses on Paul Poiret, provides important insights into how couturiers developed staging techniques derived from the performing arts, so enriching the perception of their designs. They dressed actresses both on and off stage, and developed cultures of display that established fashion as a spectacular commodity expanding from the private salons of the Parisian couture houses to wider audiences in department stores throughout Europe and America. This system, as Troy alludes to, is the foundation of cinematic tie-ins and star systems that underpinned the relationship between fashion and film cross promotional strategies throughout the twentieth century.

Importantly, the stage in the salon offered couturiers the spatial affordance of creating a grand entrance for their designs, coupled with the effect of the body in motion. This method of display enhanced the surface appearance of garments, and contributed to fashion's performance as apprehended image. As fashion historian Caroline Evans outlines in *The Mechanical Smile,* her exhaustive coverage of early fashion shows: 'there was something inherently cinematic about the fashion show ... both privilege the visual fascination of movement ... in a beguiling flow of effects and surfaces.'[14] Evans notes the many ways that film and fashion interacted in the early twentieth century. For example, from 1910, newsreels of the latest fashions from Paris couturiers including Callot Soeurs, Drecoll and Paquin were circulated worldwide to promote France's luxury industries. These short films generally portrayed house models and actresses wearing the collections within couture salons, in gardens, and in front of iconic monuments.[15]

Paul Poiret in particular is noted for his use of film, portraying mannequins modelling his lampshade tunics and trouser skirts which he showed to fashion press and public audiences on his tour of America in 1911, and again in 1913. Troy similarly notes this early fashion film as an important aspect of Poiret's promotional strategy. While he generally claimed distain for advertising, he cleverly adopted film's artistic merits to obscure his marketing techniques with a 'veneer of culture'.[16] Poiret, along with a range of couturiers since the 1870s, established the conditions of aligning fashion with art, architecture, interior design, theatre, film and other cultural products that continue to be exploited by contemporary fashion brands.[17] Drawing on the sociologist Pierre Bourdieu's theory of social distinction through taste, the use of theatrical mise-en-scène, dramatic interior architecture and staging devices by couturiers in their salons can be understood as a mode of conferring symbolic value and cultural capital on fashion garments through the consecrating discourses of the arts.[18]

While elements of the fashion show were featured in early silent cinema – for example, scenes focusing on sumptuous Lady Duff Gordon gowns in *Way Down East* (1920) – the theatrics and glamour of Parisian style fashion parades firmly entered the cinematic context in the 1930s. A number of women's films including *Vogues of 1938* (1937) and *Mannequin* (1937) used the format to disrupt the narrative and presumably enthuse female audiences to purchase the latest looks. Perhaps the most striking example of this effect occurs in George Cukor's *The Women* (1939). The fashion parade is a six-minute technicolour extravaganza showcasing Adrian designs, which somewhat disconcertingly stops the action of the otherwise black and white film. The fashions range from sportswear and swimsuits, to elaborate tea party gowns and elegant evening wear. There are nods throughout to haute couture with a number of references to Elsa Schiaparelli's designs including a swimming-cape complete with a mannequin hand clasp, eccentric hats and wide-shouldered suits with decorative epaulettes. The scene takes place in a department store, where seated guests watch on as the curtain parts and a small stage with steps appears, much akin to the design of theatrical haute couture salon interiors. Similar staging devices can also be seen in *Roberta* (1935) and *Stolen Holiday* (1937) both of which use staircases to showcase the designs of Bernard Newman and Orry-Kelly, respectively. While these fashion shows are integrated more seamlessly into the narrative than is the case with *The Women*, they perform the same role of creating an avenue for fashion consumption. In some instances, this was through direct tie-ins – as was the case for *Roberta*, where Newman designed ready-to-wear copies for Macy's.[19]

The trope of the fashion catwalk has since been incorporated in a range of fashion focused films, such as the sartorially satirical *Who Are you, Polly Magoo?* (1966), *Mahogany* (1975) in which Diana Ross stars in the rags-to-riches tail of a fashion designer, Paris fashion week docu-drama *Pret-à-Porter* (1994) and fashion world expose meets romantic comedy *The Devil Wears Prada* (2006), amongst numerous others. The staging techniques of couture fashion salons, translated to cinematic contexts, give audiences the impression that they had access to an exclusive realm. As film historian Charlotte Herzog argues:

> The dream/film offers to fulfil the wish of buying, owning and wearing the fabulous gowns … which would be impossible for many women in real life … The audience in the movie theatre can enjoy an improved social status and increased buying power equal to that of the cultural elite.[20]

In other words, drawing on Bourdieu, being exposed to the consecrating rituals of the fashion field provides audiences with a cultural knowledge of couture without having to possess the social and economic capital required to enter into such spaces. In this way, the staged fashion show on film might be understood by audiences to transcend class boundaries, reinforcing the transformative role of fashion. I argue that the staircase in particular is an architectural motif that has come to accessorize fashion across physical space, film and photographic image to represent women's transformation in a myriad of ways.

The staircase as fashion icon

By the mid-1920s, a new aesthetic of salon interior design had become de rigueur for haute couture fashion houses. Curtained stages were largely replaced by an overall modern effect of Art Deco styling that had been widely celebrated at the 1925 *Exposition Internationale des Arts Decoratifs* in Paris. Fashion and the Art Deco interior were brought together by couturiers including Maison Myrbor, Madeleine Vionnet and Jeanne Lanvin in order to cater to the desires of the modern woman.[21] Arguably, the couturière Gabrielle (Coco) Chanel and her designs epitomized this confluence of modern woman persona, the straight silhouette of the modern body, and the minimalism of modern décor more than any other fashion house. The salon at House of Chanel was a vast open space, accented by domed chandeliers and mirrored walls creating a sparkling and refracting effect. A mirrored staircase positioned between the couture salon on the first floor and the designer's second-floor apartment set it apart from other haute couture maisons of the 1920s.

The staircase at Chanel has become an iconic image of the couturière's myth. There are a multitude of publicity images, by photographers including Robert Doisneau, Cecil Beaton, Douglas Kirkland and Suzy Parker which positioned Chanel at the top of the stairs (Figure 4.1). Multiplied through mirrored panels, she is the omnipotent observer of her empire, an image cemented in the collective imagination as a symbol of fashionable modernism. Chanel's claim that 'I spent my life on the stairs' bolstered this myth, as she sat there, hidden from the audience below, to view the reception of her collections.[22] In addition to promulgating her celebrity designer persona, the mirrored staircase also served as a backdrop to her couture collections in magazines. Illustrations and photographs in *Vogue* and *Harper's Bazaar* presented the Chanel staircase as an icon of fashion: 'the famous faceted mirrored spiral staircase' was the backdrop to a jacquard velvet evening gown in 1931, a white sequin embroidered ball gown in 1937 and dinner pyjamas in 1967, amongst numerous others.[23] In these images the staircase is positioned as an entryway into the fantasy world of the Chanel lifestyle and reinforces Chanel's modern woman brand identity. As Evans observes, Chanel's stagecraft created 'a human kaleidoscope as the mannequins came down the circular staircase ... which splintered and refracted their image like a futurist painting in motion'.[24] Her interpretation

Figure 4.1 Fashion designer Gabrielle Coco Chanel sitting on the stairs in her atelier. Photo Credit: Photo by Photo 12/UIG/Getty Images.

implies reference to Marcel Duchamp's painting *Nude Descending a Staircase, No. 2* (1912) which depicts the female body in movement, active and repeated. It is a fitting analogy for Chanel's garments which materialized modernist fascinations of speed, movement and multiplicity in form and reproducibility. Chanel's collections represented in repetition across the mirrored surface of the staircase comply with her vision of creating what *Vogue* described as 'The Chanel Ford – The frock that all the world will wear'.[25]

The longevity and significance of the staircase to the Chanel brand were further reinforced by Karl Lagerfeld. In 1983, the year that Lagerfeld became director of the Chanel brand, photographs by Helmut Newton depicted Lagerfeld on the staircase in a similar mode to images of Chanel, drawing a seemingly continuous line between the two designers. The mythology of the Chanel staircase is a visual point of reference to confer the idea that Lagerfeld's succession at the house would follow in the spirit of Chanel's style. Lagerfeld alluded to this continuing design dialogue in a 2003 imagined interview in which the two faces of the Chanel brand talk to each other. Strikingly, the interview begins: 'Coco Chanel: I am watching you. The other day I saw you posing on my famous staircase … Karl Lagerfeld: Your staircase? You sold your business years before you went wherever you are now.'[26] Like Chanel, Lagerfeld posed on the staircase in various moments throughout his career, sometimes with celebrity models – including Victoria Beckham for *Elle* France in 2012.[27] More significantly, the staircase continued to be circulated as an iconic backdrop to the Chanel look. For example, a towering spiral staircase was the centrepiece to the spring show in 2006, and two curved staircases flanked an orchestra for spring 2014.

In 2019, the mirrored staircase appeared yet again as an icon of the brand's heritage, tethering another new designer at the helm, Virginie Viard, to Chanel's signature style. The fashion codes developed by Gabrielle Chanel – little black dresses, cream suiting, quilted bags, chains belts and pink tweed – which had informed Lagerfeld's collections for thirty-six years, were again reinterpreted by Viard. For the Métiers d'Art collection, presented at the Grand Palais, Viard collaborated with film director Sofia Coppola to recreate Chanel's 31 Rue Cambon apartment, the salon and mirrored staircase. An interview with Coppola for *Vogue* provides telling insights regarding how the Chanel myth is recreated through the icon of the staircase. She states that:

> It was a Chanel fantasy dream for me … I had always loved those images of the stairs – the old days at rue Cambon with Coco standing on the stairs … My main role was really the atmosphere … when I do a film, the sets have to relate to what the people are wearing – it all has to come together. So it was fun to

... incorporate the atmosphere and sets to compliment what she [Viard] was designing ... I love that she incorporates so much of the history and codes.[28]

In this way, the Chanel style coupled with the icon of the staircase provides the brand with a narrative of continuous heritage, timelessness, aura and immaterial value. Gabrielle Chanel was well aware of the benefits of providing couture clients with such experiences, as she explained in 1935:

> When my customers come to me, they like to cross the threshold of some magic place; [...] they are privileged characters who are incorporated into our legend. For them it is a far greater pleasure than ordering another suit. Legend is the consecration of fame.[29]

Viard, like Lagerfeld before her, reconstitutes the legend of Chanel through these iconic references and incorporates a further layer of cultural sanctification by collaborating with a famed film director. In this way, the staircase not only spectacularizes the fashion moment, but also symbolizes the threshold of a fantasy world that the Chanel consumer buys into. The mythology of the mirrored staircase at Chanel continues a set of cultural associations of transformation, transcendence, appearance and arrival. The architectural historian John Templar provides insight into the symbolic function of the staircase as: 'art object, structural idea, manifestation of pomp and manners, behavioural setting, controller of our gait, political icon, legal prescription, poetic fancy'.[30] To this list, I would add fashion icon – a repeated and recognizable symbol that has come to represent goddess like decent from the heavens, Cinderella moments of admiration and more generally fashion as change.

The staircases of fashion photography established their majestic and elegant associations well before Chanel refurbished her couture house. Edward Steichen's first fashion photographs of models on the stairs at Paul Poiret in 1911, published in *Art et Decoration* exploited the staircase's structure to create perspective, providing close-up and full-figure views of the fashions on display.[31] From this point, stairs became a frequent feature of Steichen's images, and in fashion photography more generally. There is an exhaustive array of images I could refer to here. Some notable examples include: George Hoyningen-Huene's 1928 image of model Bettina Jones wearing Schiaparelli-designed sweater and shorts, smoking a cigarette as she talks to a male model against the backdrop of graphic black and white steps, Richard Avedon's 1947 photograph of Renee, wearing the New Look and twirling her way down the steps at the Palace de Concord and the Liszt gown of swirling black and white patterned curves echoing the balustrades at Dior by Willy Maywald in 1948. In fact, the staircase at Dior so frequently appears in fashion photographs of the 1940s and 1950s that its image might almost rival the staircase at Chanel (Figure 4.2).

The proliferation of fashionable staircases can be understood through fashion historian Margaret Maynard's framework that positions fashion photography as an ecology of images – that is, 'a rhetorical practice, informed by provisional, external engagements and framing procedures that play with relational contrasts'.[32] In other words, fashion photography is in constant conversational reference with other fashion photographs, but also with other visual media to convey meaning and narrative, so much so that the image of fashion is just as much a commodity as the garment being depicted. Certainly, photographs such as Mike Figgis' campaign for Agent Provocateur *Kate Moss Descending* (2007) which reference the Duchamp painting, or Maywald's *Eugenie dress, Ailee Line* (1948) reminiscent of Renoir's *Woman on the Stair* (1876), are testament to

Figure 4.2 Model standing on staircase wearing a white organdie dress by Dior, Paris, March 1956. Publication: Picture Post. Photo Credit: Savitry/Picture Post/Hulton Archive/Getty Images.

this intertextual relationship. With this vast array of photographic reference points in mind, it seems clear that the staircase then can be understood as a fashion object, or accessory, in much the same way as the Eiffel Tower, yellow taxies or red telephone boxes operate as emblematic devices in photography to convey the fashionability of Paris, New York or London. The staircase, through its reoccurring image as fashionable accoutrement in photography and film, conveys a fantasy of transformation and transcendence that echoes the way that fashion operates as a product of class distinction and how its codes can be manipulated for the purposes of social mobility. The staircase, like fashion, performs the role of transition space between one state and another.

A powerful evocation of this relationship can be seen in stylist André Leon Tally's fashion editorial 'Scarlett N' the Hood' photographed by Karl Lagerfeld for *Vanity Fair* magazine in 1996. Naomi Campbell plays the role of Scarlett O'Hara from *Gone with the Wind* (1939), in a photo shoot that remakes the iconic staircase scenes from the film, with the supermodel wearing Givenchy by John Galliano. In this tableaux Tally reimagines the inherent racism and white supremacy of a film that essentially glorifies the Confederates and their support of slavery by casting a model of Afro-Caribbean decent in the role of the plantation owner's daughter. Tally's satirical take on *Gone with the Wind* is commentary on fashion and film's racial stereotyping and the lack of representation of people of colour in these spaces of glamour. The staircase in this instance represents an imaginary transformation of history, in which it is possible for a woman of colour to play 'a grandiose grand dame of the nineteenth century'. As Tally states of the photo shoot, 'I wanted people to think: *What if?* ... it was a quiet form of activism. My way of approaching diversity in the world of fashion was to communicate with the power of suggestion.'[33] The staircase in fashion photography is an emblem of change, capturing an arrested moment, whether that be the arrival of a new era of inclusiveness – as in Tally's editorial, acceptance into a new social realm as implied by photographs of grand gowns on the Dior staircase or simply the appearance of a new style. Films including *Gone with the Wind*, and many others that have fashion at their forefront, use these architectural tropes in similar ways.

Staircases in fashion film: You stepped out of a dream

As with fashion photography, Hollywood has frequently cast the staircase as stylish architectural accessory. Symbolically representing upward social mobility and the desire for transformative self-improvement, the staircase offers the opportunity to observe the fashion of leading ladies in moments that partially disrupt the narrative to create visual spectacle. Film Historian Barbara Klinger notes that Universal Studio's publicity machine identified the stairway as an architectonic site of spectacle, where: 'it takes a circular staircase to bring out a girl's sex appeal … [the staircase's entertainment value lies in] exhibiting breath taking showgirls to their best advantage.'[34] This was obviously the case for Busby Berkeley films which drew on the tradition of Florenz Ziegfeld's Broadway showgirl spectacles of costume and dance. Here again the relationship between fashion and staging devices to produce glamorous forms of entertainment is made evident, Ziegfeld hired Lady Duff Gordon to design the costumes for his showgirls in 1915. Lucile gowns were part of the attraction of seeing a Ziegfeld production (Figure 4.3). As Herzog notes, 'fashion was the theme of many musical numbers … "Maids of Mesh," … "The Laces of the World" and the "Episode of the Chiffon" were all vehicles for spectacular costumes.'[35] The fashion parade format that Lucile helped develop was transposed into the Broadway setting, which in turn, would be transposed to the feature film. The influence of the *Ziegfeld Follies* in establishing this mode of display for fashion in film should

Figure 4.3 *Ziegfeld Follies* performers dressed by Lucile (Lady Duff Gordon) (1917). Photo Credit: Bettmann/Getty Images.

not be underestimated. In addition to collaborating with Lucile to create an extravaganza of fashionable excess, the architect Joseph Urban produced sets that were equally fantastic. Aside from creating elaborate scenography praised as 'ecstasy to the eye', Urban's grand staircases were the centrepiece for numerous musical numbers, on which the dancers posed and paraded Lucile's looks.[36] These key aspects of fashion's staging became standard to the translation of the Follies style musical revue to cinema.

The motif of the stairway in Busby Berkeley films, such as *Gold Diggers of 1933* (1933), *Dames* (1934) and *Ziegfeld Girl* (1941), was a spatial construct which served as an ornamental platform for showcasing the talents of hundreds of uniform girls who danced rhythmically up and down the steps. It also provided symbolic function, conveying the social climbing element of the storyline that these films held in common – in which, typically working-class women become showgirls and attract the romantic attentions of wealthy men. The dreamlike qualities of these scenes were an escape from the realities of depression era America, offering fantasies of glamour and wealth. For example, early on in *Ziegfeld Girl*, Hedy Lamarr, Lana Turner and Judy Garland make their debut as showgirls in a Follies revue. The production features an elaborate staircase sequence in which the three women wear extravagant white goddess gowns and sparkling costumes to the strains of '*You Stepped Out of a Dream*'. As the women appear on the stairs to the words 'you are too wonderful', 'you are too marvellous', the sequence takes on the appearance of a fashion parade with showgirls wearing an array of fantastical costumes, feathered gowns, silky sheaths and gauzy confections (Figure 4.4). The relationship between fashion, staircases and the women protagonists' dreams of stardom and social mobility couldn't be clearer.

This narrative of self-improvement, common to many musicals, can also be seen in a number of Audrey Hepburn films, which similarly offer multiple moments of fashion transformation. From chauffer's daughter to sophisticated romantic interest in *Sabrina* (1954), dowdy book store assistant to glamorous model in *Funny Face* (1957) and cockney flower seller to society lady in *My Fair Lady* (1964). Each of these films rely on a Cinderella storyline of working-class girl turned elegant woman, with staircases providing moments of spectacular appearance, transcendence of class boundaries and the emergence of a more confident persona. Elegant fashions play prominent roles in arrival scenes – think Sabrina's black and white Givenchy gown glimpsed across the stair case balustrade, or the Cecil Beaton glittering sheath dress worn by Eliza Doolittle as she ascends the stairs at the Embassy ball. Grand entrances provide audiences

Figure 4.4 Hedy Lamarr, Judy Garland and Lana Turner as chorus girls wearing Adrian designed gowns in *Ziegfeld Girl* (1941). Credits: Busby Berkeley and Robert Z. Leonard (Director), Metro-Goldwyn-Mayer (Film Production). Photo Credit: Bettmann/Getty Images.

with the opportunity to 'study costume details and admire the heroine's enviable ability to use fashion as a traditional feminine path to social improvement and, of course, romantic happiness'.[37]

Perhaps the most memorable of Hepburn's fashion staircase moments occurs in *Funny Face*. The film adopts the visual language of a *Vogue* or *Harper's Bazaar* photo editorial to demonstrate the power of fashion to change the character of protagonist Jo Stanley (Hepburn) from bookish philosopher to fashionable romantic. The first scene in which Jo is unveiled as an elegant fashion model takes the familiar trope of the stage and the raising of the curtain to reveal her stiffly posed in a long white sheath dress and pink flowing cape. While we see Jo emerge according to the film's dialogue, 'not as a butterfly, but a bird of paradise', the transformation is not yet complete. Her response to the wide approval of the fashion editorial team is, 'it's wonderful, but it's not me.' This scene is followed by a series of fashion shoots in which Hepburn poses in Givenchy gowns, each more spectacular than the next, to show her growing confidence and increasing fashionability. The most dramatic of these images occurs as Jo glides down the stairs of the Louvre with *The Winged Victory of Samothrace* (200BC) behind her (Figure 4.5). Wearing a form-fitting red evening gown with gauzy wrap fluttering around her, Jo echoes the form of the ancient Grecian sculpture, as if she might fly down the stairs like the 'bird of paradise'. In this scene, we understand that Jo's fashion transformation is complete. Taking on the role of art director, she infuses the fashion shoot with her own imagination and personality. Jo has embraced her fashionable identity and career as a model, as well as her desire for love interest photographer Dick Avery (Fred Astaire).

Within these films we might understand the staircase as 'the locus of spectacularisation of the woman', as Mary Ann Doane argues, 'it is *on the stairway* that she is displayed as spectacle for the male gaze.'[38] Yet, it is also apparent that these scenes are addressing a female audience. As discussed in Chapter 1, for Doane the female spectator position is complicated, whereby women view other female bodies through the eyes of their desirability to men, but due to women's dual role as consumer and commodity she is also positioned as her own oppressor. For Doane, 'the cinematic image for the woman is both shop

Figure 4.5 Audrey Hepburn descends the Daru Staircase at the Louvre in Paris, in a scene from *Funny Face* (1957). Credits: Stanely Donen (Director), Paramount Pictures (Film Production). Photo Credit: Archive Photos/Getty Images.

window and mirror, the one simply a means of access to the other.'[39] From this perspective, the staircase is a mechanism which prompts women to examine herself as an apprehended image of admiration. Fashion, in this context, plays the crucial role of mediating desire, as the object which highlights women's beauty and sexual appeal. However, this position, which reduces female spectatorship to merely replicate an objectifying gaze fails to take into account appreciation for embodiment, that is, being in a body and transforming it through adornment for self-pleasure. In this way Jo's descent down the Louvre staircase in *Funny Face* can be understood as an opportunity to admire Hepburn's body as an object of desire, but we might also connect with the experience of wearing clothes as a method for conveying freedom of individual expression through the body.

The staircase as a site of psychological anxiety and tension has been examined by Doane in her analysis of the 'paranoid women' of melodramas and suspenseful thrillers. For Doane, films such as *The Spiral Staircase* (1946) use the staircase motif to represent the role of the patriarchy and the constraints of family, marriage or social roles. In many instances the storyline hinges on women sacrificing their desires to maintain traditional social orders. The staircase epitomizes this social order, and to not comply results in a tragic outcome.[40] The staircase in Luca Guadagnino's *I Am Love* (*Io sonno l'amore*) (2009) plays a similar role. Drawing on the tropes of the melodramatic staircase as constraint, as well as symbolic divergence from Cinderella narratives, *I Am Love* presents the staircase as a site of psychological evolution and fashion transformation in unconventional ways.

Set in Piero Portaluppi's Milanese Villa Necchi Campiglio (1932–1935), *I Am Love* is the story of Emma Recchi (Tilda Swinton), the wife of a rich industrialist who falls in love with her son's friend. The mansion, a symbol of Italian Fascist bourgeois culture, is cold and imposing – a metaphor for the Recchi family, their wealth and conservative values. Fashion plays a similarly significant role in further delineating the luxurious world of the Recchi family, with the central protagonist's costumes provided by Fendi, Hermès and Jil Sander. The staircase at the centre of this film is the epitome of Milanese style. Its marble steps and geometric carved-wood balustrade are quietly elegant, an aesthetic of austere luxury rather than brash, grandiose glamour. Its narrative function seems to serve the role of highlighting Emma's understated fashionable restraint. On each occasion Emma walks down the stairs, she is stylishly dressed and the object of admiration. The first time she glides down the steps in a Jil Sander burgundy sheath dress, we recognize her character as the 'perfect' wife and mother with a habitus of tasteful dress, complying with the conservative ideals of the family

(Figure 4.6). Yet, as the film progresses we observe that fashion plays a crucial role in conveying Emma's altered states of sexual awakening. A tangerine-hued figure-hugging dress worn when she contrives to meet her lover is in sharp contrast to the monochromatic, tailored looks of her family life.

With this sartorially symbolic register in mind, we can understand Emma's next appearance on the staircase, wearing a sophisticated pearl evening gown with dramatic Sonia Delaunay graphic stole as a form of masquerade. Her dress conveys the traditional values her family expects of her; however, the patterned stole appears as an almost Freudian slip revealing the real state of her newly discovered sensual inner life. In this scene, Emma's grand entrance is approved by the admiring gaze of her husband, Tancredi (Pippo Delbono). Unaware of her infidelity, he accepts her masquerade as the devoted wife and mother he knows, while her son, Edo (Flavio Parenti) turns away – at this point, suspicious of her affections for his friend. The tragedy that unfolds here after, with the accidental death of Emma's son after confronting her about the affair is punctuated by a final staircase scene. Racing home from Edo's funeral, Emma strips off her elegant black mourning attire and changes into her lover's work pants and jacket. Shedding the restraints of her family, her final dash down the stairs is the disavowal of her lifestyle of bourgeois capitalism, and the rigidity of her expected role as perfect wife and mother.

Figure 4.6 Tilda Swinton as Emma Recchi in *I Am Love* (*Io sonno l'amore*) (2009). Credits: Luca Guadagnino (Director), First Sun (Film Production). Screen still.

Emma's transformation is the discarding of fashion for a life of simplicity, and the removal of the mask of style to follow the desires of her authentic self. While this transformation is not without sacrificial tragedy, the reversal of the traditional fashion narrative of ascendance to a higher social status complies with other themes accentuated within the film – the decaying forces of capitalism and the patriarchy. Emma's transcendence towards love is on the level of the spirit rather than the social, affirming her self-actualization and sexual awakening over traditional gender roles and privileged economic positions. However, while the overarching narrative of *I Am Love* appears to be a feminist repudiation of the constraints of marriage, and fashion's role in contributing to the restraints of patriarchal gender roles, this message is somewhat complicated by Swinton's presence as the main protagonist due to her status as fashion icon. Film theorist Hilary Radner outlines this conundrum; Swinton is frequently featured on best-dressed lists and in high fashion publications, yet also refuses a personal interest in fashion, where 'this vexed relationship with fashion inflects Swinton's cinematic performances, enhanced by her emphasis on disguise and transformation'.[41] Fashion as masquerade provides Swinton with the means to navigate divergent roles on film and perform the nebulous persona of her celebrity status. *I Am Love* is one more fashionable transformation in a career emphasized by chameleon-like change. Despite an underlying anti-fashion narrative, *I Am Love* perpetuates a desirable fashion image, that no doubt contributed to the cultural capital of the Jil Sander brand identity, and was further enhanced by the glamorous aesthetic of architectural fetishism in the form of the Villa Necchi Campiglio. This formula has resonances for consumer culture in the staircases of fashion flagships.

Statement staircases of luxury fashion

The staircase as fashion icon has become a recognizable trope to such an extent that it is an important focal point for retail spaces. While elevators are more expedient modes of travel within retail environments, the grand staircase is a signature architectural feature that contributes to the cultural capital of fashion. Chanel's staircase at the salon on rue Cambon and the Dior staircase at the avenue Montaigne exemplify a tradition that symbolically combines high fashion with elevated status. However, this relationship has even longer standing in fashion retail environments. The first specialized department store – the Bon Marche – was known for its majestic double-revolution staircase based on that of the Paris Opera. Built in the 1870s with the input of Gustave Eiffel, the Bon Marche's ornamental ironwork interiors were impressive spaces that made the luxuries of the upper classes visible to the bourgeoisie. As architectural historian Meredith Clausen surmises, 'the grand stair drew customers upstairs, offering them an opportunity to exhibit their newly acquired attire in full view of others … The building itself was designed as a stage set, an elegant theatre for the public.'[42] Other Parisian department stores of the era – the Galeries Lafayette, Printemps and Samarataine – similarly erected theatrical staircases as the centrepiece of consumer cathedrals. The staircases at the Bon Marche are now escalators, yet still fulfil the role of consumer spectacle, where artists and architects including Nendo, Leandro Erlich and Ai Weiwei have been invited to transform electric staircases into dramatic installations (Figure 4.7). These artistic transformations of retail spaces are indicative of trends set by luxury fashion brands which have increasingly collaborated with artists, architects and interior designers to enhance fashion's cultural capital and create hybrid commerce, art and entertainment environments. Lipovetsky describes this conversion between culture and consumption practices as artistic capitalism, where aesthetic experience has become an object of mass consumption. To create immaterial value and emotional connection with fashion products, luxury brands develop 'an entire mise-en-scène' that exploits aesthetics, imagination and emotions to enhance the consumer experience and stimulate desire.[43]

Figure 4.7 Oki Sato, Nendo Studio *Ame Nochi Hana-Rain Flowers* at Le Bon Marche department store (2020). Photo Credit: Chesnot/Getty Images.

Grand entrances 103

The feature staircases of luxury flagship stores operate within this aesthetic and experiential paradigm, combining architectural theatricality, fashionable display and immaterial value to enhance brand identity. As will be discussed further in Chapter 6, since the 1990s, strategically located global flagship stores have become an important site of luxury fashion consumption experience. Prestigious locations, spectacular architecture and the widest array of designer products on display reinforce the premium position of fashion brands within the market. Flagship stores are unique shopping destinations that communicate brand exclusivity, unique identity and cultural capital. The statement staircases of flagship stores create spectacular visual impact, both as experience and image. Take for instance, the Gwenaël Nicolas designed black and white marble staircase at Dolce & Gabbana's Old Bond street boutique in London (2018). Widely celebrated in design magazines such as *Wallpaper** and *Dezeen*, the staircase is fetishized in ways not dissimilar to fashion, where the descriptions of its exotic materials and surfaces – 'Brazilian Copacabana, Indian Black Lightning, and Chinese Panda White', – are akin to fashion copy.[44] Taking centre stage within the Baroque styled interior of the boutique, photographs of the staircase position it as the spatial equivalent to a leading lady's grand entrance. Architectural historian Alice Friedman's insights regarding the ways that glamorous architecture is designed to be photographed further elucidate this analogy, where: 'the surface organisation and treatment of materials … [functions] like make-up on skin or accessories on a well-dressed body.'[45] While Friedman in this instance is referring to the mid-century modern buildings of Frank Lloyd Wright, her point that architecture takes on the glamorous veneer of fashion photography is well made, and equally applicable to the architecture of luxury consumerism. The experience of the staircase is similarly based on an ecology of fashion images and cinematic moments, a stage upon which consumers might enact their fantasies of self-transformation.

The 'starchitect' designed statement staircases of fashion flagships are understood as an expression of the celebrity architect's virtuosity, contributing to the further aestheticization of fashions on display, and providing immaterial value.[46] For example, OMA architect Rem Koolhaas' wooden staircase and undulating wave at the Prada Epicentre, New York (2000–2012) acts as boutique showcase, performance and installation space (Figure 4.8). This collaboration between Koolhaas and Prada further spectacularizes the fashion image, where the staircase becomes a gateway for Prada to associate its luxury fashions with art and theatre. The staircase is a symbolic locus of the brand's cultural capital, which is further enhanced by the creative reputation of the architect. For consumers,

Figure 4.8 Prada Epicentre staircase designed by architect Rem Koolhaas (2001). Photo credit: David LEFRANC/Gamma-Rapho via Getty Images.

this is not a staircase to perform the staging of a new image, rather it is a space to enact socio-economic means of differentiation through appreciation of a brand that recognizes the cultural significance of novel architecture.

The circulation of the Prada Epicentre stairs as an innovative cultural and commerce environment in both fashion and architecture media is indicative of the ways in which fashion retail spaces are styled to produce the appearance of glamour.[47] As Friedman observes, architectural photography and fashion photography share an aesthetic of 'theatricality, spectacle, fantasy and narrative appeal'.[48] Further, as with designer fashion, starchitect buildings – and by extension their staircases – are understood as luxury commodities, operating within the realms of authorial genius, signature style, material excess, exclusivity and expensiveness. As architectural historian Annette Condello argues, luxury architecture throughout history can be defined in terms of scale, rarity of materials, ornamentation, novelty and excessiveness.[49] The staircases of fashion flagships certainly hold these qualities in common and are fetishized in architecture and design media as destination experiences. The list of celebrated fashion staircases is extensive. Notable examples include: the Massimiliano and Doriana Fuksas vortex of whirlwind dynamic movement across four floors at Armani Fifth Avenue; Peter Marino's incorporation of installation art by Jean-Michel Othoniel, Guy Limone and Annie Morris in staircase design at Chanel New Bond Street London, Louis Vuitton Munich and Louis Vuitton Place Vendôme, David Chipperfield's geometric terrazzo staircase at Valentino, New York and Frank Gehry's deconstructionist steel staircase at Issey Miyake, New York.[50] The unique staircases of these retail environments are key components of architectural distinction to convey luxury, signifying acceptance into an exclusive inner realm, and contributing to consumer sensory experience. Key features of the luxury fashion brand identity – expensive materials, exquisite craftsmanship and unique design are also exemplified by the staircases of conspicuous architectural luxury. In this way, the signature staircase contributes to the immaterial value of fashion – an emblem of the visible and tangible power and prestige of the brand.

As this chapter has shown staircases are rich with symbolic associations of transformation, social arrival and spectacular appearance reinforced through their representation in fashion films and photography. As a space for image making and the performance of fashionable identities, the staircase enhances the captivating qualities of fashion objects, and the women who wear them. They are spaces closely associated with the creation of desire, and as such have an affinity with the store window, as will be the focus of the next chapter.

5

Windows and screens: Cinema, department stores and boutique display

Audrey Hepburn as Holly Golightly, dressed in pearls, and elegant black Givenchy dress, wistfully gazing into the store windows of the famed jewellery store in *Breakfast at Tiffany's* (1961) memorably captures the long-standing relationship between screen and window. Like film, the shop window is a space for the creation of desire. The world of fantasy interfaces with everyday life. As the *Tiffany's* scene so clearly articulates, shop windows are places for reflection and contemplation, a space to consider what pleasures a purchase might bring, and a mirror that projects our own image into dreams on display. The cinema screen as a shop window has been similarly positioned. Eckert astutely observes that films 'functioned as living display windows for all that they contained; windows that were occupied by marvellous mannequins and swathed in a fetish-inducing ambience'.[1]

As this book has shown throughout Chapters 1 to 3, a range of gender and sexual identities augmented through fashion, the interior and architecture have been made desirable to consumers through their appearance on film. The spectacle of shop windows as dreamworlds to stimulate consumer desire has been examined by numerous film and fashion historians, with many recognizing how these spaces prefigured cinema.[2] Here, I extend this history to include the lesser-known intersection between French avant-garde cinema, couture fashion and architecture, pioneered by collaborations between Sonia Delaunay and Robert Mallet-Stevens on Marcel L'Herbier's *Le Vertige* (1926) and René Somptier's *Le P'tit Parigot* (1926). I argue that a translation occurs from fashion to architecture that is activated through cinematic effect, which both Delaunay and Mallet-Stevens would also re-imagine through their individual approaches to boutique window display.

In developing the analogy between window shopping and film spectatorship as mechanisms of the fashion image, this chapter will trace the passage from arcade to cinema. Drawing on sociologist Mike Featherstone's ideas concerning how the windows and screens of consumer culture provide glamorous and sensory experiences, this chapter argues that the mutual exchange that occurs between fashion, spatial design and cinema is indicative of a system of reciprocity. The fashion image is mobilized to translate the illusionary world of film to tangible real-world desires on display. In this context, the screen and the window as mediating devices of fashion can be understood as both projection and mirror for the consumer.

Windows as screens

Shop windows as places to display goods to passers-by have been part of the urban environment since at least the fourteenth century.[3] Their development as a space of urban spectacle – in modes that replicate the theatre, art gallery and cinema – was closely related to new technologies of plate glass, electric lighting and the emergence of new retail environments such as arcades and department stores. Sophisticated window displays that enhanced a store's fashionable standing have been significant to retail practices since the eighteenth century, and the acceleration of advertising and visual merchandising that occurred in consumer cultures of the nineteenth century required window dressers to produce increasingly fantastical tableaux.[4]

By the late nineteenth century store windows were often thematized, displaying fully decorated rooms, exotic environments and theatre-like dramas. For example, L. Frank Baum, the author of the *Wizard of Oz* (1900), was a pioneering advisor to window dressers in Chicago in the 1890s and editor of trade magazine *Show Window* from 1897 to 1902.[5] Having worked in the theatre, as well as a salesman, playwright and publisher, Baum was uniquely placed to understand how narrative, spectacle and advertising might come together in the shop window to appeal to consumers. He proclaimed that windows could sell goods:

> By placing them before the public in such a manner that the observer has a desire for them and enters the store to make a purchase. Once inside the customer may see other things she wants ... the credit of the sale belongs to the window.[6]

Art historian Stuart Culver argues that Baum cleverly incorporated his understandings of consumer culture in his children's fairy-tale *The Wizard of Oz*, where the title character is able to artfully sell 'material objects that symbolise the spiritual qualities' that the Scarecrow, Tin Woodman and Cowardly Lion desire, even though they know he is a charlatan.⁷ The book, and the later 1939 film starring Judy Garland, portrays reality and dreamworlds side by side, so that even when the machinery of the fantasy is exposed, the audience still remains enchanted. Baum's book presents a narrative where 'autonomy and integrity proves to be at the same time the dramatization of an inescapable desire for an object ... that is nothing but an image'.⁸ This sentiment aptly describes how Baum also put these ideas to work in commercial contexts by promoting the concept of the 'illusion window', using the effects of mechanical wizardry to draw attention to the fantasy worlds of visual merchandising. Movement was an important component of an engaging window display, whether achieved through the use of real-life mannequins who 'vanished' to reappear wearing a new outfit, or through the use of mechanical devices to power revolving stars and fluttering butterflies. Baum urged his fellow window dressers to encourage people to 'watch the windows! People are naturally curious they will always stop to examine anything that moves.'⁹ He clearly understood window display as a form of entertainment that combined artistry, theatre and commerce to transform spectators of 'show windows' to desiring customers.

Baum's innovations in window display should be understood within the context of the female-oriented consumer culture of the period. Obviously, American cities in the early twentieth century were not the only places to develop the store window as visual spectacle. The display windows of Selfridges in London have been an integral part of the department store's retail strategy since its opening in 1909 (Figure 5.1). Established by the American entrepreneur Harry Gordon Selfridge, the eponymous department store developed a range of new retail techniques that specifically targeted female consumers. These included locating the perfume and cosmetic counters at the front of the store, a crèche, reading room and ladies restroom to entice consumers into the store for longer periods of time, and frequent fashion parades that displayed ready-to-wear garments. Window shopping was similarly promoted as a pleasurable cultural past-time, allowing women to engage in this urban experience without having to enter the premises. Early twentieth-century advertising for the store stimulated the attraction of visiting the windows by day, but also highlighted that they were

> brilliantly lit up every Evening until Midnight. These twenty-one windows, twelve of which are the largest sheets of plate glass in the world, will be frequently redressed, and will present a constant pageant of prevailing Fashion.¹⁰

Selfridges' windows – much like other department stores of the era – offered women a form of self-fulfilment, by providing a legitimate mode of independent

Figure 5.1 Selfridges windows lit up at night (1935). Photo Credit: David Savill/Topical Press Agency/Getty Images.

access to the public spaces of metropolitan culture. They also played an important role in the suffrage movement in England, providing a space for political engagement on the streets. Selfridge was a supporter of women's rights, underwriting feminist publications, encouraging protest organizers to meet in the store and displaying suffragette colours in the store's windows. Perhaps recognizing that support of the movement could also make him money, Selfridge stocked the white dresses that suffragettes adopted as their uniform. When in March 1912 women protesters broke the windows of almost 400 shops, including said department store, Selfridges did not press charges.[11]

As the case of Selfridges demonstrates, the shop window, like cinema, complicates understandings of the relationship between women and consumer culture. As outlined in Chapter 1, according to much feminist film analysis, cinema contributes to the condition where the female spectator is encouraged to participate in her own objectification and commodification while aligning herself to cultures of consumption.[12] Just as cinema offered women opportunities to consider modern identities that enacted forms of liberation and agency through mobility and self-determination, shop windows both enticed women to engage in consumption and offered opportunities for new forms of social engagement in urban life. Film historian Lauren Rabinovitz provocatively suggests that reflections in shop windows allowed for a female spectatorship – where women could participate in acts of looking not only at commodities on display, but also at herself in relation to other people participating in the urban environment. Cinema, as a development of the shop-window gaze,

> extended the legitimate public space for women to look, and it expanded their possibilities of a mobilized wandering gaze from the restrictive zone of the street window and department store to new virtual territories.[13]

The cinematic effect of shop windows can also be uncovered in Walter Benjamin's writings in the allusive montage of thoughts that is the *Arcades Project*.[14] The covered shopping passages of nineteenth-century Paris provided Benjamin with an allegory for his investigation into the spectres of modernity. Drawing on Marxist theories of commodity fetishism, Benjamin proposes the commodity on display as a phantasmagoria – a spectacle of illusion that enthrals the bourgeois class through unobtainable dream-like images and experiences that mask the 'reality' of everyday life. Identifying window shopping as the act of the male *flâneur* in search of sensation, the phantasmagoric effects of the arcade provided pleasure in looking, through a constellation of temporal associations.[15] Obliquely drawing connections between the arcade as the precursor to department stores, fashion as a structure that presides over commodity fetishism and interior spaces as phantasmagorical experiences, Benjamin brings together these 'residues of a dream world', as the constituents of a mobilized gaze of urban spectatorship.[16]

Film studies scholar, Anne Friedberg draws parallels between Benjamin's experience of the arcade as a temporal movement through space and time that produced a dream-like state and cinema spectatorship, emerging from 'the social and psychic transformation that the arcades – and the consequent mobility of *flânerie* – produced'.[17] In other words, Friedberg makes the case for the window shopping *flâneur* as the precursor to the cinema spectator, both of whom are engaged in acts of consumption. Furthermore, 'as visual experience became commodified in shop display ... and in cinema spectatorship, the fluidity of *flânerie* (once offered predominantly to men) was now offered as a pleasure to anyone'.[18]

Like the department store, cinema offered women another public space to engage in modern urban life. An experience that offered new forms of identification and the possibility to 'explore gender, racial and sexual mobility and engage in the pleasures of more fluid forms of subjectivity'.[19] These ideas are played out in French New Wave cinema director, Agnes Varda's *Cléo de 5 à 7 (Cléo from 5 to 7)* (1961) in which tensions between woman as spectacle and spectator, window shopper and female *flâneur* are made evident. The film tells the story of Cléo's (Corinne Marchand) profound transformation from self-involved woman obsessed with her own image to an alert citizen of the street. Over the course of the film we see Cléo's dual position as object/subject made evident through her engagement with windows and mirrors. For example, in a sequence where Cléo becomes enthralled by the shopfront of a millinery boutique and then admires herself through the glass and other mirrored surfaces as she tries the hats on, we understand the character to be narcissistically captivated by her own image and presented as the object of desire. This position is reinforced as she walks down the street as the subject of the admiring male gaze. However, Cléo's role as spectacle is soon overtaken, when after a moment of self-realization, she begins strolling the sensory streets of Paris absorbed by the architecture, happenings and people of the city. In a moment when she breaks her compact mirror and gives the newly bought hat to a friend, we understand Cléo is no longer the self-absorbed image, but rather the poetic *flâneuse* alert to her place in the world in relation to those around her. Her subjectivity and agency are asserted as she engages with modern urban life.

The distinction made between celebrated forms of heroic masculine *flânerie* and women's window shopping is important, where the male *flâneur*'s activity of idly wandering the arcades and city spaces, gazing as shop windows has been acclaimed as poetic figure grappling with a rapidly changing world, while the female shopper is positioned as a victim of consumptive desires.[20] These misgivings were played out in the nineteenth-century zeitgeist – Émile Zola's novel *Au Bonheur des Dames* (*The Ladies Paradise*) (1884) is the classic example describing women's enthrallment in the dreamworlds of the department store. Julien Duvivier's 1930 silent French film version of the book visually renders the *flâneuse*'s experience of shop windows and vitrines as exciting and compelling repetition of marvellous objects, including an array of exquisite fashion's paraded in the store's salon. The film's representation of women's consumptive desires echoes Rosalind Williams view that department store displays were designed to appeal to the mass public using the stylistic traits of 'repetition, variety and exoticism ... imbuing merchandise with glamour, romance, and, therefore, consumer appeal ... [as such they] generally lacked any artistic merit'.[21] However, by the 1920s shop windows in Paris were also being celebrated as a new art form, with avant-garde artists, designers and architects producing exciting effects based in technologies of the screen.

Cinematic shopfronts: Boutiques by Sonia Delaunay and Robert Mallet-Stevens

The cinematic turn in luxury fashion stores might be traced back to artist and couturière Sonia Delaunay's Boutique Simultanée which made its debut at the 1924 *Salon d'Automne* in Paris at the 'Place Publique' and was reimagined as part of the rue des Boutiques at the 1925 *Exposition des Arts Decoratifs* (Figure 5.2).[22] In both these stores Delaunay employed a kinetic window display, setting in motion a series of her patterned scarves. The roller-mechanism that powered the exhibition was created by Delaunay's artist-husband Robert. Using cinematic analogies Robert Delaunay intimates how consumer cultures of fashion and film together create enthralling visual scenes:

> In this nine-by-twelve-foot spectacle, which represents the entirety of the shop front, what Apollinaire was already calling *the art of the shop front:* possibilities of presenting a great show with many episodes ... a spool device permits a simultaneous development of coloured forms *ad finitum*.[23]

The Boutique Simultanée represented Delaunay's broader project of communicating abstract art to the consuming public through an oeuvre, which included a

Figure 5.2 Recreation of Sonia Delaunay's Boutique Simultanée at the Museum of Modern Art, Paris, 2014. The original shopfront was first presented at the 1924 Salon d'Automne. Photo Credit: Chesnot/Getty Images.

prolific array of paintings, fashionable garments, textiles, interior designs and car decoration. Delaunay cultivated a synergy between fashion, interior design, advertising and film surfaces that demonstrated her understanding of an emerging cultural moment in which modern women were visibly performing more liberated lifestyles. Her approach to the shopfront can be understood as a culmination of her ideas about the cultural experience of modernity – the embodiment of movement, rhythm, time and colour. Beginning with her first foray into fashion in 1913 with the simultaneous dress which was activated through wearing, Delaunay saw fashion as an animated surface that embraced both the temporal and the spatial. Through its abstract coloured fragments, the contours of the body were displaced beneath the garment, and when in motion, it created ever changing effects.[24] Delaunay's 1926 three-minute film, titled *L'Elegance*, makes these relationships clear. Through a series of demonstrations, Delaunay's dresses and scarves are seen in movement on model's bodies and in dynamic contrast to a series of patterned backgrounds. Film in this instance offered the designer a medium through which her geometric aesthetic approach to colour and pattern was translated across the surfaces of fashion, the interior and film.

The cinematic movement of the Boutique Simultanée shop window displays in perpetual motion made the connections between the filmic gaze and window shopping obvious. Art historian Tag Gronberg's archival study reveals that that reportage at the time regarding the shopfronts of the Place Publique described the stores as: 'luminous, like a cinematographic image' and those at the rue des boutiques, a panoramic 'film-strip' sequence of shop façades.[25] The boutique was a collaboration between Delaunay and the haute couturier Jacques Heim, selling swimwear, fur coats, hats, scarves and accessories. The striking Boutique Simultanée was Delaunay's first shopfront. Its spectacular moving surfaces brought new publicity and opportunities for her designs, and were possibly the catalyst for future collaborations with the architect Robert Mallet-Stevens. In fact, the filmic associations of Delaunay's store at the Place Publique may also have its origins in Mallet-Stevens conceptualization for the square, which showcased the latest displays of fashion and interior design by the likes of *ensemblier* René Herbst, couturière Madeleine Vionnet and Paul Poiret's Atelier Martine.[26] Their lush window displays were illuminated with dramatic lighting, framed by geometrically styled façades, reimagining the city as a cinematic set for the performance of luxuries on display. The overall effect of the various boutique windows when walking past was a dynamic show of colour, light and movement – qualities which both Delaunay and Mallet-Stevens experimented with further through the medium of film.

Mallet-Stevens' experiences as a set-designer surely influenced his approach to the boutique façade, conceiving of both forms as architectural provocations that could educate the mass public in aesthetic modernism.[27] As a pioneering advocate for modernist design in the movies, his book *Le Décor Modern au Cinema* (1928) set out his theories for screen architecture and was considered highly influential to avant-garde cinema of the period.[28] Recognizing the possibilities of cinema in promoting modern French décor to a broad and captivated audience, he argued that architecture in film 'should participate in the action – it must become an actor' through dramatic staging.[29] Mallet-Stevens' film sets for Marcel L'Herbier's *L'Inhumaine* (*The Inhuman Woman*) (1924) are considered the earliest manifestations of modernist design on screen (Figure 5.3).[30] Perhaps for the first time, viewers also became acquainted with the trope of the modern woman character living in a stylish modern house.

Figure 5.3 Robert Mallet-Stevens' set design for *L'Inhumaine* (1924). Marcel L'Herbier (Director). Credit: *Art et Decoration* July 1926: 134.

The film's central protagonist, Claire Lescot – a career driven opera singer, who rejects multiple suitors – is surrounded by the rationalist machine aesthetic of the new age. Mallet-Stevens' geometric, monochrome building façades for the film are indicative of his distinctive style epitomized by the Villa Noailles (1923–7) and residences at the rue Mallet-Stevens (1927) (Figure 5.4). These exterior architectures were integrated with interiors by Alberto Cavalcanti, and Fernand Léger, and corresponded with costumes by Paul Poiret. As a showcase of French modern art, fashion, design and architecture, *L'Inhumaine* cinematically contrived an aesthetic that was beginning to appear in the homes of the Parisian avant-garde, commercial contexts and design magazines. For example, the influence of this emerging aesthetic was relayed to readers of *Art et Decoration* in 1926 with an article outlining the innovations of costume and décor on film.[31] Mallet-Stevens' set designs for *L'Inhumaine* alongside those for *Le Vertige* (*The Living Image*) (1926) and *Le P'tit Parigot* (*The Little Parisian*) (1926) were featured as examples for readers to study for inspiration. An article in the same magazine the following year provides further insight as to how these cinematic

Figure 5.4 Robert Mallet-Stevens' residence at rue Mallet-Stevens Paris (1927). Photo Credit: Jess Berry.

effects might be translated in the home through a photographic editorial on the director Marcel L'Herbier's apartment. The impact of film sets on interior design and details as to how staging and lighting can be used in at home to enhance appearances highlight the mutually reinforcing dialogue between cinema and consumer culture. The presence of textile designs by Sonia Delaunay, a further reminder as to how film décor might appear in everyday contexts, given her involvement in L'Herbier's film *Le Vertige*.[32]

In 1926, Delaunay and Mallet-Stevens collaborated on two French avant-garde silent films, *Le* Vertige and *Le P'tit Parigot*. This collaboration may well have stemmed from an aesthetic understanding of the visual correspondences between their approach to surface and design. The aforementioned Place du Public which housed the Boutique Simultanée is not the only time that Delaunay's and Mallet-Stevens' work were seen side by side during this period. During the 1925 *Exposition des Arts Decoratifs* Sonia Delaunay's fashions and co-ordinating automobile were modelled against the backdrop of Robert Mallet-Stevens' Tourism Pavilion. Here modern geometric forms were multiplied across different surfaces and spaces to create a correspondence between fashion and architecture that highlights the photogenic qualities of both, so creating an image through which women might be compelled by the phantasmagoric dreamworld of the commodity. The relationship established between Delaunay's textiles and Mallet-Stevens' architecture as fashionable images of modern lifestyles on display that had been well publicized at the 1925 exhibition, was an entirely suitable mise-en-scène for the films that they would work on together the following year.

Interestingly, René Somptier's *Le P'tit Parigot* and L'Herbier's *Le Vertige* might be seen as catalysts for the representation of male and female types against the backdrop of modernism that have dominated twentieth-century film. As I have outlined in Chapter 1, the modernist house as the domain of the emancipated modern woman was a familiar trope that may have some antecedence in *Le P'tit Parigot* (Figure 5.5). The film features a number of dance scenes dedicated to the modern woman depicting her freedom of movement, made possible by her short skirts and patterned catsuits designed by Delaunay. The modernist set designs by Mallet-Stevens, in conjunction with Delaunay's costumes, convey frenetic action, extending the animation of the screen surface. Mallet-Stevens' photogenic architecture in *Le P'tit Parigot* casts the interior as a fashionable character attuned with the modern woman's lifestyle of increased physical, social, cultural and professional mobility. Accordingly, the lead character of *Le Vertige* appears somewhat akin to the playboy dandy discussed in Chapter 3.

Figure 5.5 Interior design by Robert Mallet-Stevens and Sonia Delaunay, *Le P'tit Parigot* (1926). Credits: René Le Somptier (Director), Luminor (Film Production). Photo Credit: ullstein bild/ullstein bild via Getty Images.

While Henri de Cassel (Jaque Catelain) wears slim fit suits for most of the film, his appearance in Delaunay's striking dressing robe in her signature abstract patterning, perfectly matched to the soft furnishings she designed for the film's interiors underscores the character's dandy image. As a sophisticated consumer of modern aesthetics on the body and in the home, Cassel's character as seducer and object of desire is further reinforced. While black-and-white film stock cannot do justice to the colours of Delaunay's designs, their geometric patterns reverberate in dynamic ways. These elements complimented Mallet-Stevens' set designs which bear resemblance to images of the architect's own apartment. A comparison between the staircase and windows surrounding the doorway of Cassel's cinema house appears very similar to the vestibule of Maison Mallet-Stevens built in 1927.[33] A fitting analogy given Mallet-Stevens' reputation as the 'dandy architect'.[34] Certainly, the film demonstrates the architect's concern for 'photogenic' styling both on and off screen.[35]

Through his collaborations with haute couturiers including Paul Poiret, Jeanne Paquin, Jacques Doucet and Sonia Delaunay, Mallet-Stevens was acutely aware of how architecture could be made into a fashionable image and that both the silver screen and photography could provide an added layer of allure to his buildings. His work on set designs, coupled with the multitude of fashion photographs taken by Thérèse Bonney of his architecture, attests to the movie star-like qualities of Mallet-Stevens designed residences and commercial spaces.[36] As art historian Richard Becherer argues, photographs of Mallet-Stevens' architecture evidence that these buildings appear to be designed like movie sets, dramatically posed and artificially lit for cinematic effect.[37] In fact, the architecture of rue Mallet-Stevens features in the Josephine Baker film *La Sirène des Tropiques* (Siren of the Tropics) (1927) where we once again witness modern architecture and the interior as backdrops to the performance of modern lifestyles. However, this cinematic quality and its links to style and glamour led the architectural critic Sigfried Giedion to denounce Mallet-Stevens' architecture as the epitome of surface fashion design.[38]

It is possible to speculate that through his collaboration with Sonia Delaunay on these films and other projects, Mallet-Stevens was able to mobilize the fashion image as a way of translating his ideals of architecture from the screen to real life, where modern women would move from imagining dreamworlds and spaces to the possibility of embodying them. As such, I propose that Mallet-Stevens' architecture of appearances was entirely appropriate for the context of the boutique façade, presenting an opportunity to provide a modern image for the city streetscape. The inter-relationship between fashion, architecture and film that appears to underpin so many of Mallet-Stevens' buildings culminate in his boutique designs for the Bally shoe company, consisting of three stores in Paris (1928), Lyons (1930), Rouen (1934) and Algiers (1937). The first of these at the boulevard de la Madeleine employed a cinematic series of eye-level window boxes, framed with chrome that protruded onto the street front inviting close inspection of the shoes on display. Illuminated at night by a cantilevered lighting strip, Mallet-Stevens' aim was to make the illusionary world of film tangibly available to passing customers. As with his film set work, Mallet-Stevens wrote a series of articles that promoted the shopfront as a new experimental space for architecture and advocated for collaboration with lighting engineers.[39] Recognizing the relationship between cinema, retail space and advertising, he promoted modern shop design that highlighted the products on display where: 'It is the passer by, enthusiastic about the shops, who will produce the most effective propaganda for modern building.'[40]

Mallet-Stevens' innovations in retail design should be considered within the context of an enthusiasm for boutique shopfronts and window display as the art gallery of the street.⁴¹ The design magazine *Art et Decoration* praised the involvement of architects and designers including Mallet-Stevens, Francis Jourdain, René Herbst and Le Corbusier in revolutionizing the shop window in the post-war period (Figure 5.6). Credited for developing a sense of mise-en-scène in window display casting objects as 'actors' within the frame, the article espouses numerous references to the cinema in the ways that lighting, movement and colour have been used to create a sensation to seduce the consumer. Outlining the influence of the 1925 *Exposition des Arts Decoratifs*, and collaboration between modern architects and fashion designers, it is clear that the synergies between these fields were recognized by design critics of the era for their important contribution to visual merchandising, but also to the beautification of the streets of Paris.⁴²

The relationship between cinema and shopping that Mallet-Stevens cultivated through his architectural approach to the boutique window should not be underestimated. His cinematic style was very likely the antecedent to much of Cedric Gibbons' work for MGM, which, as Esperdy has argued, was highly influential in cultivating a reciprocity between film and consumer culture.⁴³ As

Figure 5.6 René Herbst, Hall of Windows, Studio Siegel. Photographer uncredited. *Art et Decoration* 1927: 199.

discussed in Chapter 1, the pronounced impact of the Paris *Exposition des Arts Decoratifs* in 1925 on Gibbons' set design brought Art Deco to the American public. In addition, Becherer makes the carefully argued point that Greta Garbo's modernist home in *The Kiss* was directly copied by Cedric Gibbons from photographs of the Maison Mallet-Stevens' living room and hallway that he had seen published in Francis Jourdain's book *Intérieurs* (1929) held in the MGM art library.[44] As such, it is not inconceivable that Gibbons was also inspired by Mallet-Stevens' acumen in bringing together screen and window in ways that had the ability to cultivate consumers. Certainly, MGM studio publicists had an inkling of the potential for silver screen tie-ins. As Esperdy contends, photographs of Gibbons' set designs from *The Wizard of Oz* were sent to architecture and decorating magazines in the hope that the dreamworlds of the cinema might enter the reality of American homes.[45] From 'The Carol Lombard in Macy's Window' to 'Queen Christina Tie-ups', the relationship between Hollywood cinema and consumer culture has been well documented, and the examples of window displays in department stores and boutiques that have made reference to film sets to promote fashions and other products are numerous. Mass-produced copies of garments seen on screen and sold in 'Cinema Shops' and in-store concessional spaces, often designed by Hollywood costumers such as Orry-Kelly were advertised in fan magazines such as *Photoplay* as studio styles worn by the stars.[46] However, the synergy between screen and window is not just a matter of selling remakes of film costumes as fashionable dress to consumers. The proliferation of fashionable images mobilized through cinema and advertising made luxury seemingly more accessible and desirable, and was compounded by the effect of glamorous settings in the cinema theatre, the department store and the boutique.

The glamour of surfaces

The sociologist, Mike Featherstone argues that 'both the cinema and the department store fostered dreams of luxury lifestyles' transforming the surfaces of things through glamour, where 'glamour operates as a force that can make things appear more alluring and splendid, better than they really are'.[47] For Featherstone, glamour is transformative. Unlike beauty which is perceived as inherent, glamour is an image that can be cultivated, and a veneer that can be attached to objects and people.[48] The screen and the shop window then, provide this glamorous surface to fashion, offering an intensified aesthetic experience through distance – the boundary between self and desired object is mediated by a surface that is, in itself, glamorous. The shimmering qualities of light amplified by screen and glass window cultivate the allure of products on display. The implication being, that when consumers engage with these beguiling objects through purchasing and bodily interaction, a new sensory experience will be produced, one which goes beyond a simple engagement with image and surface, transforming the consumer into a more alluring version of the self.

This idea is clearly encapsulated through the reciprocal relationship between cinema, department store and the Ziegfeld showgirl type of Busby Berkeley's films of the 1930s and 1940s. As identified in Chapter 4, the *Follies* showgirl was a spectacle of extravagant fashion and set design that produced a fantasy of glittering transformation, where working-class shop girls became stars. Press releases relating to the theatre showgirls, which could be equally applied to their role on film, described the *Follies* as 'life's show windows ... the glorified girls, the galaxy of stars, and the marvellous scenic effects and costumes, we hold up to the world all the elaborateness and beauty that are to be associated with the shop window of life'.[49] The spectacular synergy between set design and costume of the *Follies* shows was due to the vision of architect Joseph Urban. Dramatic lighting, elaborate decorative surfaces and grand scale proscenium framing were developed by Urban as shared strategies between sites of consumption. Lavish display underpins his oeuvre which includes *Ziegfeld Follies* productions (1914–1932), film sets for *The Young Diana* (1922) and *Under the Red Robe* (1923), and proposed designs for the Bedell Store façade, New York (1928) and Kaufmann's Department store, Pittsburg (1928) as well as the ostentatious resort Mar-a-Lago (1924–1927).

The commodification of showgirl style went beyond the theatre stage and the cinema screen and was promoted in department store displays and themed windows that appropriated the *Follies* exotic dream-like scenes to enhance the appearance of fashion items.[50] For example, photographer Sam Hood's image of a display window featuring MGM *Ziegfeld Girl* promotional material from 1941, situated alongside ready-to-wear fashion garments, and a suggested home dressmaking project provides consumers with instruction in how to achieve glamorous transformation in everyday life (Figure 5.7). The translation from screen to window and possible purchase illustrated here is not achieved through the shimmering sequins and ostentatious feathers of Hollywood costume. Rather, the association between screen-style and the staged vitrine makes more affordable interpretations of fashion appear as a fantasy within reach. While the store window might be understood here as yet

Figure 5.7 Sam Hood, *Ziegfeld Girl* display window using MGM promotional material (1941). Photo Credit: State Library of New South Wales.

another example of how cinema and fashion commoditises women's bodies through the construction of glamorous surfaces, it also makes visible the ways in which the cinema and the department store made fashion, glamour and luxury 'comparably more attainable and democratic' feeding aspirations of social mobility.[51]

The shop girl turned showgirl narrative that *Ziegfeld Girl* portrayed can be understood within the broader context of a range of films that play into working-class women's fantasies of socio-economic 'rags to riches' fashion transformation. The department store as transitional space for the shop girl to become model, designer, or attract the attentions of wealthy romantic interest was frequently portrayed in depression era films such as *Mannequin* (1937) and *The Women* (1939). The cliché of this storyline has rendered it open to alternative and ironic interpretations. For example, Jacques Demy's musical *Les parapluies de Cherbourg* (*The Umbrellas of Cherbourg*) (1964) takes the shop girl romance as its premise, yet throughout highlights the hyper-artificial nature of the genre through the aesthetic of the highly saturated, stylized surfaces of the shop interiors and costumes. Catherine Deneuve as shop girl Genevivèe inhabits the space of the shop window. Her dress in this scene harmonizes with the wallpaper that surrounds her so that we are at once aware of her glamorous façade, but also the blatant falsity of the situation. The narrative that emerges is an unwanted pregnancy to her lover and subsequent marriage to a rich older man whom she doesn't love. The fairy tale ending is incomplete, while she lives a luxurious lifestyle the waning of her desire lingers – perhaps not unlike the purchase of the commodity and the sheen of glamour that disappears once it leaves the shop. A more recent example of the subverted shop girl narrative is the queer love story portrayed in *Carol* (2015) discussed in Chapter 3. Clearly the currency of the department store and boutique as transformative space still holds currency.

Display and digital fashion futures

Fashion-focused films such as *The Great Gatsby* at Harrods and Tiffany & Co (2013) (Figure 5.8), James Bond at Harrods (2012) and *The Grand Budapest Hotel* at Prada (2014) are examples of how film tie-ins and display windows continue to operate in contemporary contexts. Film directors and production

Figure 5.8 Baz Luhrmann (Director) and Catherine Martin (Production Designer) at the unveiling of Tiffany's Fifth Avenue windows inspired by their adaptation of *The Great Gatsby* (2013). Photo Credit: Andrew H. Walker/Getty Images for Tiffany & Co.

designers with recognizable cinematic styles have also been invited to conceive of window displays that bring their aesthetic vision to the street, with Baz Luhrmann and Catherine Martin creating 'Baz Dazzled' Christmas windows for Barneys in 2014, and Nitin Desai's makeover of Selfridges to replicate the exotic and spectacular world of Bollywood in 2002. Drawing on the aesthetic of films such as *Hum Dil De Chuke Sena* (1999), in addition to store windows Desai designed a dancefloor made with marigolds in Selfridges Atrium, peacocks and garlands covering the main entrance, and redecorated the Food Hall with Persian carpets, life-size pieces of tropical fruit and decorative canopies. Film-screenings, fashion-shows and in-store performances of Indian dance and music were also part of this marketing strategy aimed at engaging London's large Hindi community.[52] Beyond these traditional forms of visual merchandising, short fashion films, the digital mainstay of contemporary fashion advertising have further entrenched the relationship between shop window and screen.

The intersection between digital fashion film and retail display can be found in collaborations between SHOWstudio and department stores. In 2000, the British fashion photographer Nick Knight launched the digital platform to showcase fashion as a performative moving image. SHOWstudio was conceived as a creative space outside the constraints of traditional advertising and print media. The fashion films that were produced in the early years of the website were abstract and experimental, focusing on how techniques such as slow motion and montage editing might create sensorial representations of fashion.[53] Highlighting the materiality of fashion and the flow of fabric as a haptic visual experience activated by the motion of the body, films such as those by Ruth Hogben for Gareth Pugh *Pitti Immagine* in 2011, or more recently Nick Knight for Valentino F/W 2021 *Of Grace and Light,* have their origins in the early 'cinema of attractions'.[54] In particular, Loie Fuller in the *Danse Serpentine* – a hand-painted film depicting the dancer's swirling fabric movements by the Lumière Brothers from 1896 – appears to be an inspiration for many of the SHOWstudio films which attempt to convey fashion collections as visual spectacles of light, colour, texture and movement. The SHOWstudio approach to the presentation of fashion has in many ways supplanted the traditional catwalk show as a vehicle for promotion with its ability to infiltrate social media and video streaming sites to reach a vast global audience. In addition to being the first platform to live stream a runway show – with Alexander McQueen's Spring/Summer 2020 *Platos Atlantis* collection – it has been at the forefront of innovating new modes of fashion display through the moving image.

Consumer interest in fashion films, such as those by SHOWstudio, and more obviously branded content by luxury labels, should be understood within the context of immaterial consumption. That is, the increasing consumption of images of fashion mediated through screens, facilitated by the internet and mobile devices. In addition, the windows of computers and mobile screens have replaced the store front of shopping experiences, where the digital *flâneur* of the virtual shop window is provided with an inexhaustible array of products to behold, anywhere, at any time. As Featherstone argues, 24/7 consumption has changed the rhythms of everyday life and social behaviour. The seductive pleasures of screen browsing have replaced in-store bricks and mortar experiences for many consumers, algorithms designed to curate consumption to individual tastes, and habits influence decisions and as a result, reduce opportunity for contemplation and reflection.[55] In this way the screen window obscures the mirror effect of the shop window, the invitation for consumers to look and consider 'is this me?' is supplanted by data gathering devices that offer continuous affirmations to consumers that 'this is you'.

Recognizing the potential to disrupt traditional approaches to window display and reach a wider audience both Selfridges and Harrods have collaborated with SHOWstudio to produce digital content fashion films that intersect with their displays. The first of these collaborations was with Selfridges on The Masters project in 2014. Showcasing capsule collections by fashion designers including Stella McCartney, Jean Paul Gaultier, Yoji Yamamoto, Roberto Cavalli and Paul Smith among others, each was celebrated in a dedicated Oxford street window display inspired by a different film genre. For example, Cavalli's fashions as the master of glamour appeared in the context of a 1930s woman's film, and Yamamoto's clothes were displayed in a sci-fi setting reminiscent of *Blade Runner* (1982). In conjunction with the store windows, SHOWstudio's Marie Schuller produced a promotional fashion film stylistically encapsulating the work of each of the designers that screened in the department store's cinema.[56] Selfridges' creative director Linda Hewson described the relationship between the department store and cinema, where: 'Shopping is a fun form of escape, so to offer our customers access to the escapist power of cinema within Selfridges makes for a great combination.'[57] The success of this approach and the increasing need for fashion retailers to act as content producers saw Selfridges launch Hot Air, its own broadcasting channel for film. Selfridges' resident film maker Katherine Ferguson has explored themes such as unconventional beauty, non-binary ways of dressing, ethical fashion consumption and radical luxury to produce striking visual content for the department store's platform.[58]

The possibilities for digital technology and film to provide new innovative retail experiences are explored in SHOWstudio x Harrods 'Future of Fashion' project for Spring/Summer 2021. This programme of events included online content streaming the season's latest fashions; virtual panel discussions via zoom to examine how fashion has been transformed by the digital revolution; and street-level display windows showcasing a series of SHOWstudio curated installations. As Knight explains, the digital imperatives of fashion's future have become increasingly clear: 'Fashion is going through total and long overdue change, and our planet demands that fashion must be sustainable.'[59] The digital activation of fashion required due to the 2020 global pandemic necessitated new approaches to fashion consumption, opening up yet further opportunities for the fashion film, yet as the Harrods windows imply the physical activation of space still has its place.

While the fashion media has become increasingly saturated with digital content, the narrative abilities of display windows still remain an important part of retail branding. As will be discussed further in Chapter 6, many luxury fashion brands have undergone an 'artification' process, where by collaborations with contemporary artists, architects, designers and film makers have contributed to the cultural capital of brand identities. Shop windows have been a key site for this process to be made visible to consumer audiences. Louis Vuitton have been pioneers in the field of luxury branded artistic collaboration, with notable examples including Dan Flavin's minimalist neon lights in 2011, Yayoi Kusama's coloured dot patterns obliterating the surfaces of window displays in 2012, and Jeff Koons' inflatable bunny replicas and stainless-steel balloon versions of the LV logo in 2017. These artists share attention to surface and effect in common. Their approach is akin to the surface spectacle of pop art rather than deeply conceptual concerns, so suited to these commercial contexts. The department store Selfridges has also engaged with a range of artists to produce window displays for their London store. While many of their store windows displays have been artistic interpretations of branded fashions, in the spirit of the suffragette windows of the early 1900s, political content has also featured. Twenty-first century issues are explored with displays devoted to the scourge of ocean plastics, sustainable fashion and the possibilities of genderless fashion. In this way, contemporary store windows not only invite consumption but also offer the possibility for contemplation beyond the imperative to buy. The physical properties of spectacular window display still appear to be important in engaging consumers. Mediatecture, interactive, touchscreen and hologram display windows are increasingly infiltrating retail environments. However, the prevalence of fantastical visual merchandising that employs the traditional methods of lighting and tableaux styling to enhance the dramatic presentation of fashion and everyday consumer objects suggests the interface between the glass front and the just out of reach commodity continues to create the necessary mise-en-scène for cultivating desire. As Featherstone contends, 'consumer culture constantly seeks to transcend the sensational and banal image overload' employing experiential techniques that promise 'sensory fulfilment' where 'the promise of luxury goods merges with that of works of art'.[60] As I have outlined here, the window display is capable of mirroring the aesthetics of avant-garde art forms, and the experience of cinematic movement and narrative, these immersive qualities become even more pronounced in the interiors of fashion flagships – as will be the focus of the next chapter.

6

Dream spaces: Film sets as fashion flagships and experiential retail environments

Experiential consumption is central to the luxury brand model of retail, whereby the consumer is invited to engage with shopping practices alongside contemporary art and architecture. Fashion retail environments are spaces where real-world consumption intersects with fantasy to create symbolic value for goods. Sensory, emotional, interpersonal and aesthetic experiences are just as important to the consumer as the tangible purchase. In this context, the mise-en-scène of film provides narrative associations and cultural capital for fashion and lifestyle items that appeal to consumer affirmations of identity. Drawing on the sociologist, Gilles Lipovetsky's concept of aesthetic capitalism, this chapter examines how fashion brands have adopted scenographic style. That is, the staged space of retail interiors and architecture are similar to cinematic set design, facilitating brand storytelling through framing, and display to spatially reinforce marketable brand identities.[1]

The commodification of history and nostalgia through film tie-ins has become an integral part of luxury brand strategies of 'artification'. Brands including Prada, Fendi, Gucci and Ralph Lauren have not only provided costumes for cinema, and created their own short fashion films, they have also incorporated the spectacular staging techniques of the cinema to enhance fashion flagships and brand extension retail spaces. These brands construct a contemporary language of nostalgia for past moments in time, reproducing heritage indicators mediated through cinematic mise-en-scène to create innovative retail environments. As such they offer consumers the ultimate imaginary film experience, spatially reconfiguring nostalgia through the layering of cinematic references, styles and surfaces.

Brand heterotopias: Storytelling through interior design

Visual storytelling is essential to developing immaterial value for luxury fashion brands. The experience of fashion spaces through an ecology of images and films produces narrative appeal, where real and fictive spaces collide. Innovative retail spaces are not just the backdrop to fashion, they are essential to creating luxury brand mythologies and meanings that can be understood within the context of this glamorous architecture. As Lipovetsky and Veronica Manilow argue, the 'artification' of retail space enables consumers to see shopping as an aesthetic encounter, a culturally edifying pleasure in which 'the shopper feels improved by the experience'.[2] While haute couture has engaged with cultural experiences including art, theatre, film, performance and architecture since its beginnings in the mid-nineteenth century, these practices have become increasingly important to the development of luxury fashion brand identities. The 'democratisation' of luxury – that is, the availability of luxury in broad socio-economic contexts – along with the aestheticization of everyday life has led luxury brands to adopt increasingly spectacular differentiation techniques in order to construct themselves as exclusive and desirable.[3] In addition, e-commerce has challenged luxury brands to create increasingly distinctive and atmospheric entertainment experiences for consumers in bricks-and-mortar spaces. Fashion historians Peter McNeil and Giorgio Riello suggest that providing a unique experience in the acquisition of luxury has become just as important as the object itself. Luxury brands are

> [i]nvesting more in highly visible retail spaces ... the 'luxury element' comes from the experience of having purchased the good from a luxury shop ... an experience which is worth as much if not more than the product itself.[4]

As such luxury brands participate in what economists B. Joseph Pine and James Gilmore define as the experience economy – in which retailers attempt to fulfil feeling, sensation and self-realization needs through escapist, aesthetic and entertainment experiences. For Pine and Gilmore, 'an experience occurs when a company intentionally uses services as the stage, and goods as props, to engage consumers in a way that creates a memorable event'.[5] Fashion flagship stores, along with their interconnected branded cultural spaces – art galleries, museums, cafés and restaurants – allow consumers to interact with the brand on a multi-sensory level that goes beyond simply shopping in the boutique. These brand extension spaces often operate to reinforce luxury fashion brand heritage.

This aspect of brand identity is multifaceted. It can include authentic narratives that develop around the origin story of the brand, its history and values, but can also extend more broadly to 'borrowed' heritage – for example 'country-of-origin' effects, collaboration with cultural producers, or architectural spaces that lend their heritage stories to the brand by association.[6] As Uche Okonkwo argues, 'most luxury brands are built on a foundation of history and heritage. However, the evolving luxury market requires an adaptation of the traditional outlook of luxury brands to a modern stance'.[7] 'Artification' strategies provide this further layer of heritage, where cultural producers become part of the value chain and renew the brand's image by imparting creative credibility.[8] It is clear that contemporary art is the dominating field of aesthetic stimulation for luxury brand conglomerates to ensure differentiated positioning within the market. Numerous scholars have recognized that flagship stores have engaged with the display techniques of museums and art galleries to sanctify the shopping experience, and have reinforced this relationship by expanding this analogy to also include contemporary art within the retail environment and affiliated art foundations.[9] However, within this context, there is scarce scholarship on the influential role of cinematic experiences in retail environments, despite a long-standing association.[10] Here, I am interested in the ways in which luxury fashion brands adopt cinematic references as heritage indicators, borrowing stylistic qualities of film to enhance retail experiences.

It is useful to consider fashion film retail environments in the context of what I term 'brand heterotopias'. As introduced in Chapter 3, Michel Foucault's concept of a 'heterotopia' is a space that deviates from the ordinary spaces we inhabit through a disruption in time and place. Foucault identifies theatres and cinemas as heterotopias, 'capable of juxtaposing in a single real place several spaces, several sites that are in themselves incompatible'.[11] By extrapolation, flagship stores which adopt cinematic references in the staging of their fashions can be seen to combine different spaces and times. They do this in ways that merge past and present – through heritage indicators in contemporary collections; are both isolated but penetrable – in their exclusivity and differentiation from everyday shopping contexts; and juxtapose illusion with the real – through the evocation of fantasy film narratives in bricks-and-mortar stores. Extending this concept, 'brand heterotopias' are places where luxury brands create their own fantastical worlds of experience that are heavily reliant on 'inter-spatial' layering – the film set, cinematic narrative, art gallery, café, heritage collection, archive and fashion boutique meld together to create a unique cultural consumption environment available to a limited elite audience.

The recent trend of creating brand heterotopias by incorporating intimate size cinemas in luxury retail stores is just one example of how film has increasingly infiltrated the shopping experience. For example, Gucci Garden in Florence, Italy provides shoppers with a range of inter-spatial experiences dedicated to promoting the Gucci brand's luxury heritage. Housed in the historic Palazzo della Mercanzia, Gucci Garden opened in 2018 as a concept space with multiple branded cultural contact points to engage with. In addition to the ground floor boutique, there is a museum display of the Gucci leather and garment archive harking back to the 1920s, a series of exhibition spaces for the presentation of rotating contemporary art, a restaurant presided over by three-Micheline-star chef Massimo Bottura, and a cinema auditorium. As a Gucci Garden didactic describes of the Galleria: it 'is above all a place combining the real with the imaginary … embracing history, objects, anecdotes and geography … ready to be reactivated in constellations rich with future in which past meets present'.[12] Through this statement Gucci's multifaceted approach to heritage is made clear, where both authentic and borrowed indicators are activated. For example, Gucci Garden's presence in a Palazzo just a stone's throw from the Medici residence suggests the brand's deep Florentine roots and patronage of the arts.[13] In fact, the brand was established in 1921 and their artification strategy began in 2015. The boutique – which features antique furniture, and vintage–inspired wall paper styled on Gucci's floral scarf designs from the 1960s – reinterprets previous aesthetic cues as the backdrop to contemporary collections. The museum adopts a similar approach, displaying the archive thematically to reiterate the relationship between the past and present. Through this array of heritage indicators Gucci celebrates the mythology of their origin story, and their relationship to Italian style and craftsmanship updating these elements to connect with more current cultural products.

In this context, the thirty-seat Cinema da Camera – a plush red-velvet lined auditorium – is suggestive of a contemporary interpretation of past movie theatres, providing audiences with an experience of exclusivity and glamour (Figure 6.1). The films on show are generally examples of Italian art house cinema such as Marco Ferreri's *La Donna Scimmia* (1964), or more recent experimental film – such as Josh Blaaberg's *Distant Planet: The Six Chapters of Simona* (2019) about the world of Italo disco. In this way, the brand attempts to connect its existent heritage indicators with Italian cinematic heritage, in order to provide consumers with unique, immersive cultural experiences that are suggestive of long-lasting values and timeless appeal. Gucci Gardens is part of the brand's 'artification' strategy. Since the appointment of Alessandro Michele as creative director in

Figure 6.1 Cinema da Camera, Gucci Gardens, Florence. Photo Credit: Jess Berry (2019).

2015, Gucci has attempted to enhance the symbolic and aesthetic attributes of the brand through a range of artistic endeavours including collaborations with artists Trouble Andrew and Daito Manabe, sponsored exhibitions, and patronage of women in the film industry. This strategy has proved to be incredibly successful, with Gucci holding the place of most valuable Italian fashion brand in 2019.[14] I contend that Gucci's appropriation of cinema as a heritage indicator within retail design is indicative of an approach to history and nostalgia that has been adopted by a range of luxury brands. This approach is similar to cinema's treatment of heritage as a style. As discussed in Chapter 3, heritage cinema 'savours the qualities and presence of dwellings, costumes, artworks, objects', as Richard Dyer adeptly explains, 'history is a discipline of enquiry into the past; heritage is an attitude towards the legacy of the past'.[15] With this in mind, I argue that luxury fashion brands reinterpret history as heritage and nostalgia and treat these as stylish surfaces where past and present, real and imaginary spatial experiences are manipulated for aesthetic, entertainment and escapist effects.

Cinemas in flagship stores, as heritage branded attractions appear to be an emerging trend. Louis Vuitton's Maison Etoile (2012) is housed in Rome's first cinema. The nineteen-seat screening room is dedicated to the history of Cinnecita film studios and also displays the collection of trunks made for Wes Anderson's *The Darjeeling Limited* (2007). Shanghai Tang's refurbishment of Cathay Theatre Hong Kong (2013) is an original Art Deco cinemas still in operation that also displays fashion apparel arranged to represent movie scenes. The movie theatre as an entertaining flagship artification strategy can be understood more broadly as a form of in-store exhibition. In the case of Gucci, Louis Vuitton and Shanghai Tang cinematic heritage is a somewhat tenuous link, a symbolic borrowing of style through association rather than deeply embedded in the brand's history. Conversely, the museum at the Salvatore Ferragamo flagship store in Florence, Italy draws on the country-of-origin effect of 'Made in Italy' branding, in conjunction with the fashionable symbolic economy of the city, and history of cinematic collaboration to develop an 'authentic' situated heritage experience.

Salvatore Ferragamo began his career in Hollywood with the 'Boot Shop' he opened in 1923 where he provided footwear for a number of movie stars including Mary Pickford and Gloria Swanson. Having established his expertise within the film industry, in 1927 he moved to Florence to rebrand his business based on the city's historical reputation of fine leather craftsmanship, opening a store in the medieval building Palazzo Spini Feroni. From this location Ferragamo was able to continue his work with Hollywood through the Rifreddi studios in Florence, and the Cinecitta studios in Rome, where a number of Hollywood blockbusters and Italian productions were made. As 'shoemaker to the stars' Ferragamo made custom footwear for actresses including Marilyn Monroe, Audrey Hepburn and Sofia Loren cementing the brand's stylish cinematic heritage.[16] The Salvatore Ferragamo brand has continued this association, producing shoes for films including *Evita* (1996), *Ever After: A Cinderella Story* (1998) and *Australia* (2008).

Exhibitions at the museum have reinforced this cinematic heritage since its opening in 1995 including 'Cinderella: The Shoe Rediscovered' (1998), 'Audrey Hepburn. A Woman. The Style' (1999), 'Shoes and Famous Feet' (2000), 'Australia: Behind the Scenes' (2009), 'Greta Garbo' (2010) and 'Marilyn' (2013).[17] The museum's exhibitions as brand extension strategy within the fashion flagship create a rich visual experience for consumers to engage with the brand's extensive archive, enriching their understanding of the brand's history, artisanal qualities and cinematic ties. For example, the museum's most recent cinema exhibition

'Italy in Hollywood' (2018–19) connects the Salvatore Ferragamo brand mythology to the broader narrative, celebrating the influence of Italian creatives on the American film industry during the early twentieth century (Figure 6.2). The shoemaker's impact on Hollywood costume is positioned alongside the work of screen stars such as Lina Cavalieri and Rudolph Valentino. The culmination of the exhibition is an array of Ferragamo shoes displayed against the backdrop of striking black-and-white stills that create the atmosphere of a film set, immersing audiences in Ferragamo's cinematic heritage.[18] To coincide with the exhibition the brand produced a capsule collection of shoes based on those worn by Mary Pickford, Gloria Swanson, Joan Crawford and Rudolph Valentino so that consumers might personally experience the style of these fashionable screen

Figure 6.2 *Italy in Hollywood* exhibition Museum Salvatore Ferragamo (2018). Photo Credit: Jess Berry.

stars. In this way the museum, in concert with the flagship store creates a brand heterotopia where historical archive, cinematic dream-space, nostalgic revelry and boutique shopping come together. The past is made present through this inter-spatial layering, bestowing heritage as a desirable immaterial value that has continuity in the here-and-now.

Incorporating entertainment experiences in the form of the movie theatre or film costume exhibition is not the only way that fashion flagships have engaged with the spatial possibilities of cinema. Lipovetsky and Manilow illuminate this relationship: 'long-time luxury blends with the rhythm of the screen, the logic of heritage combines with the extreme mobility of images, and brand's lastingness fuses with the mind set of a Hollywood movie.'[19] Inspiration from set design and cinematic scenography is even more prevalent within the fashion flagship store heritage paradigm, providing consumers with highly engaging immersive experiences.

Film sets as fashion flagships, experiential retail spaces and the commodification of history and nostalgia

Ralph Lauren's Rhinelander Mansion refurbished by Naomi Leff in 1986 was the first flagship store to actively engage with filmic fantasy as a whole of brand merchandising strategy. Throughout his career, Lauren's collections have been influenced by cinema – think English sportswear from *Chariots of Fire* (1981), the preppy look of *Dead Poets Society* (1989) or safari inspiration from *Out of Africa* (1985). As *Vogue* fashion journalist Joan Juliette Buck explains:

> The clothes of Ralph Lauren are a form of cinema; they fulfil the private function known in movies as the backstory – telling you who you are, and who you were, and where you come from – and the public function of demonstrating these things to other people.[20]

Of the many cinematic collections the brand has produced, *The Great Gatsby* has endured as an ongoing aesthetic style in garments, interior design and advertising.[21] The designer's involvement in creating Jay Gatsby's (Robert Redford) suits and shirting for Jack Clayton's 1974 film adaptation of *The Great Gatsby* has consistently underpinned the brand's identity. As Ralph Lauren describes:

> I was doing Gatsby long before *The Great Gatsby* came out. That's what I did. It was glamorous. When people couldn't understand what I did I would talk about Gatsby – it was the era of the jackets with belted backs, of flannel suits.[22]

Apart from a signature style that fit neatly with the film's affluent aesthetic, the designer's origin story seemed to mirror the Gatsby mythology. Lauren's transformation from Ralph Lifshitz – the son of a Russian Jewish émigré who grew up in the Bronx – to the all-American, entrepreneur of a multi-billion-dollar fashion empire is the personification of the American dream of self-made success that underpins the F. Scott Fitzgerald novel. While Jay Gatsby's fate is a tragic one, and ultimately a story of disillusionment with conspicuous consumption and the underlying problems of economic and social inequity, Ralph Lauren's appropriation of the Gatsby identity focuses on stylish glamour, wealth and the possibility of making one's dreamworld a reality. Like Chanel – who epitomized her brand identity and the modern woman lifestyle through her persona, fashion and the retail experiences of her salon interiors – Ralph Lauren has composed a consistent image of aspirational success. This image of wealth and privilege germinated in the 1970s when he convinced the department store Bloomingdale's to place all of his merchandise together in the mode of mise-en-scène, rather than dispersed in separate departments. The concession was decorated with accoutrements such as walking sticks, chesterfield sofas and alligator skin luggage, creating a version of the gentleman's club as retail environment.[23] Lauren would go onto exploit these lifestyle branding strategies and ready-made heritage indicators even further with the Rhinelander Mansion flagship store.

The Rhinelander Mansion, commissioned in 1895 by Gertrude Rhinelander-Waldo, was a large private residence designed in French Renaissance and Gothic revival styles by Kimball and Thompson architects.[24] Leff's renovation of the American pedigree site maintained many of its original features and combined these with cinematic styling to create an image of an aristocratic manor house. Mahogany wood panelling, moulded ceilings and chandeliers are accented by velvet drapery, period furnishings, equestrian scenes in gilt frames, Persian rugs and leather sofas. These sumptuous surroundings are the backdrop to Ralph Lauren menswear, accessories and homewares (Figure 6.3). As Lauren describes of the store: 'I am not just selling clothes. I am selling a world, a notion of style. I'm offering a philosophy of life.'[25] The world that Lauren is selling is the American dream of aspirational luxury. Through reference to *Gatsby* set decorations, Ralph Lauren constructed a heritage for the brand, simulating an aristocratic lifestyle of a bygone era. Adapting cinematic narrative for brand storytelling purposes is inherent to the Ralph Lauren experience and promotional strategy, as described in branded content:

> For Ralph it was all about the environment, we were providing the context, the movie that was in his head ... No expense was spared on evocative window displays and cinematically staged interiors ... Ralph Lauren never really thought

Figure 6.3 Bedroom decorated by Ralph Lauren as part of his new Home Collection New York. LIFE 1986. Photo Credit: Dirck Halstead/The LIFE Images Collection via Getty Images/Getty Images.

of himself as a designer, but as someone who tells stories through his clothes. And he never thought of the mansion on 72nd street as a store. It was an environment, a club and an atmosphere that created context around his brand, allowing him to tell a story in a clearer and more powerful way.[26]

The aesthetically refined heritage cues inherent throughout the store, coupled with the *Gatsby* references are a savvy strategy that appeals to Ralph Lauren's aspirational luxury for upper-middle-class consumers. The scenography of the Rhinelander Mansion is ultimately the story of upward social and economic mobility, bringing the accoutrements of the aristocracy within perceptible reach for the nouveaux riches. The styling of Ralph Lauren 'looks' as complete ensembles, enhanced by the atmospheric settings of branded homewares, and accented by vintage props, creates a ready-made lifestyle of intergenerational wealth. Ralph Lauren European Creative Director, Ann Boyd explains that:

> People wanted to put entire room sets on their charge cards, and just pantechnicon everything to their home counties, from the Edwardian-style bathrooms that look as though the Windsors have just popped out, to bedrooms Biggles would be happy to crash into.[27]

Ralph Lauren is not the only fashion brand to benefit from *The Great Gatsby's* heady aesthetic of 1920s glamour redefined for contemporary tastes. Director Baz Luhrmann's 2012 adaptation was heralded as a fashion and style extravaganza, with evening dresses designed by Miuccia Prada and men's tailoring by Brooks Brothers.[28] Prada's costume designs for *The Great Gatsby* are in line with the brand's larger marketing strategy of artistic patronage and development of short film advertisements to enhance fashion's immaterial value. Prada's designs for the film were derived from the brand's 2010 and 2011 archive. They appealed to costume production director Catherine Martin as fashionable garments that were not historically accurate, yet were coherent with the 1920s era – so fitting with the film's overall mise-en-scène. In this instance, fashion and the interior are treated as glamorous and alluring surfaces and the 1920s as a lavish and dazzling fantasy world of consumption. Martin provides insight into this collaboration, expounding that: 'Baz [Luhrmann] and Miuccia [Prada] have always connected on their shared fascination with finding modern ways of releasing classical and historical references from the shackles of the past.'[29] This treatment of the past is typical of fashion, which constantly seeks to reinterpret previous styles for contemporary audiences, empty of historical meaning. The Prada gowns, along with production stills and sketches, were exhibited on the staircase at the Prada Epicentre, New York as part of the flagship store's cultural programme in 2012, so incorporating the film into the brand's heritage of cultural capital achieved through cinematic reference (Figure 6.4).

In addition to fashion commodity tie-ins, Luhrmann's *Gatsby* also produced a range of interior design furnishings. Based on the lavish Art Deco style staging of the film, Martin collaborated with Designer Rugs to create a series of lush graphic hand-knotted floor-coverings, as well as a range of geometric wallpapers and fabrics for Mokum. Presumably, consumers could re-create the *Gatsby* aesthetic and experience in their own homes in much the same way that Art Deco cinema of the 1920s and 1930s promoted interior design innovations to women audiences, as described in Chapter 1. Martin's refurbishment of the Fitzgerald Suite at The Plaza Hotel, New York included examples of these commercially designed furnishings, creating a further layer of intertextual referencing where The Plaza featured as one of the film's locations. Martin's Fitzgerald Suite might be understood as a brand hererotopia in the same way as the Ralph Lauren *Gatsby* inspired flagship store. Through the contemporary referencing of past historic styles, mediated through cinematic set design, and combined with a mythologizing narrative of a glamorous character, an illusory 'dream-space' is made a tangible experience for consumers. This type of inter-spatial layering of

Figure 6.4 Catherine Martin and Miuccia Prada Dress Gatsby at Prada Epicentre, New York (2013). Photo Credit: Dimitrios Kambouris/Getty Images for Prada.

retail environments, that rely on cinematic references to create experiences that intersect the real and the fictitious have become an increasingly prevalent brand strategy for luxury fashion that extend beyond traditional boutiques.

Perhaps the most obvious example of this idea is Wes Anderson's Bar Luce (2015), at Fondazione Prada, Milan (Figure 6.5). Expanding Prada's universe of artistic patronage, the foundation is the culmination of the brand's image consisting of: spectacular 'starchitect' designed space – Rem Koolhaas transformed the former distillery with a new architecture that interacts with existing buildings; engagement with contemporary art and film as brand aligned cultural capital – including permanent exhibitions by Robert Gober, Louise Bourgoise and Jean-Luc Godard; and celebration of auteur cinema directors –

Figure 6.5 Wes Anderson, Bar Luce at Fondazione Prada, Milan. Photo Credit: Jess Berry (2018).

including Wes Anderson, Roman Polanski and Steve McQueen. In this context, Bar Luce is a reminder of Prada's engagement with digital fashion film as a branded cultural product. Wes Anderson short films *Prada Candy* (with Roman Coppola in 2013) and *Castello Cavalcanti* (2013) are just two examples of a suite of Prada branded content by auteur directors, including examples by Roman Polanski, Yang Fudong and Ridley Scott.

The Bar Luce, like Anderson's films, is rich with intertextual references, the most obvious being the retro 1950s style of *Castello Cavalcanti*, the story of an America racing car driver (Jason Shwartzman) who crashes his vehicle in a tiny Italian village that happens to be his ancestral home. The Prada produced short film, in which nothing of significance occurs, appears to be as much about the aesthetic experience of the café – with its nostalgic Formica table-tops and palate of pastel green, bright red and yellows – as it is a homage to Federico Fellini's *Amarcord* (1973) and *La Dolce Vita* (1960). Bar Luce plays on these nostalgic references along with Milanese style – pale pink terrazzo floors, seating arrangements of pale green upholstery, Gio Ponti coffee machine, wood panelling and Formica counter. Wallpaper depicting the Galleria Vittorio Emanuele shopping arcade makes reference to Prada's origins and their restoration of Milanese architectural heritage. A Cavalcanti pin-ball machine, situated along the back wall of the café, is a nod to the director's previous Prada collaborations and the aesthetic inspiration for the décor. Another game, dedicated to Steve Zizzou of Anderson's *The Life Aquatic* (2004), is suggestive of his broader cinematic oeuvre. Anderson's signature aesthetic – highly stylized sets, fashion conscious wardrobes and carefully curated props – makes his film's nostalgic spectacles rich in surface detail. Anderson's cinema is abundant with memorable fashion ensembles, such as: Margo Tenenbaum (Gwyneth Paltrow) wearing a Fendi fur coat, Lacoste tennis dress and Hermès Birkin bag in *The Royal Tenenbaums* (2001); *The Life Aquatic's* Steve Zizzou's (Bill Murray) Adidas Sneakers; the Louis Vuitton custom-monogrammed luggage of *The Darjeeling Limited*; and Prada designed luggage for Tilda Swinton's Madame D. along with coats worn by Willem Dafoe and Ralph Fiennes in *The Grand Budapest Hotel* (2014). This proliferation of luxury fashion references contributes to Anderson's style-conscious resume, making him a suitable auteur director for commercial fashion film. Anderson's attention to spatial details in these films is similarly highly stylized and atmospheric. Intense colour schemes, vintage style furniture and decorative features combine to create a highly artificial aesthetic of nostalgia. For example, the pink, purple and red colour scheme, and Art Deco ornamentation of the Grand Budapest Hotel in its 1930s incantation, recalls the department stores, café's, hotels and other glamorous spaces of the era.

With its candy-tone hues and elaborate architecture it appears much like a cake – not dissimilar to the Mendl's patisseries that form part of the plot. The aesthetic is based on an invented history and idea of Europe, which has resonance in reality but also conveys a dream-like quality. Production designer Adam Stockhausen articulates this process:

> We were trying to make the most of the architecture that was around us … we used an existing shell of a department store … to become the hotel. Then we put a set dressing on top of that, and props on top of that, to draw out the specifics of the history and period, even though, … it's sort of an invented history. Then we started inventing things to layer on top of that … From there the film started to develop a richness and history of its own.[30]

This layering of surfaces to create an artificial history and nostalgia for an imagined hotel in Anderson's film can be compared to the atmosphere of Bar Luce. Its intertextual cinematic references both to his own films and those of Italian New Wave directors – Vittorio De Sica and Luchino Visconti – transport the bar's patrons to the fantasy world of cinematic style.[31] As Anderson describes of his interior design, 'I do think it would make a pretty good movie set, I think it would make an even better place to write a movie. I tried to make it a bar I would want to spend my own non-fictional afternoons in.'[32] Here, Anderson alludes to Bar Luce as a heterotopic space situated between reality and imagination. The everyday experience of the bar or café becomes an extraordinary evocation of the alternative world of the silver screen and a real space where consumers might act out their film fantasies.

Fondazione Prada's Bar Luce is just one example of many restaurants and cafes that have been incorporated into luxury brand heterotopias. The Gucci Osteria, Ralph's Coffee – the 1950s themed Ralph Lauren eatery, and Fendi café at Harrods, are indicative of how luxury brands are attempting to create all-encompassing lifestyle offerings. Predictably, cinematic references have found their place in this context as well. For example, India Mahdavi's pastel-hued interior designs for Laudrée appear to be based on Sofia Coppola's version of *Marie Antoinette* (2006). Perhaps even more evocative than being able to devour macaroons surrounded by the twenty-first-century aesthetic equivalent to the patisserie loving French queen's boudoir, is the possibility to eat breakfast at Tiffany's. The Blue Box Café at Tiffany & Co flagship store New York provides consumers with an imaginary and immersive experience of the 1961 film *Breakfast at Tiffany's*. Eating in-store was not a real possibility for Holly Golightly (Audrey Hepburn). Instead, her breakfast was alfresco – a take-away coffee and croissant while perusing the store windows, dressed in a Givenchy black gown and layers of pearls, wistfully dreaming of what might be. The Blue Box café offers a more gourmet selection of food than the film – smoked salmon, lobster salad and petit fours, consumed while surrounded by the brand's trademark blue décor and tableware available through the Tiffany's homeware collection. These elements combine to create a luxury branded experience of the New York highlife that Holly Golightly dreamed of. Similar to Bar Luce, this brand heterotopia exemplifies how the imaginary worlds of cinema are exploited by luxury brands through borrowed heritage indicators.

As these examples show, consumer experiences of these spaces do not need to be true to an original film scene, rather, they need only be indicative of cinematic style, providing a compelling image that is 'Instagrammable' so that visitors can display their conspicuous consumption through social media. In this way, brand extension into café, bar, cinema and gallery spaces provide 'non-traditional consumers of the brand' with opportunities to engage with luxury fashion at a more affordable price-point.[33] Like flagship stores, these experiential retail environments become tourist destinations, accessible to a broader demographic of aspirational luxury consumers. Furthermore, cinematic spatial references offer an approachable entry point to these consumers. As popular mass-media entertainment, film is arguably a more readily available cultural experience than contemporary art. In addition to the inter-spatial layering of film scenography with brand identity markers, these brand extension environments also benefit from a 'country-of-origin-effect' whereby the cultural mythologies of fashion cities – for example, Milan in the case of Bar Luce, and New York in the case of the Blue Box Café – are also embedded within brand heterotopias.

The aforementioned examples: Prada, Gucci and Salvatore Ferragamo all use Italian taste, craft tradition, historic architecture and cinematic heritage as iconic elements to leverage brand identity and cultural capital in ways that are both 'authentic' and 'borrowed'. Through this process, cultural products can be subsumed by the luxury brand in ways that can obscure the cultural work's original intent. Take for example the case of Ralph Lauren's borrowing of the *Gatsby* narrative, where the text's original critique of the empty pursuit of pleasure is transformed into a glamorous image of conspicuous consumption through luxury branding. This is not a new mode of operation for the fashion system, which consistently appropriates cultures, images and styles for its own purposes, emptying them of their original meaning and transposing them into the dreamworld of surface glamour. In recent decades fashion brands have been held to account for their misinterpretation and disregard for appropriated cultures and the exploitative power differentials that are at play within this system.[34] Within this context it is important to consider the ways that fashion brands use the glamour of film to obfuscate history through their appropriation of contentious heritage sites as well as the philanthropic role they can play in preserving heritage.

Since 2012, the Italian government has sought patronage from luxury fashion brands to provide the funds for the maintenance and restoration of the country's civic monuments.[35] Examples of this in Rome alone include Tod's cleaning of the Colosseum, Bulgari's restoration of the Spanish Steps and Gucci's restyling of the Tarpeian Rock. The benefits of heritage patronage for luxury fashion brands are emblematic – association with historical sites of cultural importance lends prestige through values of distinction, timelessness, exclusivity and classical aesthetics. For governments and local economies, this type of patronage helps to keep investment, employment, craftsmanship and tourism within the city or country through the preservation of culture. Fendi's patronage and restoration of the Trevi Fountain (2013–15), Palazzo Civiltà Italiana (2013–15) the site of Fendi headquarters, and a seventeenth-century Palazzo in Rome to house its flagship store are examples of a philanthropic strategy that traverses both preservation and problematic appropriation of contentious heritage. In the case of Fendi's involvement in the restoration of the Trevi Fountain and Palazzo Civiltà Italiana, these sites have further layers of symbolic value as images of glamour due to their presence in Federico Fellini's *La Dolce Vita* (1960), and the *Boccaccio '70* (1962) episode '*The Temptation of Dr Antonio*' (Figure 6.6).

According to fashion historian Eugenia Paulicelli, Fellini's films helped shape Rome, and Italy as a 'laboratory of style, aesthetics and creative innovation'.[36] Costume and set-designer Piero Gherardi styled *La Dolce Vita* like a series of fashion photographs that accentuate Italian glamour. For example, the journalist

Figure 6.6 Anita Eckberg on the set of *Boccaccio '70* segment 'Le tentazioni del dottor Antonio' (1961) against the backdrop of Palazzo Civiltà Italiana, directed by Fedrico Fellini. Photo Credit: Vittoriano Rastelli/Corbis via Getty Images.

Marcello Rubini's (Marcello Mastrioianni) alluring masculinity is accentuated through a series of tailored slim-fit suits accessorized with dark sunglasses. Sylvia (Anita Ekberg) equals his erotic appeal dressed in a black strapless gown that clings provocatively to her voluptuous body as she takes a sensual bath in the Trevi Fountain. Ekberg's look is copied in *Boccaccio '70* in which she wears a similar figure-hugging evening gown embellished with sparkling gems while walking the streets in front of Palazzo Civiltà Italiana haunting Dr Antonio's dreams. Fendi is among numerous fashion brands including Dolce & Gabbana, Prada and Valentino who have found inspiration in *La Dolce Vita*, the Trevi Fountain and Ekberg's velvet gown. However, Fendi's branding strategy of drawing on the cultural capital of cinematic Rome through the patronage of Trevi Fountain and Palazzo Civiltà Italiana has embedded these associations within the brand's heritage to the extent that it might lay special claim to classic Italian cinema.

Widely reported in the fashion press with reference to *La Dolce Vita*, in July of 2016 a glass catwalk was installed over the Trevi Fountain's waters to perform a spectacular fashion show in celebration of Fendi's 90th anniversary and the completion of the restoration of the monument.[37] Fendi's claim to the iconic cinematic style of Rome is further encapsulated in the brand's recasting of Palazzo Civiltà Italiana (also known as Colosseo Quadrato) from Fascist monument to fashionable image.[38] In 2017, Fendi cemented the relationship between the brand, Palazzo Civiltà Italiana and cinema with the opening of a year-long exhibition 'Fendi Studios' dedicated to showcasing the brand's appearance in films such as *And the Ship Sails On* (1983), *The Grand Budapest Hotel* and *I Am Love*. Other exhibitions at Palazzo Civiltà Italiana including 'A New Rome' (2016) and 'The Artisans of Dreams' (2016) have similarly presented the brand's relationship to Roman architecture and film.[39] More recently, the brand's Roman Holiday collection (2019) advertising campaign referenced the Audrey Hepburn 1953 film as well as Fellini's cinema, with a short fashion-film featuring Kiernan Shipka and Christian Coppola romping around the arches and steps of Palazzo Civiltà Italiana and against the backdrop of the Trevi fountain. Fendi's restyling of Palazzo Civiltà Italiana through its association with film can be understood within the context of other fashion brands who have rebranded historic buildings within the frame of architectural luxury.

Fendi has sought to de-couple Palazzo Civiltà Italiana from its roots in Fascist architectural propaganda by highlighting the building's aesthetic appeal. Initially commissioned by Mussolini, the monument was designed by Giovanni Guerrini, Ernesto L. Padula and Mario Romano, as the centrepiece to the 1942 world fair which never eventuated. It was to serve as a symbolic image of Mussolini's 'new

Roman Empire, the present and the future legitimised by the past, and for both imperial Rome's "empire" signified order, authority, civilisation'.[40] The building has featured as a metaphor for these same conservative and oppressive social values in Roberto Rossellini's *Roma Città Aperta* (1945), the aforementioned *Boccaccio '70*, Bernado Bertolucci's *Il Conformista* (1970) and Peter Greenaway's *The Belly of an Architect* (1987) among others. While Fendi celebrated these films as part of the building's cinematic heritage in exhibitions and publications, it has glossed over Palazzo Civiltà Italiana's rationalist glorification of a dictatorship to focus purely on the building as an emblem of the brand's ties with Rome. In a statement that should be understood as a different form of propaganda, the brand claims that, for Italians the building is 'completely deloaded, empty of any significance of that period'.[41] Certainly Fendi went about 'deloading' the building from its Fascist heritage by seamlessly integrating its classical Roman arches and modernist geometric structure into a reoccurring fashionable image. The arches of Palazzo Civiltà Italiana, in marble sculptural relief, accent the red marble staircase at the Palazzo Fendi flagship store in Rome, and have appeared in various incantations in Fendi flagship stores globally (Figure 6.7). They have also featured as the

Figure 6.7 Fendi New York Flagship Boutique, Madison Aveue (2015). Photo Credit: Gilbert Carrasquillo/GC Images via Getty Images.

backdrop to fashion shows, window displays and advertising campaigns. As former creative director Karl Lagerfeld explained of Fendi's 2014/2015 advertising campaign: 'I chose Palazzo Civiltà Italiana because it is one of the most graphic buildings in the world and one of the most famous buildings of modern Rome. This campaign expresses what Fendi is about ... It is very Roman, it is luxurious but at the same time it has a modern and young approach.'[42]

Just as Mussolini appropriated Rome's traditional architecture as a symbol of his Fascist government's political power legitimized by a perceived link to Imperial Rome, Fendi as fashion brand employs these forms as a symbol of its Roman heritage, imperial wealth and fashionable authority. History, disassociated from its ugly bits, becomes a luxury commodity. The architectural critic Owen Hatherly astutely pinpoints the problem:

> Fascist architecture, fashion, Fendi, all part of a history of amoral, elite good taste ... However, to assume that this is little more than a game with aesthetics, a play on history, is to assume that fascism is ancient, dead history in Italy. It isn't ... its architecture should remain tainted.[43]

Fendi's recasting of an architecture that might be considered to be 'evil' due to its fascist heritage also sits within the context of fashion's glamorous architecture that is primarily in the service of spectacle. For architectural critics such as Miles Glendinning, architecture that is in the service of capitalism and fashion collapses boundaries of public and private, commerce and culture, where architecture becomes a brand and is no longer built for the purposes of the social and the civic.[44] These critiques echo those aimed at the glamorous architecture of cinema as discussed in Chapter 2.

Luxury fashion brands such as Fendi assert their constructed cultural authority through the appropriation of heritage spaces, creating 'improved' versions of the past through cinematic styling. This approach might be understood more broadly in the context of what Lipovetsky describes as the global period of 'cinematographization' where nothing can escape the mediation of screens, so that cinema remains identifiable everywhere and 'the real world grows closer to its celluloid image'.[45] In this way cinema can be understood to orient our experience of everyday life, providing an imaginary experience that redefines our relationship to the real. Boutiques, 'imitate the magic universe of the cinema. Now people go to luxury stores to live their lives in a show or a film – just like a movie star.'[46]

The scenography of fashion flagship stores and brand extension spaces, in conversation with staircases and shop windows, have been at the forefront of cinematic styling that influences a range of other retail sectors. For example, the beauty brand Aesop's flagship store in Chelsea London is inspired by Ken Adam's designs for James Bond lairs while the Rome store is a collaboration with *I Am Love* director Luca Guadagnino; Mak Mak restaurant in Hong Kong cites Wes Anderson and Wong Kar-Wai's *In the Mood for Love* as inspiration; while the Darial concept store in Barcelona claims the 1963 film *The Leopard* as its cinematic source.[47] Cinema imaginaries as retail spaces have become fashionable to such an extent that it is now common for designers to reference the aesthetic styles of multiple films in one-space to create cinematic mise-en-scène. Take for example, India Mahdavi's styling of the REDValentino flagship store in London (2016) (Figure 6.8). Inspired by the domestic interiors of films such as Jacques Tati's *Mon Oncle* (1958) and Blake Edwards' *The Party* (1968), Mahdavi's design for Valentino incorporates brass-rimmed circular mirrors, a graphic-patterned floor and blush pink armchairs to function, as she describes, 'somewhere in between reality and fiction, function and dreams'.[48] While these particular cinematic influences may not be familiar to the Valentino consumer, the retail space is staged like a film set to stage a brand's transformational narrative. As Mahdavi further explains of her approach: 'I like to be transported. I like to feel like I am elsewhere. That's a strength of movies, and I like to think that's what I do with my work too.'[49]

Figure 6.8 India Mahdavi interior for RED Valentino London Flagship store, 2016. Photo Credit: David M. Benett/Getty Images for Red Valentino.

In this way, we might understand brand heterotopias as layering multiple film imaginaries, spatial typologies and time frames, to produce a dreamworld entirely open to the shopper's interpretation. As these spaces increasingly form the backdrop to consumer 'Instagrammable' moments on social media, brand narratives and experiences become embedded in individual histories and memories. Brand heritage comes closer and closer to being inextricably linked to the values and heritage of the consumer.

Conclusion

Throughout this book, I have sought to investigate the aesthetic and conceptual alignment of fashion, interior design and architecture as mediated through film. This relationship has proved to be a significant component of the representation of gender and sexual identity on screen and to have shaped consumer cultures. The overlapping histories of these disciplines provide rich aesthetic, and sociocultural context for understanding how these forms operate in the present moment which is now saturated with moving images. Yet this history has many deep and serious omissions. The under-representation of people of colour and paucity of non-Western film examples throughout this book is a problem. It is a problem embedded in the fashion system, which privileges white, slim, youthful bodies, and it is a problem of Western cinema which has a similarly poor history of racially diverse representation. *Vogue* magazine did not show a woman of colour on its cover until Donyale Luna for the March 1966 British addition. With few exceptions, the racial homogeneity of luxury fashion on runways and in magazines was not redressed in any meaningful way until 2007 when Naomi Campbell and Iman launched a campaign against racism in the industry.[1] In 2020, 41 per cent of catwalk models in major spring fashion shows were non-white, meaning there is still much room for improvement.[2] Given the historical lack of non-white bodies in mainstream fashion media it is perhaps unsurprising that Hollywood cinema has often overlooked these bodies in their representation of glamour also. While diverse actors have become more prevalent in films since the 1980s, these are rarely roles in which people of colour wear designer fashions in opulent surroundings. Simply put, Western ideals of luxurious glamour are spectacularly lacking when it comes to representing diverse bodies in cultures of fashion and space. My purpose then in this conclusion is to signal spaces in my argument where current and future research could address these under-represented identities.

Josephine Baker, as the first Black woman to star in a major motion picture – *Siren of the Tropics* (*La Sirène des Tropiques*) (1927) – has been the subject of much scholarship examining the entertainer's racial representation on screen. While fashion and architecture have often formed part of this discourse – intriguingly, Adolf Loos imagined an unbuilt zebra-striped house for the actress – there is scope to further examine her oeuvre.³ Take for example Baker's performance in *Princess Tam Tam* (1935), a Pygmalionesque story that sees Baker as Alwina transformed from a poor homeless Tunisian girl to being passed off as African royalty in Parisian society. A climactic scene set in a luxurious nightclub sees Alwina overcome by the desire to dance to the beat of a drum. She storms the Follies–type showgirl review that is occurring on stage, strips off her extravagant gold-lame evening gown, races down the stage's central spiral staircase and proceeds to perform a frantic 'Danse Sauvage' that Baker was famous for. As I argue in Chapter 4, the staircase is here again a fashionable site for transformation. However, rather than indicating a glittering moment of glamorous make-over leading to the transcendence of class boundaries that we see with Audrey Hepburn in *My Fair Lady,* Alwina's undressing is portrayed as a return to her 'wild' African roots. Scholar of African-American studies Anne Anlin Cheng, makes the compelling argument that Baker's body in this film is represented as a surface, upon which the audience projects their primitivist fantasies. Further, she astutely recognizes the connection between tropes of nakedness, dress and undress that circle understandings of Baker's performances and the extraordinary black and white skein cladding of Loos' Baker House.⁴ Baker's films encapsulate numerous tensions regarding the representation and stereotyping of racialized female sexuality on screen as well the ways that fashion might be manipulated to interrogate white supremacy – themes that continue to have resonance in contemporary contexts.

At the time of writing, the prospect of the forthcoming James Bond film *No Time to Die,* due for release in October 2021 has the potential to redress some of the tensions of gendered representation that I have exposed in relation to spy films, as well as highlight the previous racist characterizations that have previously plagued the franchise. British-born actress of Jamaican heritage, Lashana Lynch, plays the role of a 007 operative Nomi, who inherits the secret agent role while Bond (Daniel Craig) is in exile. What the Nomi character will bring to the Bond suite of films is yet unknown. However, Lynch's 2020 interview with *Harper's Baazar* intimates that her role is 'revolutionary', and that she has the opportunity to 'challenge narratives' regarding stereotypical representations of race, gender and 'toxic masculinity'.⁵ How fashion, interior design and architecture will be deployed to convey her character's interiority, and to subvert these stereotypes by circumventing the prevailing image of the playboy dandyism of Bond is a question for future study. As I have argued in Chapter 2, the dandy suit as a symbol of spy sex appeal has links to the bachelor pads of *Playboy* magazine and their promotion of fashionable, luxurious and technologically advanced consumer desires through Bond films. There appears to be some clues to the subversion of this trope in the cinema trailer, which portrays Nomi as fashionably clad in a safari-suit jacket. This styling opens the possibility for fashion scholars to further consider the relationship between colonialism and the African diaspora as a pertinent thread of the dandy suit, and how this has been represented in cinematic contexts. As Monica L. Miller argues, black dandyism is a subversive style that uses clothing, gesture and wit to reimagine and manipulate the performance of racial identity.[6]

Miller's analysis of Isaac Julien's film *Looking for Langston* (1989), for example, offers salient insights regarding how the queer black dandy's self-fashioning of the tuxedo represents a stylish and revolutionary redefinition of blackness and masculinity. A poetic rendition of 1920s queer Harlem's speakeasy nightclub scene and its artistic underground, *Looking for Langston*'s visual stylization resonates with my argument regarding how queer ways of seeing the surfaces of fashion and space can produce heterotopic experiences where individuals are free to perform gender and sexuality outside of heteronormative identities. As Miller argues, 'Julien's effort to visualize a queer aesthetic of blackness is visionary … [where costume is essential to] this beauty and its life affirming potential.'[7] As a queer heterotopia *Looking for Langston*'s Harlem clubs have their present-day equivalent in the contemporary ball room scenes of *Paris Is Burning* that I examine in Chapter 3. Both share the quality of creating space where queer people of colour can perform their identities through glamorous and spectacular fashions in ways that transcend systems of exclusion and oppression.

The representation of glamorous and fashionable racially and ethnically diverse peoples and identities in cinema is a largely untapped lifestyle and consumer market for luxury brands to engage. The box-office success of the Hollywood film *Crazy Rich Asians* (Chu, 2018) is testament to audience's desire for the centring of people of colour in historically white positions of focus and power.[8] While the film has been criticized for reductive stereotyping, it is the only US studio produced film since *The Joy Luck Club* (Wang, 1993) to have an all Asian cast, that focuses on contemporary characters.[9] The luxury lifestyles of the protagonists are represented through couture wardrobes by Prada and Dior as well as a range of South-East Asian designers including Michael Cinco, Khoon Hooi, LORD's Tailor and Aston Blake. Widely reported in the design press as fashionably equivalent to *Sex and the City*, with settings that evoke decadent

Gatsbyesque glamour, *Crazy Rich Asians* demonstrates the transnational mixing of styles common to globalized fashion markets.[10] Interior styling of the Singaporean homes featured throughout the film combine ornamental William Morris wallpaper with Chinese lacquered furniture, ornate porcelain vases and Peranakan patterned rugs. These types of decorative surfaces are often common to films set in South East Asia. As Rosalind Galt contends, 'pretty aesthetics', are a defining feature of contemporary world cinema, where decorative surfaces are often understood within the context of colonialism, exoticism and Orientalism, and have been denigrated in relation to modernist design aesthetics.[11]

Galt's argument regarding film studies' disavowal of surface style in relation to certain identity positions, particularly the feminine and the queer has been reiterated throughout this book. In particular, I have attempted to develop this position by exposing how the relationship between fashion and spatial design provide rich and complex insights to audience's understandings of narrative and character development, particularly as they relate to gender and sexuality. In recognizing the visual pleasure associated with viewing fashion and the interior on screen and how these surfaces might help diverse gender and sexual identities enact forms of personal agency, this book has sought to instate the confluence between fashion and spatial design as an integral area for design studies. With Galt's refrain that transnational film cultures are uniquely placed to present 'a cinematic ethics of worldliness through the resonance of the decorative image' in mind, it is clear that there is much further work that can be done to examine the ways that fashion and the interior interact to produce racially and ethnically diverse positions on screen.[12] The Orientalist fashion and interiors of films such as *Shanghai Express* (1932), *Daughter of the Dragon* (1931) and *The World of Suzie Wong* (1960) should certainly be the topic of critical study to further expose Hollywood's compulsion towards exotic and erotic fantasies in the screen representation of Asian cultures. Conversely, appreciation of the aesthetic approach taken to surface in *The Scent of Green Papaya* (*Mùi đu đủ xanh*) (Hung, 1993) which examines the beauty of everyday domesticity in Vietnam, or the exuberant costumes and extravagant sets of Bollywood romances, *Devdas* (Sanjay Leela Bhansali, 2002) and *Monsoon Wedding* (Mira Nair, 2001) amongst a multitude of others, would contribute rich insights to this emergent field of study.[13]

In addition to positioning the intersection of fashion and spatial design as culturally significant I have also examined them as a commercial phenomenon mediated by film. By revealing how fashion, the interior and architecture work in tandem to translate cinematic style to real-world retail contexts I have shown how these forms acquire value and meaning through modes of consumption.

As I have identified in Chapter 6, the commodification of history and nostalgia through film tie-ins has become an integral 'artification' strategy for luxury lifestyle brands. By introducing the concept of 'brand heterotopias' I have highlighted the ways that inter-spatial layering produces past and present, real and imaginary experiences manipulated for aesthetic, entertainment and escapist effects. Luxury brands exploiting these qualities have the potential to become inextricably linked to the values and heritage of the consumer.

Within this context, luxury brands have been critiqued for the appropriation of cultural styles and histories, exploiting these forms for their own profit. For example, Ralph Lauren's Safari Home Collection inspired by *Out of Africa* produced colonial chic Hollywood Africa through animal skin rugs and wicker chairs, displacing diverse cultures and erasing political conflict through fashionable furniture. Equally, global fashion conglomerates such as Chanel and Dior bring the design homogeneity of Euro-lux minimalism to flagship stores throughout Asia and the Middle East. While there is the opportunity to engage with localized aesthetics, architects and designers, luxury brands appear committed to producing uniform spaces around the globe. In light of the *Crazy Rich Asians* success story, surely, if luxury brands were to adopt transnational styling that thoughtfully collaborates with and appropriately renumerates local and traditional designers to produce aesthetics appropriate to different cultural contexts, a lucrative new dimension to tourist-driven flagship shopping would emerge.

There is also the possibility for retail spaces to bring politically engaged content to their audiences. As I have argued in Chapter 5, with regard to the relationship between shop windows and screens, while these spaces are complicit in the commodification of bodies, they can also facilitate forms of social mobility, participation in the urban environment and legitimize ways of looking that have been empowering. The history of the department store window in relation to the suffragette movement is indicative of how these spaces might produce democratic political engagement. The fashion system is in many ways complicit in the oppression that results from systemic racism, socio-economic inequity, labour exploitation and gentrification through socio-spatial control. If nothing else, the breaking of department store and luxury fashion windows by political protesters in recent times is a powerful reminder of resistance against such forms of systemic inequity, the analysis of which is yet to find its contemporary fashion studies scholar.

The explosion of new media, globally circulated through social media platforms, internet video channels and video sharing apps has made cinematic style in the form of branded fashion entertainment and short fashion film ubiquitous. Luxury fashion conglomerates, designers and traditional fashion media are producing an inexhaustible range of digital content on screen for consumers to engage with. The pioneering platform SHOWstudio has not only led the way in terms of integrating fashion-film content in retail space, and supplanting fashion catwalks with digital spectacles of fashion in motion, they have also demonstrated dedication to creating content that includes people of diverse racial backgrounds. By representing models such as Adwoa Aboah, Chris Lee, Ming Xi and Jourdan Dunn in haute couture editorial photographs and films, as well as proving discussion panel platforms to address issues of racial equity, and showcasing the talent of diverse creatives, SHOWstudio provides some reckoning with fashion-film's embedded racist structures.[14]

This type of fashion content has disrupted the fashion media environment that until the beginning of the new millennium was largely dominated by traditional fashion magazines such as *Vogue* and *Harper's Bazaar*. The impact of entertainment streaming services such as Netflix, HBO and Amazon Prime has equally challenged Hollywood, creating film and television series as well as showcasing world cinema to hundreds of million subscribers worldwide. The result is more diverse content that features people from a wide range of races, ages and sexual orientations responding to audience demand. There is much scope within these offerings for future research to examine the intersection between lavish interiors, luxury fashion and glamorous architecture as they relate to diverse bodies in examples such as *Bridgerton* (2020), *Selfmade* (2020), *The Fabulous Lives of Bollywood Wives* (2020) and *The House of Flowers* (2020). It is clear that the advent of digital content has forever altered the ways that fashion, interiors and architecture are consumed as images.

Throughout this book I have focused on examples that are largely from the realm of luxury and designer fashion rather than that of everyday streetwear. Similarly, examples of interiors and architecture have by and large complied with an interest in design aesthetics and the construction of glamour. There is much scope for future scholarship to examine quotidian examples of the intersection between fashion and spatial design as they relate to gender and sexual identities as performed by everyday people, documented as smartphone video and uploaded to sites such as YouTube, Instagram and TikTok. Around the world, women in particular, are inviting internet strangers into their bedrooms and bathrooms as they perform the gender rituals of styling outfits and applying make-up. Intimate spaces are the location in which the construction of the masquerades of feminine appearance is exposed.

As I outline in Chapter 1, such representations can be seen to both limit and reinforce gender roles and objectified positions. As a genre, these bodily maintenance videos expose the labour of femininity and broadly comply with traditional patriarchal ideals of beauty. In her analysis of the artist Cindy Sherman's photographic masquerade self-portraits, Susan Best provides perceptive interpretation that might also be applied to the women performing these make-over videos: 'Like types in a pantomime ... they are both recognisable and exaggerated for effect ... [they are] compliant and yet commanding, self-possessed while also coming undone.'[15] As she suggests, the performance of femininity is complicated, consisting of both pleasure and pain. Internet influencers take up the role of movie star, compelling spectators to participate in their own objectification and commodification. Yet, just as I argue in relation to the bedrooms and bathrooms of *Dinner at Eight* and *The Women*, these intimate settings and fashionable performances can also provide instances that operate outside traditional modes of regulated femininity through representations of diverse bodies as well as through strategies of irony and parody. An example of this is the drag queen Valentina (James Andrew Leyva), performing the six-hour make-up ritual that it takes her to transform from Latin American man into 'rich white woman'.[16] Throughout the video Valentina advises that the secret to beauty is 'feeling your fantasy' and makes a series of jokes about the constructed nature of femininity. The sparkling white bathroom setting and slinky white robe in which she performs this fantasy is not dissimilar to the mise-en-scène of Hollywood films. As an advertorial for the make-up products she uses, Valentina's transformation video has its origins in Max Factor advertising film tie-ins. As a glamorous performance of gender transformation by a non-white person using fashion and the interior to frame her star image – 'take that Gwyneth Paltrow' – this video is just one of many across social media that might open up new understandings of cinematic style.

My aim with this book has been to expose the relationship between fashion, interior design and architecture as mediated by film beyond surface style. By closely examining how these surfaces can reveal rich and complex understandings of the ways in which gendered identity formation intersects with the consumer cultures of design and cinema, I have argued for their combined significance beyond the superficial. As I have outlined here, there are many omissions in this book, especially in relation to understanding skin as another surface that has contributed to the representation of gendered and sexual identities in fashion film.[17] There are inevitably many more omissions that future scholarship might contend with.

Notes

Introduction

1. Deborah Nadoolman Landis, *Dressed: A Century of Hollywood Costume Design* (New York: HarperCollins, 2007): 6.
2. For a full account of Art Nouveau design in cinema see Lucy Fischer, *Cinema by Design: Art Nouveau, Modernism and Film History* (New York: Columbia University Press, 2017).
3. *Theatre* magazine cited in Sumiko Higashi, *Cecil B. DeMille and American Culture: The Silent Era* (Berkeley: University of California Press, 1994): 144.
4. Louise Wallenberg, *Fashion and Modernity*, trans. Rune Engebretsen (London: Bloomsbury, 2019): 83–100.
5. Rosalind Galt, *Pretty: Film and the Decorative Image* (New York: Columbia University Press, 2011): 11.
6. Ibid., 2.
7. Jess Berry, *House of Fashion: Haute Couture and the Modern Interior* (London: Bloomsbury, 2018).
8. Lucy Fischer, *Designing Women: Cinema, Art Deco and the Female Form* (New York: Columbia University Press, 2003).
9. See Lesley Jackson, *The New Look Design in the Fifties* (London: Thames and Hudson, 1998).
10. For insightful discussion regarding the New Look silhouette in *Rear Window* see Sarah Street, 'The Dresses Had Told Me: Fashion and Femininity in Rear Window', in *Alfred Hitchcock's Rear Window*, ed. John Belton (Cambridge: Cambridge University Press, 2000). For discussion regarding architecture in Hitchcock films see: Steven Jacobs, *The Wrong House: The Architecture of Alfred Hitchcock* (Rotterdam: 010 Publishers, 2007).
11. John Potvin, 'The Velvet Masquerade: Fashion, Interior Design and the Furnished Body', in *Fashion, Interior Design and the Contours of Modern Identity*, eds. Alla Myzelev and John Potvin (Oxon and New York: Routledge) 2016: 11.
12. Berry, *House of Fashion*.
13. For an historical account of the architectural emergence of interiority see Ewa Lajer-Burcharth and Beate Söntgen, 'Introduction: Interiors and Interiority', in *Interiors and Interiority*, eds. Ewa Lajer-Burcharth and Beate Söntgen (Berlin and Boston: Degruyter, 2016): 1–13.

14 Joan Riviere, 'Womanliness as a Masquerade', *The International Journal of Psychoanalysis*, 10 (1929): 303–13.
15 Mary Ann Doane, 'Film and the Masquerade: Theorising the Female Spectator', *Screen*, 23:3–4 (1982): 74–87; Judith Butler, *Gender Trouble: Feminism and the Subversion of Identity* (New York: Routledge, 1999).
16 Penny Sparke, *The Modern Interior* (London: Reaktion Books, 2008).
17 For discussion of haute couture in cinema see Stella Bruzzi, *Undressing Cinema: Clothing and Identity in the Movies* (London: Routledge, 1997).
18 Pamela Church Gibson, 'The Fashion Narratives of Tom Ford: *Nocturnal Animals* and Contemporary Cinema', *Fashion Theory*, 21:16 (2017): 644.
19 Pamela Church Gibson, *Fashion and Celebrity Culture* (London: Bloomsbury, 2012).
20 Nick Rees-Roberts, *Fashion Film: Art and Advertising in the Digital Age* (London: Bloomsbury, 2018).
21 For discourse on set design and art direction see Leon Barsacq, *Caligari's Cabinet and Other Grand Illusions* (New York: Little Brown, 1976); Beverly Heisner, *Hollywood Art: Art Direction in the Days of the Great Studio* (London: St James Press, 1990); Tim Bergfelder, Sue Harris and Sarah Street, *Film Architecture and the Transnational Imagination: Set Design in 1930s European Cinema* (Amsterdam: Amsterdam University Press, 2007).
22 See for example: Sarah Street, *Costume and Cinema* (London and New York: Wallflower, 2001); Sarah Berry, *Screen Style: Fashion and Femininity in 1930s Hollywood* (Minneapolis and London: University of Minnesota Press, 2000); Anne Massey, *Hollywood beyond the Screen* (Oxford and New York: Berg, 2000).
23 Adrienne Munich (ed.), *Fashion in Film* (Bloomington: Indiana University Press, 2011); Rachel Moseley (ed.), *Fashioning Film Stars: Dress Culture and Identity* (London: British Film Institute, 2005); Jane Gains and Charlotte Herzog (eds.), *Fabrications: Costume and the Female Body* (London: Routledge, 1990).
24 Bruzzi, *Undressing Cinema*.
25 Merrill Schleier, *Skyscraper Cinema: Architecture and Gender in American Film* (Minneapolis and London: University of Minnesota Press, 2009).
26 See for example, Katherine Shonfield, *Walls Have Feelings: Architecture, Film and the City* (London: Routledge 2000); and Richard Koeck and Les Roberts (eds.), *The City and the Moving Image* (London: Palgrave Macmillan, 2010).
27 David Clarke (ed.), *The Cinematic City* (Hoboken: Taylor & Francis, 1997); Mark Lamster (ed.), *Architecture and Film* (New York: Princeton Architectural Press, 2000).
28 Pamela Robertson Wojcik, *The Apartment Plot: Urban Living in American Film and Popular Culture, 1945–1975* (Durham: Duke University Press, 2010).
29 For more in the Eames' involvement in the *Moon Is Blue* see Pat Kirkham, 'Living in a Modern Way in *The Moon Is Blue*: Mid-Century Modern Architecture, Interiors and Furniture', *Interiors*, 10:1–2 (2019): 103–22.

30 For a brief history of the professions of set design and production design see Pat Kirkham and Sarah A. Lichtman (eds.), *Screen Interiors: From Country Houses to Cosmic Heterotopias* (London: Bloomsbury, 2021). For monographs on influential set/production designers see: Howard Gutner, *MGM Style: Cedric Gibbons and the Art of the Golden Age of Hollywood* (Lanham: Rowman and Littlefield, 2019); Christopher Frayling, *Ken Adam and the Art of Production Design* (London: Faber and Faber, 2005).

31 Donald Albrecht, *Designing Dreams: Modern Architecture and the Movies* (New York: Harper and Row, 1986); Fischer, *Cinema by Design*; Fischer, *Designing Women*.

32 Kirkham and Lichtman (eds.), *Screen Interiors*.

33 Laura Mulvey, 'Visual Pleasure and Narrative Cinema', *Screen*, 16:3 (1975): 6–18; Mary Ann Doane, *Femme Fatales: Feminism, Film Theory, Psychoanalysis* (London and New York: Routledge, 1991).

34 Michel Foucault, 'Of Other Spaces, Utopias and Heterotopias [1967]', *Architecture/Mouvement/Continuite*, 5 (October 1984): 1–9.

35 Jean Whitehead, *Creating Interior Atmosphere: Mise-en-scène and Interior Design* (London and New York: Bloomsbury, 2018).

36 Pierre Bourdieu, *Distinction: A Social Critique of Judgement through Taste*, trans. Richard Nice (London: Routledge, 1984).

37 Mike Featherstone, 'Luxury Consumer Culture and Sumptuary Dynamics', *Luxury: History, Culture and Consumption*, 1:1 (2015): 47–69.

38 Gilles Lipovetsky and Veronica Manlow, 'The "Artialization" of Luxury Stores', in *Fashion and Imagination*, ed. Jo Teunissen (Arnheim: ArtEZ Press, 2007): 154–67.

Chapter 1

1 Here I use the term woman's film loosely. For more precise definitions and extended discussion see Jeanine Basinger, *A Woman's View: How Hollywood Spoke to Women 1930–1960* (Connecticut: Wesleyan University Press, 1995); Mary Ann Doane, *The Desire to Desire: The Woman's Film of the 1940s* (Bloomington: Indiana University Press, 1987).

2 Charles Eckert, 'The Carole Lombard in Macy's Window', *Quarterly Review, of Film and Video*, 3:1 (1978): 7.

3 Ibid., 5.

4 Mary Louise Roberts, 'Samson and Delilah Revisited: The Politics of Women's Fashion in 1920s France', *The America Historical Review*, 98:3 (1993): 684.

5 Mulvey, 'Visual Pleasure and Narrative Cinema', 6–18.

6 Luce Irigaray, *This Sex Which Is Not One* (Ithaca: Cornell University Press, 1985): 84.

7 Mary Ann Doane, 'The Economy of Desire: The Commodity Form in/of the Cinema', in *Movies and Mass Culture*, ed. John Belton (London: The Athlone Press, 1996): 121.
8 Elizabeth Wilson, *Adorned in Dreams: Fashion and Modernity* (London: I.B Tauris, 2003).
9 Liz Conor, *The Spectacular Modern Woman: Feminine Visibility in the 1920s* (Bloomington: Indiana University Press, 2004): 29.
10 See for example: Janey Place, 'Women in Film Noir', in *Women in Film Noir*, ed. Anne Kaplan (London: BFI Publishing, 1992); Doane, *Femme Fatales*.
11 Susan Best, 'Rethinking Visual Pleasure: Aesthetics and Affect', *Theory Psychology*, 17:5 (2007): 508.
12 It is important here to note that the term 'Art Deco' was only attributed to the style in 1966, denoting an eclectic range of features in design and architecture that emerged in France between the wars. A shared aesthetic of streamlining, geometric forms, often combining elements of the classical and the modern underpins the style that was first widely exhibited at the 1925 Parisian *Exposition des Arts Decoratifs et Industriels Moderns*.
13 Fischer, *Designing Women*, 104–5.
14 See Kenneth A. Yellis, 'Prosperity's Child: Some Thoughts on the Flapper', *American Quarterly*, 21:1 (1969): 44–64; and Roberts, 'Samson and Delilah Revisited', 684.
15 For this extended argument refer to Berry, *House of Fashion*.
16 Christina Wilson, 'Cedric Gibbons: Architect of Hollywood's Golden Age', in *Architecture and Film*, ed. Mark Lamster (New York: Princeton Architectural Press, 2000): 103–109; Howard Mandelbaum and Eric Myers, *Screen Deco* (Santa Monica: Hennessey and Ingalls, 2000).
17 Fischer, *Designing Women*.
18 'Le Pavillion d'Elegance', *L'Illustration* (Juin 1925): 34. All translations are mine unless otherwise stated.
19 Francis Jourdain cited in Jean-Pierre Berthomé, 'Les Décorateurs du Cinema muet en France', *1895. Mille huit cent quatre-vingt-quinze*, 65 (2011): 109.
20 See Leon Moussinac, 'Le Décor et Le Costume au Cinema', *Art et Decoration*, 50 (Juillet-Decembre 1926): 129–39; Rene Chavance, 'Chez un Cinéaste', *Art et Decoration*, 52 (Juillet-Decembre 1927): 43–8; 'Un décor du film de Marcel L'Herbier', *Art et Decoration*, 47 (Janvier-Juin 1925): 152–4.
21 Henri Bidou, 'A l'Exposition Internationale des Arts Decoratifs et Industriels Moderns. Le Décor de la vie moderne', *Vogue* (France) (1 June 1925): 35.
22 Press Release *Our Dancing Daughters* cited in Mandelbaum and Myers, *Screen Deco*, 33.
23 Cited in Heisner, *Hollywood Art*, 77.
24 Cedric Gibbons cited in Mayme Ober Peak, 'Every Home's a Stage', *Ladies Home Journal*, 50:7 (1933): 25.

25 Ibid.
26 'Miss Crawford of Hollywood Back with the Spoils of Paris', *Vogue* (America) (15 October 1932): 64–5; 'Joan Crawford', *Town & Country* (November 1945): 118.
27 Hobe Erwin cited in Gutner, *MGM Style*, 128.
28 'Lingerie for a New Season', *Vogue* (America) (October 1932): 98.
29 Joan Collins cited in Samantha Barbas, *Movie Crazy: Fans, Stars and the Cult of Celebrity* (New York: Palgrave Macmillan, 2000): 150.
30 Hilary Hinds, *A Cultural History of Twin Beds* (London: Bloomsbury, 2019): 111.
31 For further discussion of Doris Day's representation of sexuality on screen in *Pillow Talk* see Tamar Jeffers McDonald, *Doris Day Confidential: Hollywood, Sex and Stardom* (London: I.B. Tauris, 2013).
32 Wong Kar-Wai cited in Paul Arthur, 'Film Reviews: *In the Mood for Love*', *Cineaste*, 26:3 (2001): 41.
33 Anne Troutman, 'The Modernist Boudoir and the Erotics of Space', in *Negotiating Domesticity: Spatial Productions of Gender in Modern Architecture*, eds. Hilde Heynen and Gulsum Bayder (London and New York: Routledge, 2005): 296.
34 Ed Lilley, 'The Name of the Boudoir', *Journal of the Society of Architectural Historians*, 53:2 (1994): 193–8.
35 Georgina Downey and Mark Taylor, 'Impolite Reading and Erotic Interiors of Eighteenth Century France', in *Designing the French Interior: The Modern Home and Mass Media*, eds. Anca I. Lasc, Georgina Downey and Mark Taylor (London and New York: Bloomsbury, 2015).
36 Troutman, 'The Modernist Boudoir and the Erotics of Space', 301.
37 Emmanuelle Dirix, 'Birds of Paradise: Feathers, Fetishism and Costume in Classical Hollywood', *Film, Fashion and Consumption*, 3:1 (2014): 24.
38 See for example: Helena Leigh, 'The Cosmetic Urge', *Harper's Bazaar* (August 1931): 114, 116, 118,120; Helena Leigh, 'The Cosmetic Urge', *Harper's Bazaar* (July 1930): 100, 102, 104–5; Helena Leigh, 'The Cosmetic Urge', *Harper's Bazaar* (February 1932): 86, 88, 94.
39 Paul Iribe, 'The Audacious Note of Modernism in the Boudoir', *Vogue* (America) (15 June 1919): 58–9.
40 Helen Appleton Read, 'Twentieth Century Decoration', *Vogue* (America) (19 January 1929): 76–7, 100, 106.
41 'The Rising Tide of White Decors: Lace and Linen in the Boudoir', *Harper's Bazaar* (August 1931): 74–5.
42 Michael Adcock, 'Remaking Urban Space: Baron Haussmann and the Rebuilding of Paris, 1851–1870', *University of Melbourne Library Journal*, 2:2 (1996): viewed on 13 January 2020, https://museumsandcollections.unimelb.edu.au/__data/assets/pdf_file/0008/1624850/adcock.pdf
43 For a more nuanced discussion of nineteenth-century bathing scenes in painting see Georgina Downey, 'Bathrooms: Plumbing the Canon- the Bathtub Nudes

of Alfred Stevens, Edgar Degas and Pierre Bonnard Reconsidered', in *Domestic Interiors*, ed. Georgina Downey (London and New York: Bloomsbury, 2013).

44 Cecil B. DeMille cited in Virginia Postrel, *The Power of Glamour: Longing and the Art of Visual Persuasion* (New York: Simon & Schuster, 2013): 188.
45 Cecilia de Mille Presley and Mark A. Vieira, 'The Wickedest Movie in the World: How Cecil B. DeMille made *The Sign of the Cross*', *Bright Lights Film Journal* (18 December 2014): viewed on 8 January 2020, https://brightlightsfilm.com/wickedest-movie-world-cecil-b-demille-made-sign-cross/#.XhZ9RpIzaS4
46 Anthea Callen cited in Downey, 'Bathrooms: Plumbing the Canon', 120.
47 Christian Esquevin, *Adrian: Silver Screen to Custom Label* (New York: Monacelli Press, 2008).
48 Simone de Beauvoir, 'Brigitte Bardot and the Lolita Syndrome', *Esquire* (August 1959): 36.
49 Mulvey, 'Visual Pleasure and Narrative Cinema', 11.
50 Ginette Vincendeau, 'The Old and the New: Bridget Bardot in 1950s France', *Paragraph*, 15:1 (1992): 89.
51 Mari Ruti, *Feminist Film Theory and Pretty Woman* (London and New York: Bloomsbury, 2016): 148.
52 Hilary Radner, *Neo-Feminist Cinema: Girly Films, Chick Flicks and Consumer Culture* (London: Routledge, 2010): 33.

Chapter 2

1 Robert Mallet Stevens cited in Bergfelder, Harris and Street, *Film Architecture and the Transnational Imagination*, 58.
2 Alice T. Friedman, *American Glamour and the Evolution of Modern Architecture* (New Haven and London: Yale University Press, 2010).
3 Joseph Rosa, 'Tearing Down the House: Modern Homes in the Movies', in *Architecture and Film*, ed. Mark Lamster (New York: Princeton Architectural Press, 2000): 159.
4 Steve Cohan, *Masked Men: Masculinity and the Movies in the Fifties* (Indiana: Indiana University Press, 1997); Yvonne Tasker, *Spectacular Bodies: Gender, Genre and the Action Cinema* (London: Routledge 1993).
5 Steve Neale, 'Masculinity as Spectacle: Reflections on Men and Mainstream Cinema', *Screen*, 24:6 (1983): 2–16.
6 Stella Bruzzi, *Men's Cinema: Masculinity and Mise-en-Scene in Hollywood* (Edinburgh: Edinburgh University Press, 2013).
7 Berry, *House of Fashion*.
8 Joel Sanders, 'Introduction', in *Stud: Architectures of Masculinity*, ed. Joel Sanders (New York: Princeton Architectural Press, 1996): 11–25.

9 Adolf Loos cited in Beatriz Colomina, 'The Split Wall: Domestic Voyeurism', in *Sexuality and Space*, ed. Beatriz Colomina (New York: Princeton Architectural Press, 1992): 90.
10 Friedman, *American Glamour and the Evolution of Modern Architecture*, 6.
11 George Wagner, 'The Lair of the Bachelor', in *Architecture and Feminism*, eds. Debra Coleman, Elizabeth Danze and Carol Henderson (New York: Princeton Architectural Press, 1996): 185.
12 For discussion regarding the contradictory nature of modernism as a stereotypically 'masculine' architecture see Joel Sanders (ed)., *Stud: Architectures of Masculinity* (New York: Princeton Architectural Press, 1996); Mark Wigley, *White Walls, Designer Dresses: The Fashioning of Modern Architecture* (Cambridge, MA: MIT Press, 1995).
13 Robert Boyle cited in Jacobs, *The Wrong House*, 310.
14 Adolf Loos, 'Ornament and Crime [1908]', in *Adolf Loos Ornament and Crime: Selected Essays*, ed. Adolf Opel (California: Ariadne Press, 1998).
15 See Janet Stewart, *Fashioning Vienna: Adolf Loos's Cultural Criticism* (London: Routledge, 2000); Beatriz Colomina, 'Sex, Lies and Decoration: Adolf Loos and Gustav Klimt', *Thresholds*, 37 (2010): 70–81.
16 Adolf Loos cited in Rebecca Houze, 'From Weiner Kunst im Hause to the Wiener Werkstätte: Marketing Domesticity with Fashionable Interior Design', *Design Issues*, 8:1 (2002): 22.
17 Adolf Loos cited in Beatriz Colomina, 'The Split Wall: Domestic Voyeurism', 94.
18 The general understanding of the dandy figure is often equated with foppish extravagant dress. However, in fashion history the dandy is understood as having reformed male attire in the 1800s by wearing the precursor to suiting – buckskin trousers, white linen and a dark frock coat. This approach to men's dress was reserved, practical and understated compared to the peacocks and macaronis of the Regency period. See Christopher Breward, *The Suit: Form Function and Style* (London: Reaktion, 2016); Wilson, *Adorned in Dreams*; Ellen Moers, *The Dandy: Brummell to Beerbohm* (London: Secker and Warburg, 1960).
19 Doane, 'Film and the Masquerade', 82.
20 Butler, *Gender Trouble*.
21 Anne Hollander, *Sex and Suits: The Evolution of Modern Dress* (London: Bloomsbury, [1994] 2016): 64.
22 Johnathan Faiers, *Dressing Dangerously: Dysfunctional Fashion in Film* (New Haven and London: Yale University Press, 2013): 227.
23 Ulrich Lehmann, 'Language of Pursuit: Cary Grant's Clothes in Alfred Hitchcock's North by Northwest', *Fashion Theory*, 4:4 (2000): 467–85.
24 Todd McEwen, 'Cary Grant's Suit', *Granta: The Magazine of New Writing*, 94 (2006): 119.

25 Ibid., 123.
26 Andrew Spicer, 'Sean Connery: Loosening his Bonds', in *British Stars and Stardom: From Alma Taylor to Sean Connery*, ed. Bruce Babbington (Manchester: Manchester University Press, 2001): 220–1.
27 Everett Mattlin, 'Off the Cuff', *GQ: Gentleman's Quarterly*, 36:3 (1966): 8, 12, 14, 18, 28. 12
28 See for example: 'Trevor Howard: Operation Savile Row', *GQ: Gentleman's Quarterly*, 36:1 (1966): 96–7; 'Monte Christo Advertisement', *GQ: Gentleman's Quarterly*, 35:1 (1965): 51; 'Stetson Shoe Advertisement', *GQ: Gentleman's Quarterly*, 37:4 (1967): 128.
29 Pamela Church Gibson, 'From Style Icon to Fashion Victim: Masculinity and Spectacle in the James Bond Franchise', *Vestoj: The Platform for Critical Thinking on Fashion*, 7 (2017): viewed on 5 December 2018, http://vestoj.com/from-style-icon-to-fashion-victim/
30 Ibid.
31 Tom Ford cited in Llewella Chapman, 'Fitting Fleming's Hero like a Savile Row Suit: The Tailoring of James Bond', in *From Bloefeld to Moneypenny: Gender in James Bond*, ed. Steven Gerrard (Bingley: Emerald Publishing, 2020): 69.
32 Viki Karaminas and Adam Geczy, *Fashion and Masculinities in Popular Culture* (London: Routledge, 2007): 38.
33 A.M. Marple, 'The Impassioned Palate of James Bond', *GQ: Gentleman's Quarterly*, 33:5 (1963): 36, 40, 78, 80, 162.
34 Becky Conekin, 'Fashioning Playboy: Messages of Style and Masculinity in the Pages of Playboy Magazine, 1953–1963', *Fashion Theory*, 4:4 (2000): 459.
35 'The Progressive Dinner Party', *Playboy* (January 1965): 107.
36 Pam Cook and Claire Hines, 'Sean Connery is James Bond: Re-Fashioning British Masculinity in the 1960s', in *Fashioning Film Stars: Dress, Culture, Identity*, ed. Rachel Moseley (London: British Film Institute, 2005).
37 Reyner Banham cited in Bill Ogersby, 'The Bachelor Pad as Cultural Icon', *Journal of Design History*, 18:1 (2005): 99.
38 Sparke, *The Modern Interior*.
39 For an account of women's influence on modernist architecture see Alice T. Friedman, *Women and the Making of the Modern House* (New York: Abrams, 1998).
40 John Potvin, *Bachelors of a Different Sort: Queer Aesthetics, Material Culture and the Modern Interior in Britain* (Manchester: Manchester University Press, 2014): 13.
41 'Playboy's Penthouse Apartment', *Playboy*, 3:10 (October 1956): 54.
42 Wojcik, *The Apartment Plot*, 92–4.
43 Ibid., 96.
44 'Playboy's Penthouse Apartment', 59.
45 Susan R. Henderson, 'Bachelor Culture in the Work of Adolf Loos', *Journal of Architectural Education*, 55:3 (2002): 125.

46 Ibid., 130.
47 Colomina, 'Sex, Lies and Decoration: Adolf Loos and Gustav Klimt', 79.
48 Walter Benjamin. 'Paris: Capital of the Nineteenth Century' [1939], *Perspecta*, 12 (1969): 163–72.
49 Steve Rose, 'James Bond: The Enemy of Architecture', *The Guardian* (4 November 2008): viewed on 22 May 2018, https://www.theguardian.com/artanddesign/2008/nov/04/james-bond-architecture
50 Frayling, *Ken Adam*, 175.
51 'A Playboy Pad: Pleasure on the Rocks, review of John Lautner, Elrod House', *Playboy*, 18:11 (November 1971): 151–1, 208.
52 Sigfried Giedeon, *Space, Time and Architecture* (Cambridge: Harvard University Press, 1967): xxxii.
53 Lehmann, 'Language of Pursuit: Cary Grant's Clothes in Alfred Hitchcock's North by Northwest', 467–85.
54 Robertson Wojcik, *The Apartment Plot*, 133.
55 R.W Connell cited in Potvin, *Bachelors of a Different Sort*, 29.
56 Colomina, 'Sex, Lies and Decoration: Adolf Loos and Gustav Klimt', 77; regarding Loos homophobia see Beatriz Colomina, *Privacy and Publicity: Modern Architecture as Mass Media* (Cambridge: Cambridge University Press, 1994).
57 See Richard Dyer, *The Culture of Queers* (New York: Routledge, 2001) regarding style as a queer survival strategy.

Chapter 3

1 Throughout this chapter I deploy 'queer' as a term that can encapsulate identities that resist traditional heteronormative categories, where appropriate specific identities, for example lesbian, gay, trans are used.
2 Harry M. Benshoff and Sean Griffin, *Queer Images: A History of Gay and Lesbian Film in America* (Lanham: Rowman & Littlefield, 2006): 66.
3 For a comprehensive discussion on definitions of Camp see Fabio Cleto, 'Introduction: Queering the Camp', in *Camp: Queer Aesthetics and the Performing Subject*, ed. Fabio Cleto (Ann Arbor: The University of Michigan Press, 1999): 1–42.
4 Susan Sontag, 'Notes on Camp [1964]', in *Camp: Queer Aesthetics and the Performing Subject*, ed. Fabio Cleto (Ann Arbor: The University of Michigan Press, 1999): 55.
5 Jack Babuscio, 'Camp and the Gay Sensibility', in *Queer Cinema, the Film Reader*, ed. Harry Benshoff and Sean Griffin (London: Routledge, 2004).
6 Mark Booth, *Camp* (London and New York: Quartet, 1983).

7   Janet Jakobsen, 'Queer Is? Queer Does? Normativity and the Problem of Resistance', *GLQ: A Journal of Lesbian and Gay Studies*, 4:4 (1998): 511–36.
8   Svetlana Boym, 'Nostalgia and Its Discontents', *The Hedgehog Review*, 9:2 (2007): 7.
9   Tamara de Szegheo Lang, 'The Demand to Progress: Critical Nostalgia in LGBTQ Cultural Memory', *Journal of Lesbian Studies*, 19:2 (2015): 230–48.
10 For a comprehensive overview of queer representation in film see Benshoff and Griffin, *Queer Images: A History of Gay and Lesbian Film in America*.
11 Richard Dyer, *The Culture of Queers* (London and New York: Routledge, 2002): 205, 211.
12 Gilad Padva, *Queer Nostalgia in Cinema and Pop Culture* (Hampshire and New York: Palgrave Macmillan, 2014).
13 Allain Daigle, 'Of Love and Longing: Queer Nostalgia in Carol', *Queer Studies in Media & Popular Culture*, 2:1 (2017): 199–211 makes a similar argument; however, I extend this to focus specifically on how the relationship between fashion and the interior in queer film creates a heterotopic space.
14 Christopher Reed, 'Imminent Domain: Queer Space in the Built Environment', *Art Journal*, 55:4 (1996): 69.
15 See David Ansen, 'Gucci Goo', *Newsweek* (7 December 2009): 23, 68; Naomi Fry, 'Surface Matters: Todd Haynes's Carol Mistakes Aesthetics for Meaning', *The New Republic* (13 November 2015): viewed on 5 December 2018, https://newrepublic.com/article/123221/todd-hayness-carol-mistakes-aesthetics-meaning; Peter Bradshaw, 'Laurence Anyways- Review', *The Guardian* (30 November 2012): viewed on 13 January 2019, https://www.theguardian.com/film/2012/nov/29/drama-transgender
16 Todd Haynes cited in Benshoff and Griffin, *Queer Images: A History of Gay and Lesbian Film in America*, 204.
17 Haynes director's commentary 2002 cited in Nishant Shahani, *Queer Retrosexualities: The Politics of Reparative Return* (Maryland: Lehigh University Press, 2011): 65.
18 For further discussion regarding the relationship between Modernism, film, colour and decorative surface see Rosalind Galt, *Pretty: Film and the Decorative Image*; and David Bachelor, *Chromophobia* (London: Reaktion, 2000).
19 Kirsten Moana Thompson, 'Falling in (to) Colour: Chromophilia and Tom Ford's *A Single Man* (2009)', *The Moving Image*, 15:1 (2015): 75.
20 Brett Farmer, *Spectacular Passions: Cinema, Fantasy, Gay Male Spectatorships* (Durham: Duke University Press, 2000): 175.
21 Potvin, *Bachelors of a Different Sort*, 17.
22 Ibid., 23.
23 Eve Kosofsky Sedgwick, *Epistemology of the Closet* (Berkeley: University of California Press, 1990): 70.

24 Aaron Betsky, *Queer Space: Architecture and Same-Sex Desire* (New York: William Morrow and Company, 1997): 16–17.
25 Foucault, 'Of Other Spaces, Utopias and Heterotopias', 1–9.
26 Angela Jones, 'Queer Heterotopias: Homonormativity and the Future of Queerness', *Interalia: A Journal of Queer Studies*, 4 (2009):1–20.
27 Phyllis Nagy interviewed by Terry Gross, 'Carol, Two Women Leap into an Unlikely Love Affair', *NPR Movie Interviews* (6 January 2016): viewed on 2 November 2018, https://www.npr.org/templates/transcript/transcript.php?storyId=462089856
28 Victoria L. Smith, 'The Heterotopias of Todd Haynes: Creating Space for Same Sex Desire in Carol', *Film Criticism*, 42:1 (2018): viewed on 2 November 2018, https://quod.lib.umich.edu/f/fc/13761232.0042.102?view=text;rgn=main I extend Smith's argument to consider other encounters with mirrors.
29 Foucault, 'Of Other Spaces, Utopias and Heterotopias', 4.
30 Betsky, *Queer Space: Architecture and Same-Sex Desire*, 17.
31 Fabio Cleto, 'The Spectacles of Camp', in *Camp: Notes on Fashion*, ed. Andrew Bolton (New York: The Metropolitan Museum of Art, 2019): 17.
32 I refer here to Laurence with female pronouns in accordance with the film's position that she has always identified as woman.
33 Judith Butler, *Gender Trouble: Feminism and the Subversion of Identity* (New York: Routledge, [1990] 1999).
34 Nick Rees-Roberts, 'Fade to Grey: Dolan's Pop Fashion and Surface Style', in *ReFocus: The Films of Xavier Dolan*, ed. Andre Lafontaine (Edinburgh: Edinburgh University Press, 2019): 220.
35 Judith Butler, *Bodies That Matter: On the Discursive Limits of Sex* (New York: Routledge, 1993): 137.
36 *Paris Is Burning* has been screened at multiple Fashion Film festivals and programmes including Fashion On Film, ACCMI Melbourne 2018; Fashion and Film Festival Arnhem 2007, Copenhagen Fashion Film 2016 amongst others. It has also frequently featured in fashion media such as *Dazed, Vogue and Vanity Fair*.
37 *Paris Is Burning* has been the subject of widespread critical debate. See bell hooks, *Black Looks: Race and Representation* (New York and London: Routledge, 2015); Butler, *Bodies That Matter*; Lucas Hilderbrand, *Paris Is Burning: A Queer Film Classic* (Vancouver: Arsenal Pulp Press, 2013).
38 Foucault, 'Of Other Spaces, Utopias and Heterotopias', 3.
39 For thorough analysis of ballroom culture see Marlon M. Bailey, *Butch Queens: Gender, Performance and Ballroom Culture in Detroit* (Ann Arbor: The University of Michigan Press, 2013).
40 Other examples include a fashion feature in New York lifestyle magazine *Details*, and a 1989 Thierry Mugler Paris runway show incorporating voguers. See Hilderbrand, *Paris Is Burning: A Queer Film Classic*.

41 Church Gibson, *Fashion and Celebrity Culture.*
42 Ibid., 99.
43 See Church Gibson, *Fashion and Celebrity Culture*; Rees-Roberts, *Fashion Film.*
44 Dyer, *The Culture of Queers,* 206.
45 Ibid.
46 Ibid., 217–18.
47 Sarajane Hoare, 'Actors Tweeds', *Vogue* (Britain) (November 1987): 270–6.
48 Rees-Roberts, 'Fade to Grey: Dolan's Pop Fashion and Surface Style', 217.
49 Shayne Leverdière and Xavier Dolan, 'Xavier Dolan', *L'Uomo Vogue,* 456 (December 2014): viewed on 1 July 2020, https://www.vogue.it/en/uomo-vogue/cover-story/2014/12/dolan
50 Alasdair McLellan, Xavier Dolan for Louis Vuitton Mens Summer 2016 short film, viewed on 20 October 2020, https://www.youtube.com/watch?v=EfxGl_JfPuw
51 Hannah Rochelle and Lucy Pavia, 'What's Now: Big Screen Chic', *Instyle* (December 2015): 171–2.
52 Robert Sullivan, 'Dramatic Effect: Reel Talk', *Vogue* (December 2015): 180, 182.
53 Diane Waldman, 'From Midnight Shows to Marriage Vows', *Wide Angle,* 6:2 (1984): 48.
54 Jane Gaines, 'The Queen Christina Tie-ups: Convergence of Show Window and Screen', *Quarterly Review of Film and Video,* 11:1 (1989): 43.
55 Ibid., 50.

Chapter 4

1 Gilles Lipovetsky, *The Empire of Fashion: Dressing Modern Democracy*, trans. Catherine Porter (Princeton and Oxford: Princeton University Press, 1994): 26.
2 Ibid., 29.
3 See Rosalind Williams, *Dream Worlds: Mass Consumption in Late Nineteenth Century France* (Berkeley: University of California Press, 1982); Caroline Evans, *Fashion at the Edge: Spectacle, Modernity and Deathliness* (New Haven and London: Yale University Press, 2003).
4 Berry, *Screen Style: Fashion and Femininity in 1930s Hollywood*; Caroline Evans, *The Mechanical Smile: Modernism and the First Fashion Shows in France and America, 1900–1929* (New Haven and London: Yale University Press, 2013); Charlotte Herzog, 'Powder Puff Promotion: The Fashion Show-in-the-Film', in *Fabrications: Costume and the Female Body*, eds. Jane Gains and Charlotte Herzog (London: Routledge, 1990).
5 Tamar Jeffers McDonald, *Hollywood Catwalk: Exploring Costume and Transformation in American Film* (New York: I.B Tauris, 2010), also makes the case

for staircases as sites of transformation however her argument does not extend to recognizing the fashionable iconicity of staircases in photography and retail environments as I do here.

6   See Nancy J Troy, *Couture Culture: A Study in Modern Art and Fashion* (Massachusetts: Massachusetts Institute of Technology, 2003); Evans, *The Mechanical Smile*.
7   Lady Duff Gordon, *Discretions and Indiscretions* (New York: Frederick A Stokes, 1932).
8   Joel H. Kaplan and Shiela Stowell, *Theatre and Fashion: Oscar Wilde to the Suffragettes* (Cambridge: Cambridge University Press, 1994): 119.
9   Duff Gordon, *Discretions and Indiscretions*, 78.
10 Berry, *Screen Style: Fashion and Femininity in 1930s Hollywood*, 47.
11 Robert Forest Wilson, 'The House of Nicole Groult', *Vogue* (America) (January 15 1927): 20, 116, 120.
12 Robert Forest Wilson, 'The House of Lucien Lelong', *Vogue* (America) (October 15 1925): 33–6; Robert Forest Wilson, 'The House of Bechoff', *Vogue* (America) (February 15 1927): 23–4, 136; 'The House of Jean Magnin', *Vogue* (America) (March 15 1927): 52, 170.
13 Troy, *Couture Culture*.
14 Evans, *The Mechanical Smile*, 247.
15 A selection of these films can be viewed online 'Paris Fashions', *British Pathé* (1909): viewed on 20 July 2020, https://www.britishpathe.com/video/paris-fashions-4
16 Troy, *Couture Culture*, 228.
17 Berry, *House of Fashion*.
18 Bourdieu, *Distinction: A Social Critique of Judgement through Taste*.
19 'Leading Stores Exploit Fashions from Roberta', *The Film Daily* (15 March 1935): 16.
20 Herzog, 'Powder Puff Promotion: The Fashion Show-in-the-Film', 154–5.
21 For an extensive discussion Berry, *House of Fashion*. Here I focus on and develop the analysis of the staircase.
22 Gabrielle Chanel cited in Lisa Chaney, *Coco Chanel: An Intimate Life* (New York: Penguin, 2011): 202.
23 'L'Escalier des Glaces Chez Chanel', *Vogue* (France) (1 August 1931): 41; Francois Kollar, 'Escalier chez Chanel' (1937) (Photograph); 'Chanel-Her Famous New Dinner Pyjamas', *Vogue* (America) (15 November 1965): 116–17.
24 Evans, *The Mechanical Smile*, 129.
25 'The Debut of the Winter Mode', *Vogue* (America) (October 1926): 69.
26 Karl Lagerfeld, 'Karl Chats with Coco', *Harper's Bazaar* (March 2003): 226.
27 Karl Lagerfeld (photographs), 'La Reign Victoria', *Elle* (France) October 2012, 167.
28 Steff Yotka, 'Sofia Coppola Goes behind the Scenes at Chanel in a New Documentary', *Vogue* (10 July 2020): viewed on 20 July 2020, https://www.vogue.com/article/sofia-coppola-goes-behind-the-scenes-at-chanel-in-a-new-documentary

29 Gabrielle Chanel cited in Justine Picardie, *Coco Chanel: The Legend and the Life* (London: HarperCollins, 2010): 1.
30 John Templar, *The Staircase: History and Theory* (Massachusetts: MIT Press, 1998): x.
31 Edward Steichen's first fashion photographs illustrated in Paul Cornu, 'L'Art de la Robe', *Art et Decoration* (Avril 1911): 103–7.
32 Margaret Maynard, 'The Fashion Photograph: An Ecology', in *Fashion as Photograph*, ed. Eugenie Shinkle (London: I.B Tauris, 2010): 55.
33 André Leon Tally, *The Chiffon Trenches* (London: HarperCollins, 2020, e-book location 1911).
34 Universal Studios press cited in Barbara Klinger, *Melodrama and Meaning: History, Culture and the Films of Douglas Sirk* (Bloomington and Indianapolis: Indiana University Press, 1994): 60.
35 Herzog, 'Powder Puff Promotion: The Fashion Show-in-the-Film', 137.
36 *New York Times* cited in John Loring, *Joseph Urban* (New York: Abrams, 2010): 31.
37 Gaylyn Studlar, 'Chi-Chi Cinderella: Audrey Hepburn as Couture Countermodel', in *Fabrications: Costume and the Female Body*, eds. Jane Gains and Charlotte Herzog (London: Routledge, 1990): 165.
38 Original emphasis, Doane, *The Desire to Desire*, 136.
39 Ibid., 33.
40 Ibid.
41 Hilary Radner, 'Transnational Celebrity and the Fashion Icon: The Case of Tilda Swinton Visual Performance Artist at Large', *European Journal of Women's Studies*, 23:4 (2016): 401.
42 Meredith L. Clausen, 'The Department Store: Development of the Type', *Journal of Architectural Education*, 39:1 (1985): 20–9, 24.
43 Giles Lipovetsky, 'On Artistic Capitalism', *Crash Magazine*, 65 (3 April 2015): viewed on 3 August 2020, https://www.crash.fr/on-artistic-capitalism-by-giles-lipovetsky-crash-65/
44 Laura Hawkins, 'Step Up: Dolce & Gabbana's Staircase is Ahead of the Curve', *Wallpaper** (11 January 2018): viewed on 3 August 2020, https://www.wallpaper.com/fashion/dolce-and-gabbana-marble-design-awards-2018
45 Friedman, *American Glamour and the Evolution of Modern Architecture*, 6.
46 The term 'starchitect' is used commonly to refer to famous architects of signature buildings, for example Frank Gehry, and Rem Koolhaas. See Adam Shar, 'Libeskind in Las Vegas: Reflections on Architecture as a Luxury Commodity', in *Critical Luxury Studies: Art, Design and Media*, eds. John Armitage and Joanne Roberts (Edinburgh: Edinburgh University Press, 2016): 151–76.
47 Kazyz Varnelis, 'Prada and the Pleasure Principle', *Log*, 6 (2005): 129–36.
48 Alice T. Friedman, 'American Glamour 2.0: Architecture, Spectacle and Social Media', *Consumption, Markets and Culture*, 20:6 (2017): 575.
49 Annette Condello, *The Architecture of Luxury* (Surrey: Ashgate, 2014).

50 Marcus Fairs, 'Armani 5th Avenue by Massimiliano and Doriana Fuksas Architects', *Dezeen* (23 February 2009): viewed on 10 August 2020, https://www.dezeen.com/2009/02/23/armani-5th-avenue-by-massimiliano-doriana-fuksas-architects/; James Tarmy, 'The Stair Master: How Peter Marino Turns Simple Steps into Amazing Art', *Bloomberg* (23 November 2016): viewed 10 August 2020, https://www.bloomberg.com/news/articles/2016-11-22/amazing-staircase-designs-in-peter-marino-art-architecture; Dan Howarth, 'David Chipperfield's Valentino Flagship Store Opens in New York', *Dezeen* (11 September 2014): viewed on 10 August 2020, https://www.dezeen.com/2014/09/11/david-chipperfield-valentino-flagship-store-fifth-avenue-new-york/; Joyce Caruso, 'Gehry Downtown', *Artnet* (8 July 2001): viewed on 10 August 2020, http://www.artnet.com/magazine/news/caruso/caruso8-7-01.asp

Chapter 5

1 Eckert, 'The Carol Lombard in Macy's Window', 4.
2 See Anne Friedberg, *Window Shopping: Cinema and the Postmodern* (Berkeley: University of California Press, 1994); Doane, *The Desire to Desire*; Lauren Rabinovitz, *For the Love of Pleasure: Women, Movies and Culture in Turn-of-the Century Chicago* (New Jersey: Rutgers University Press, 1998).
3 David Clark, 'The Shop Within?: An Analysis of the Architectural Evidence for Medieval Shops', *Architectural History*, 43 (2000): 58–87.
4 See Claire Walsh, 'Shop Design and the Display of Goods in Eighteenth Century London', *Journal of Design History*, 8:3 (1995): 157–76; Anca I Lasc, 'The Traveling Sidewalk: The Mobile Architecture of American Shop Windows at the Turn of the Twentieth Century', *Journal of Design History*, 31:1 (2018): 24–45.
5 Lasc, 'The Traveling Sidewalk'.
6 L. Frank Baum, *The Art of Decorating Dry Goods Windows and Interiors* (Chicago: Show Window, 1900): 146.
7 Stuart Culver, 'What Manikins Want: *The Wonderful Wizard of Oz* and the Art of Decorating Dry Goods Windows', *Representations*, 21 (Winter 1988): 97.
8 Ibid., 98.
9 L. Frank Baum cited in Rabinovitz, *For the Love of Pleasure*, 78.
10 T. Friedelson, 'Selfridges by Night', 20 March 1909, advertisement reproduced in Erika D. Rappaport, 'A New Era of Shopping: The Promotion of Women's Pleasure in London's West End, 1909–1914', in *Cinema and the Invention of Modern Life*, eds. Leo Charney and Vanessa Schwartz (Berkeley: University of California Press, 1995): 141.
11 Jane Chapman, 'The Argument of the Broken Pane: Suffragette Consumerism and the Newspapers', *Media History*, 21:3 (2015): 238–51.

12 Doane, *The Desire to Desire*.
13 Rabinovitz, *For the Love of Pleasure*, 79.
14 Walter Benjamin, *The Arcades Project*, trans. Howard Eiland and Kevin McLaughlin (Cambridge and London: Harvard University Press, 1999); see also Susan Buck-Morss, *The Dialectics of Seeing: Walter Benjamin and the Arcades Project* (Cambridge and London: MIT Press, 1991).
15 Walter Benjamin, 'Paris: Capital of the Nineteenth Century', *Perspecta*, 12 (1969 [1935]): 163–72.
16 Ibid., 172.
17 Friedberg, *Window Shopping*, 68.
18 Ibid., 147.
19 Mike Featherstone, 'The Flâneur, the City and Virtual Public Life', *Urban Studies*, 35:5/6 (1998): 919
20 Ibid., 909–25.
21 Williams, *Dream Worlds*, 70.
22 I have also outlined the cinematic experience of window displays created by Sonia Delaunay and Robert Mallet-Stevens in Berry, *House of Fashion*. Here, I revisit this material to focus more specifically on the pair's film collaborations and the possible inter-relationship with their store designs.
23 Robert Delaunay cited in Arthur Cohen (ed.), *The New Art of Colour: The Writings of Robert and Sonia Delaunay*, trans. David Schapiro and Arthur Cohen (New York: Viking Press, 1978): 140.
24 Radu Stern, *Against Fashion: Clothing as Art* (Massachusetts: The MIT Press, 2004).
25 Henri Clouzot cited in Tag Gronberg, *Designs on Modernity: Exhibiting the City in 1920s Paris* (Manchester and New York: Manchester University Press, 1998): 88.
26 See my previous analysis in Berry, *House of Fashion*, 138–44.
27 Bergfelder, Harris and Street, *Film Architecture and the Transnational Imagination*, 58.
28 Robert Mallet-Stevens, *Le Décor Modern au Cinema* (Paris: Charles Massin, 1928).
29 Robert Mallet-Stevens, 'Le Cinema et les arts: L'Architecture', *Les Cahiers du Mois Cinema*, 16–17 (1925): 95 cited in Richard Becherer, 'Past Remembering: Robert Mallet-Stevens's Architecture of Duration', *Assemblage*, 31 (1996): 16.
30 Barsacq, *Caligari's Cabinet and Other Grand Illusions*, 43.
31 Moussinac, 'Le Décor et le Costume au Cinema', 129–39.
32 Rene Chavance, 'Chez un Cineaste', *Art et Decoration* (Juillet–Decembre 1927): 43–8.
33 Photographs of Mallet-Steven's home feature in Leon Werth, 'L'Architecture Intérieure et Mallet Stevens', *Art et Decoration* (Janvier–Juin 1929): 177–88.
34 Helmut Weismann, 'Let Architecture Play Itself: A Case Study', in *The City and the Moving Image*, eds. Richard Koeck and Les Roberts (London: Palgrave Macmillan, 2010): 253–70.

35 See Richard Becherer, 'Picturing Architecture Otherwise: The Voguing of the Maison Mallet-Stevens', *Art History*, 23:4 (2000): 559–98.
36 For more extensive discussion regarding the role of Therese Bonney in producing fashionable images of interior design in the 1920s see Berry, *House of Fashion*.
37 Becherer, 'Picturing Architecture Otherwise: The Voguing of the Maison Mallet-Stevens'.
38 Sigfried Giedion's critiques of Mallet-Stevens' architecture as cited in Wigley, *White Walls Designer Dresses*, 75.
39 See Robert Mallet-Stevens, *Le Décor de la rue, les magazines, les étalages, les stands d'exposion, les éclairages* (Paris: Les Éditions de Parade, 1927); Robert Mallet-Stevens, 'L'éclairage et l'architecture modern', *Lux* (Janvier 1928): 6–9.
40 Robert Mallet-Stevens, *Le Décor de la rue, les magazines, les étalages, les stands d'exposion, les éclairages*, 3.
41 For discussion on of boutique shopfronts as the art of the street see Louis Cheronnet, 'Boutiques Nouvelles A Paris', *Art et Decoration* (Juillet–Decembre 1928): 113–20.
42 Pierre Migennes, 'De L'Étalage', *Art et Decoration* (Juillet–Decembre 1929): 97–111.
43 Gabrielle Esperdy, 'From Instruction to Consumption: Architecture and Design in Hollywood Movies of the 1930s', *The Journal of American Culture*, 30:2 (2007): 198–211.
44 Becherer, 'Picturing Architecture Otherwise: The Voguing of the Maison Mallet-Stevens', 562.
45 Esperdy, 'From Instruction to Consumption'.
46 See Eckert, 'The Carol Lombard in Macy's Window'; Gaines, 'The Queen Christina Tie-ups'; Esperdy, 'From Instruction to Consumption'.
47 Mike Featherstone, 'Luxury Consumer Culture and Sumptuary Dynamics', *Luxury: History, Culture and Consumption*, 1:1 (2015): 52.
48 Ibid., 47–69.
49 *Pictorial Review* (May 1925): 13 cited in Linda Mizejewski, *Ziegfeld Girl: Image and Icon in Culture and Cinema* (Durham and London: Duke University Press, 1999), 101.
50 Ibid.
51 Massey, *Hollywood beyond the Screen*, 41.
52 Hannah Booth, 'Shopping in Bollywood', *Design Week* (2 May 2002): 19–23.
53 See Rees-Roberts, *Fashion Film* for further discussion regarding the influence of SHOWstudio on digital fashion film.
54 Cinema of attractions is the term used to describe early silent cinema that focused on illusion and abstraction rather than narrative. See Tom Gunning, 'The Cinema of Attraction: Early Film, Its Spectator and the Avant-Garde', in *Early Cinema: Space, Frame, Narrative*, ed. Thomas Elsaesser (London: BFI, 1990): 56–62; Ruth Hogben, *Gareth Pugh Pitti Immagine #79 2011* (13 January 2011): viewed on 3 October 2020, https://www.showstudio.com/projects/gareth_pugh_pitti_immagine_79_2011;

Nick Knight, *Valentino Haute Couture F/W 2021: Of Grace and Light* (22 July 2020): viewed on 3 October 2020, https://www.showstudio.com/projects/of-grace-and-light/fashion-film?autoplay=1

55 Mike Featherstone, 'Consumer Culture and Its Futures: Dreams and Consequences', in *Approaching Consumer Culture*, ed. Evgenia Krasteva-Blagoeva (Cham: Springer, 2018): 1–46.
56 Marie Schuller, *SHOWstudio x Selfridges – The Maters* (21 August 2014): viewed on 3 October 2020, https://www.youtube.com/watch?v=cbsN4lv8Uaw
57 Jacob Stolworthy, 'Selfridges to Open in Store Cinema', *The Telegraph* (4 September 2014): viewed on 28 September 2018, https://www.telegraph.co.uk/culture/film/film-news/11075378/Selfridges-to-open-in-store-cinema.html
58 *Selfridges Hot Air*, viewed on 3 October 2020, https://www.selfridges.com/AU/en/features/welove/
59 'SHOWstudio and Harrods Present the Future of Fashion', (18 September 2020): viewed on 3 October 2020, https://www.showstudio.com/news/showstudio-and-harrods-present-future-fashion
60 Featherstone, 'Luxury Consumer Culture and Sumptuary Dynamics', 59.

Chapter 6

1 Whitehead, *Creating Interior Atmosphere*.
2 Lipovetsky and Manlow, 'The "Artialization" of Luxury Stores', 165.
3 See Lipovestky, *The Empire of Fashion* regarding the democratization of the fashion system; Jean Baudrillard, *Simulations* (New York: Semiotext(e), 1983) for discussion on the aestheticization of everyday life.
4 Peter McNeil and Giorgio Riello, *Luxury: A Rich History* (Oxford: Oxford University Press, 2016): 237.
5 B. Joseph Pine II and James H. Gilmore, 'Welcome to the Experience Economy', *Harvard Business Review* (July–August 1998): viewed on 20 August 2020, https://hbr.org/1998/07/welcome-to-the-experience-economy
6 Floriana Iannone and Francesco Izzo, 'Salvatore Ferragamo: An Italian Heritage Brand and its Museum', *Place Branding and Public Diplomacy*, 13:2 (2017): 163–75; Uche Okonkwo, *Luxury Fashion Branding* (London: Palgrave, 2007).
7 Okonkwo, *Luxury Fashion Branding*, 109.
8 Jean-Noël Kapferer, 'The Artification of Luxury: From Artisans to Artists', *Business Horizons*, 57 (2014): 371–80.
9 See Louise Crewe, *The Geographies of Fashion: Consumption, Space and Value* (London: Bloomsbury, 2017); Silvano Mendes and Nick Rees-Roberts, 'New French Luxury: Art, Fashion and the Re-Invention of a National Brand', *Luxury*, 2:2 (2015): 53–69.

10 See Lipovetsky and Manlow, 'The "Artialization" of Luxury Stores', 154–67, who identify the emergence of the 'cinematographization' of retail space as a relationship that deserves to be pursued further.
11 Foucault, 'Of Other Spaces, Utopias and Heterotopias', 6.
12 Wall text for Gucci Garden Galleria, Gucci Garden, Florence, Italy.
13 The Medici family patronage of the arts is recognized for being responsible for the majority of Florintine art during the Renaissance.
14 Gioria Sepe and Alessia Anzivino, 'Guccification: Redefining Luxury through Art – the Gucci Revolution', in *The Artification of Luxury Fashion Brands* (Cham: Palgrave, 2020): 89–112.
15 Dyer, *The Culture of Queers,* 206.
16 Maria Carmela Ostillio and Sarah Ghaddar, 'Salvatore Ferragamo: Brand Heritage as Main Vector of Brand Exension and Internationalization', in *Fashion Branding and Communication*, eds. Byoungho Jin and Elena Cedrola (New York: Palgrave, 2017): 73–99.
17 'Previous Exhibitions', *Museo Salvatore Ferragamo* (2020): viewed on 20 August 2020, https://www.ferragamo.com/museo/en/usa/exhibitions/archive/
18 'Italy in Hollywood', *Museo Salvatore Farragamo,* curated by Giuliana Musico and Steffania Ricci, 24 May 2018–10 March 2019.
19 Lipovetsky and Manlow, 'The "Artialization" of Luxury Stores', 165.
20 Joan Juliette Buck, 'Everybody's All-American', *Vogue* (America) (February 1992): 203.
21 See collections for spring/summer 2012, spring/summer 2019; 'Ralph Lauren Advertisement', *Vogue* (America) (October 2010): C2 1–7.
22 Ralph Lauren cited in Kathleen Baird-Murray, *Vogue on Ralph Lauren* (New York: Abrams, 2015): 41.
23 Teri Agins, *The End of Fashion* (New York: HarperCollins, 2009): 87.
24 Christopher Gray, 'From a Mysterious Mansion to a Ralph Lauren Store', *The New York Times* (7 October 2010): viewed on 19 August 2020, https://www.nytimes.com/2010/10/10/realestate/10scapes.html
25 Ralph Lauren cited in Jon Roth, 'Dream House: How Ralph Lauren Created a Retail Revolution on Maddison Avenue', *Ralph Lauren*: viewed on 19 August 2020, https://www.ralphlauren.com.au/en/style-guide/dream-house
26 Ibid.
27 Ann Boyd cited in Baird-Murray, *Vogue on Ralph Lauren,* 84.
28 Tom Shone, 'Great Expectations', *Vogue* (America) (May 2013): 246–55, 314.
29 Emma Ciufo, 'Miuccia Prada Unveils Great Gatsby Costumes', *Harper's Bazaar* (22 January 2013): viewed on 20 August 2020, https://www.harpersbazaar.com.au/fashion/miuccia-prada-unveils-great-gatsby-costumes-7451
30 Adam Stockhausen cited in Matt Zoller Seitz, *The Wes Anderson Collection: Grand Budapest Hotel* (New York: Abrams, 2015): 160.

31 Wes Anderson, 'Bar Luce', in *Quaderno Fondazione Prada #8* (Milan: Fondazione Prada, 2016): 48.
32 Ibid.
33 Karinna Nobbs, Christopher Moore and Mandy Sheridan, 'The Flagship Format within the Luxury Fashion Market', *International Journal of Retail & Distribution Management*, 40:12 (2012): 923.
34 Susan B. Kaiser, *Fashion and Cultural Studies* (London and New York: Bloomsbury, 2012).
35 Coral Moera Hernandez, 'Patronage, Public Relations and Philanthropy: Fendi for Fountains Case Study', *Revista de Communication Vivat Academia*, 18:133 (2015): 80–124.
36 Eugenia Paulicelli, 'Reframing History: Federico Fellini's Rome, Fashion and Costume', *Film, Fashion and Consumption*, 8:1 (2019): 72.
37 Lauren Alexis Fisher, 'Inside Fendi's Breathtaking Couture Show at Rome's Trevi Fountain', *Harper's Bazaar* (8 July 2016): viewed on 24 August 2020, https://www.harpersbazaar.com/fashion/fashion-week/news/a16573/fendi-couture-show-at-trevi-fountain/; Nicole Phelps, 'Fall 2016 Fendi', *Vogue* (8 July 2016): viewed on 24 August 2020, https://www.vogue.com/fashion-shows/fall-2016-couture/fendi
38 See Paola Somma, 'The Palazzo Civiltà Italiana: From Fascism to Fashion', in *The Routledge Companion to Italian Fascist Architecture: Reception and Legacy*, eds. Kay Bea Jones, Stephanie Pilat (Oxon and New York: Routledge, 2020): 79–91; and Jena Loncar, 'F is for … Fluctuating Symbolism: The Palazzo Civiltà Italiana and its Shifting Meaning', in *The Routledge Companion to Italian Fascist Architecture: Reception and Legacy*, eds. Kay Bea Jones, Stephanie Pilat (Oxon and New York: Routledge, 2020): 92–110. While both of these chapters make similar arguments, they do not examine its presence in film as here.
39 'Fendi Studios Exhibition Celebrates Close Bond between Fendi and the Cinema', *LVMH* (30 October 2017): viewed on 20 August 2020, https://www.lvmh.com/news-documents/news/fendi-studios-exhibition-celebrates-close-bonds-between-fendi-and-the-cinema/
40 Philip Morgan, *Italian Fascism: 1915–1945* (London: Palgrave McMillan, 2004): 143.
41 Fendi CEO Pietro Beccari cited in Somma, 'The Palazzo Civiltà Italiana: From Fascism to Fashion', 79.
42 Karl Lagerfeld cited in Loncar, 'F is for … Fluctuating Symbolism: The Palazzo Civiltà Italiana and Its Shifting Meaning', 99.
43 Owen Hatherly, 'Fendi Vidi Vici: When Fashion Flirts with Fascism', *The Architectural Review* (3 March 2015): viewed on 20 August 2020, https://www.architectural-review.com/essays/fendi-vidi-vici-when-fashion-flirts-with-fascism
44 Miles Glendinning, *Architecture's Evil Empire: The Triumph and Tragedy of Global Modernism* (London: Reaktion, 2010).

45 Lipovetsky and Manlow, 'The "Artialization" of Luxury Stores', 165. See also Giles Lipovetsky and Jean Serroy, *L'Ecran Global: Culture-médias et Cinéma à l'âge Hypermoderne* (Paris: Seuil, 2007).

46 Lipovetsky and Manlow, 'The "Artialization" of Luxury Stores', 165.

47 Elise Romano, 'Aesop Channels Bond in London's Most Instagrammable Store', *DMARGE* (18 November 2017): viewed on 4 September 2020, https://www.dmarge.com/2017/11/aesop-london-flagship.html; Alice Morby, 'NC Design & Architecture Hides Hong Kong Restaurant behind Grocery Stall', *Dezeen* (17 February 2016): viewed on 4 September 2020, https://www.dezeen.com/2016/02/17/nc-design-architecture-mak-mak-hong-kong-restaurant-hidden-behind-thai-grocery-stall/; Ali Morris, 'Gold Palm Trees Adorn the Monochromatic Interior of Darial Concept Store in Barcelona', *Dezeen* (25 November 2019): viewed on 4 September 2020, https://www.dezeen.com/2019/11/25/darial-store-barcelona-djaba-diassamidze/

48 India Mahdavi, 'REDValentino Sloan Street London', *indiamahdavi.com* (2016): viewed on 4 September 2020, https://india-mahdavi.com/project/red-valentino-sloan-street/

49 India Mahdavi cited in Fiona McCarthy, 'Shared Vision', *Wish: The Australian Magazine* (March 2020): 46.

Conclusion

1 Brandi Thompson Summers, 'Race as Aesthetic: The Politics of Vision, Visibility and Visuality in Vogue Italia's "A Black Issue"', *QED: A Journal in QLBTQ Worldmaking*, 4:3 (2017): 81–108.

2 Morgan C. Schimminger, 'Report: Racial Diversity Ticks Up Slightly, Size, Age and Gender Representation all Drop for Fashion Month Spring 2021', *The Fashion Spot* (19 October 2020): viewed on 5 January 2021, https://www.thefashionspot.com/runway-news/858789-diversity-report-fashion-month-spring-2021/

3 For discussion on Josephine Baker and fashion see: Jennifer Sweeny-Risko, 'Fashionable "Formation": Reclaiming the Sartorial Politics of Josephine Baker', *Australian Feminist Studies*, 33:98 (2018): 498–514; Benneta Jules-Rosette, 'Spectacular Dress: Africanisms in the Fashions and Performances of Josephine Baker', in *African Dress: Fashion, Agency, Performance*, eds. Karen Tranberg Hansen and D. Soyini Madison (London: Bloomsbury, 2013). For discussion on Loos Baker House imagined for the entertainer see: Colomina, 'The Split Wall: Domestic Voyeurism', 73–130; Anne Anlin Cheng, *Second Skin: Josephine Baker and the Modern Surface* (London: Oxford, 2011).

4 Anne Anlin Cheng, 'Skin Fashion: Josephine Baker and Dressing Race', *Nka: Journal of Contemporary African Art*, 37 (2015): 6–15.

5 Yrsa Daly-Ward, 'Women of the Year: Lashana Lynch on Making History as the First Black Female 007', *Harper's Bazaar* (3 November 2020): viewed on 23 November 2020, https://www.harpersbazaar.com/uk/culture/culture-news/a34517814/lashana-lynch-black-female-007-interview/
6 Monica L. Miller, *Slaves to Fashion: Black Dandyism and the Styling of Black Diasporic Identity* (Durham and London: Durham University Press, 2009).
7 Ibid., 228.
8 Lori Kindo Lopez, 'Racism and Mainstream Media', in *Race and Media: Critical Approaches*, ed. Lori Kindo Lopez (New York: New York University Press, 2020): 13–26.
9 Olivia Khoo, 'Writing about Transnational Cinema: Crazy Rich Asians,' in *Writing About Screen Media*, ed. Lisa Patti (Oxon and New York: Routledge, 2020): 75–8.
10 Jasmine Ariel Ting, 'The Crazy Rich Style of *Crazy Rich Asians*,' *Vanity Fair* (14 August 14 2018): viewed on 23 November 2020, https://www.vanityfair.com/style/2018/08/the-crazy-rich-style-of-crazy-rich-asians; Cathy Whitlock, 'Here's Why all the Sets in *Crazy Rich Asians* Look so Authentic and, Well Rich', *Architectural Digest*, 9 August 2018, available 23 November 2020, https://www.architecturaldigest.com/story/crazy-rich-asians-sets
11 Galt, *Pretty: Film and the Decorative Image*.
12 Ibid., 304.
13 For discussion of Bollywood costume and fashion see Deepsikha Chatterjee and Cheri Vasek, 'Bollywood: Cross Pollination between Film Costumes and Fashion', *Fashion Practice*, 12:2 (2020): 219–44.
14 See for example SHOWStudio, 'Rejecting the White Gaze: Black Photographers in Fashion', (31 October 2020): viewed on 5 January 2020, https://www.showstudio.com/projects/black-history-month/panel-discussion-the-future-of-fashion-photography?autoplay=1; 'A Certain Romance' (24 October 2019): viewed on 5 January 2020, https://www.showstudio.com/projects/certain-romance; 'Tino Kamal Cry' (16 November 2019): viewed on 5 January 2020, https://www.showstudio.com/projects/cry
15 Susan Best, 'From Representation to Affect: Beyond Postmodern Identity Politics in Feminist Art', in *A Companion to Feminist Art*, eds. Hillary Robinson and Maria Elena Buszek (New Jersey: John Wiley and Sons, 2019): 415.
16 Valentina, 'How Valentina from RuPaul's Drag Race Becomes Fabulous', (23 June 2017): viewed on 5 January 2020, https://www.vogue.com/article/valentina-rupauls-drag-race-hair-makeup
17 See Anlin Cheng, *Second Skin* for an excellent treatise on skin as a cinematic surface.

Filmography

In accordance with the content of the book the filmography lists production designers/art directors, set designers and costume designers.

A Single Man. Dir. Tom Ford. Prod Des. Dan Bishop. Set. Amy Wells. Cos. Arianne Phillips. Perf. Colin Firth, Julianne Moore. Fade to Black, 2009.

Adam's Rib. Dir. George Cukor. Art Dir. Cedric Gibbons, Hobe Erwin. Cos. Walter Plunkett. Perf. Katherine Hepburn, Spencer Tracy. MGM, 1949.

All That Heaven Allows. Dir. Douglas Sirk. Set. Russel A. Gausman, Julia Heron. Cos. Bill Thomas. Perf. Jane Wyman, Rock Hudson. Universal International Pictures, 1955.

Amarcord. Dir. Federico Fellini. Prod. Des. Danilo Donati. Cos. Danilo Donati. Perf. Magali Noel, Bruno Zanin. F.C. Produzioni, 1973.

American Gigolo. Dir. Paul Schrader. Set. George Gaines. Cos. Giorgio Armani, Bernadene C. Mann. Perf. Richard Gere, Lauren Hutton. Paramount Pictures, 1980.

And the Ship Sails On. Dir. Federico Fellini. Prod Des. Dante Ferretti. Set. Francesca Lo Schiavo. Cos. Maurizio Millenotti. Perf. Fressie Jones, Barbara Jefford. Rai 1, 1983.

Au Bonheur des Dames. Dir. Julien Duvivier. Set. Christian Jaque, Fernand Delattre. Cos. Gerlaur Marthe Pinchard. Perf. Dita Parlo, Ginette Maddie. Le Film d'Art, 1930.

Australia. Dir. *Baz Luhrmann.* Prod Des. Catherine Martin. Set. Beverly Dunn. Cos. Catherine Martin (Salvatore Ferragamo). Perf. Nicole Kidman, Hugh Jackman. Twentieth Century Fox, 2008.

Barbarella. Dir. Roger Vadim. Prod. Des. Mario Garbuglia. Cos. Jacques Fonteray, Paco Rabanne. Perf. Jane Fonda, John Phillip Law. Marianne Productions and Dino de Laurentis Cinematografica, 1968.

Belle de Jour. Dir. Luis Bunuel. Set Robert Clavel. Cos Helene Nourry (Yves Saint Laurent). Perf. Catherine Deneuve, Jean Sorel. Paris Film Productions, 1967.

Blade Runner. Dir. Ridley Scott. Art Dir. David L. Snyder. Set. Linda DeScenna. Cos. Michael Kaplan, Charles Knode. Perf. Harrison Ford, Sean Young, Daryl Hannah. Warner Bros., 1982.

Breakfast at Tiffany's. Dir. Blake Edwards. Set. Sam Comer, Ray Moyer. Cos. Hubert de Givenchy, Edith Head. Perf. Audrey Hepburn, George Peppard. Jurow-Shepherd, 1961.

Boccaccio '70- 'Le Tentazioni del Dottor Antonio' (The Temptation of Dr Antonio) (episode). Dir. Federico Fellini. Prod Des. Piero Zuffi. Cos. Piero Zuffi. Perf. Anita Ekberg, Peppino De Filippo. Cineriz, 1962.

Call Me by Your Name. Dir. Luca Guadagnino. Art Dir. Roberta Federico. Set. Muriel Chinal, Sandro Piccarozzi, Violante Visconti di Modrone. Cos. Giulia Piersanti. Perf. Arnie Hammer, Timothee Chalamet. Frenesy Film Company, 2017.

Camille. Dir. Ray Smallwood. Art Dir. Natacha Rombova. Cos. Natacha Rombova. Perf. Rudolph Valentino, Alla Nazimova. Nazimova Productions, 1921.

Carol. Dir. Todd Haynes. Art Dir. Jesse Rosenthal. Prod Des. Judy Becker. Set. Heather Loeffler. Cos. Sandy Powell. Perf. Cate Blanchett, Rooney Mara. The Weinstein Company, 2015.

Casino Royale. Dir. Martin Campbell. Prod. Des. Peter Lamont. Cos. Brioni, Lindy Hemming. Perf. Daniel Craig, Eva Green. Eon Productions, Columbia Pictures, 2006.

Castello Cavalcanti (short). Dir. Wes Anderson. Prod Des. Stefano Maria. Set. Cristina Onori. Cos. Milena Canonero. Perf. Jason Schwartzman, Giada Colagrande. Prada, 2013.

Chariots of Fire. Dir. Hugh Hudson. Art Dir. Jonathan Amberston. Cos. Milena Canonero. Perf. Ben Cross. Enigma Productions, 1981.

Cléo de 5 à 7 (Cléo from 5 to 7). Dir. Agnes Varda. Art Dir. Bernard Evans. Cos. Alyette Samazeuilh. Perf. Corinne Marchand. Cine-Tamaris, 1962.

Crazy Rich Asians. Dir. Jon M. Chu. Prod. Des. Nelson Coates. Set. Andrew Baseman. Cos. Mary E. Vogt. Per. Constance Wu, Henry Golding. Warner Bros., 2018.

Dames. Dir. Ray Enright, Busby Berkeley. Art Dir. Robert Haas. Cos. Orry-Kelly. Perf. Joan Blondell, Ruby Keeler. Warner Bros., 1934.

Dangerous Liasons. Dir. Stephen Frears. Art Dir. Gavin Bocquet, Gerard Viard. Set. Gerard James. Cos. James Acheson. Perf. Glenn Close, John Malkovich. Lorimar Film Entertainment, Warner Bros., 1988.

Danse Serpentine (Serpentine Dance). Dir. Louis Lumiere. Perf. Lois Fuller. Lumiere, 1896.

Daughter of the Dragon. Dir. Lloyd Corrigan. Cos. Edith Head. Perf. Anna May Wong, Warner Oland. Paramount Pictures, 1931.

Dead Poets Society. Dir. Peter Weir. Prod. Des. Sandy Veneziano. Set. John Anderson. Cos. Nancy Konrardy. Perf. Robin Williams, Robert Sean Leonard. Touchstone Pictures, 1989.

Devdas. Dir. Sanjay Leela Bhansali. Prod. Des. Nitin Chandrakant Desi. Cos. Abu Jani, Sandeep Khosla, Neeta Lulla. Perf. Shah Rukh Khan, Aishwarya Rai Bachchan. Red Chillies Entertainment, Mega Bollywood, 2002.

Diamonds Are Forever. Dir. Guy Hamilton. Prod. Des. Ken Adam. Set. John Austin, Peter Lamont. Cos. Anthony Sinclair, Donfeld. Perf. Sean Connery, Jill St. John, Charles Gray. Eon Productions, 1971.

Dinner at Eight. Dir. George Cukor. Art Dir. Cedric Gibbons, Hobe Erwin. Cos. Adrian. Perf. Jean Harlow, John Barrymore. MGM, 1933.

Distant Planet: The Six Chapters of Simona (Documentary). Dir. Josh Blaaberg. Prod. Jaqueline Edinbrow, James Galey. Frieze and Gucci, 2019.

Dr. No. Dir. Terrance Young. Prod. Des. Ken Adam. Cos. Anthony Sinclair, Tess Prendergast. Perf. Sean Connery, Ursula Andress, Joseph Wiseman. Eon Productions, 1962.

Dynamite. Dir. Cecil B. DeMille. Art Dir. Cedric Gibbons, Mitchell Leisen. Cos. Adrian. Perf. Kay Johnson, Conrad Nagel. MGM, 1929.

Ever After: A Cinderella Story. Dir. Andy Tennant. Set. Judy Farr. Cos. Jenny Beavan (Salvatore Ferragamo). Perf. Drew Barrymore, Anjelica Huston. Twentieth Century Fox, 1998.

Evita. Dir. Alan Parker. Set. Philippe Turlure. Cos. Penny Rose (Salvatore Ferragamo). Perf. Maddona. Hollywood Pictures, 1996.

Far from Heaven. Dir. Todd Haynes. Art Dir. Peter Rogness. Prod Des. Mark Friedberg. Set. Ellen Christiansen. Cos. Sandy Powell. Perf. Julianne Moore, Dennis Quaid. Focus Features, 2002.

Funny Face. Dir. Stanley Donen. Art Dir. George W. Davis. Set. Sam Comer. Cos. Edith Head, Hubert De Givenchy. Perf. Audrey Hepburn, Fred Astaire. Paramount Pictures, 1957.

Gareth Pugh Pitti Immagine #79 (short). Dir. Roth Hogben. SHOWstudio, 2011.

Gilda. Dir. Charles Vidor. Art Dir. Stephen Goosson, Van Nest Polglase. Set. Robert Priestly. Cos. Jean Lois. Perf. Rita Hayworth, Glenn Ford. Columbia Pictures, 1946.

Gold Diggers of 1933. Dir. Mervyn LeRoy. Art Dir. Anton Grot. Cos. Orry-Kelly. Perf. Joan Blondel, Aline Macmahon, Warren William. Warner Bros., 1933.

Goldfinger. Dir. Guy Hamilton. Prod Des. Ken Adam. Cos. Anthony Sinclair, Elsa Fennell. Perf. Sean Connery, Honor Blackman, Gert Frobe. Eon Productions, 1964.

Gone with the Wind. Dir. Victor Flemming. Art Dir. Lyle R. Wheeler. Set. Howard Bristol. Cos. Walter Plunkett. Perf. Vivien Leigh, Clark Gable. Metro-Goldwyn-Mayer, 1939.

Grand Hotel. Dir. Edmund Goulding. Art Dir. Cedric Gibbons. Cos. Adrian. Perf. Greta Garbo, John Barrymore, Joan Crawford. Metro Goldwyn Mayer, 1932.

Heartbeats. Dir. Xavier Dolan. Art Dir. Xavier Dolan. Set. Delphine Gelinas. Cos. Xavier Dolan. Perf. Monia Chokri, Niels Schneider, Xavier Dolan. Mifilifilms, 2010.

How to Marry a Millionaire. Dir. Jean Negulesco. Art Dir. Leland Fuller, Lyle R. Wheeler. Set. Stuart A. Reiss, Walter M. Scott. Cos. Travilla. Perf. Marilyn Monroe, Betty Grable, Lauren Bacall. Twentieth Century Fox, 1953.

Hum Dil De Chuke Sena. Dir. Sanjay Leela Bahnsali. Art Dir. Nitin Desai. Cos. Shabina Khan, Neeta Lulla. Perf. Aishwarya Rai Bachchan, Salman Khan. Bhansali Films, 1999.

I Am Love (Io sonno l'amore). Dir. Luca Guadagnino. Prod. Des. Francesca Di Mottola. Set. Monica Sironi. Cos. Antonella Cannarozzi. Perf. Tilda Swinton, Flavio Parenti. First Sun, 2009.

Il Conformista (The Conformist). Dir. Bernardo Bertolucci. Prod. Des. Ferdinando Scarfiotti. Set. Maria Paola Maino. Cos. Gitt Magrini. Perf. Jean-Louis Trintignant, Stefania Sandrelli. Mars Film, 1970.

In the Mood for Love (Fa yeung nin wah). Dir. Wong Kar-Wai. Prod. Des. William Chang. Cos. William Chang. Perf. Maggie Cheung, Tony Chiu-Wai Leung. Block 2 Pictures, 2000.

L'Atalante. Dir. Jean Vigo. Art Dir. Francis Jourdain. Perf. Dita Parlo, Jean Daste. Gaumont-Franco Film-Aubert, 1934.

La Dolce Vita. Dir. Federico Fellini. Prod. Des. Piero Gherardi. Cos. Piero Gherardi. Perf. Marcello Mastroianni, Anita Ekberg. Riama Film, 1960.

La Donna Scimmia (The Ape Woman). Dir. Marco Ferreri. Art Dir. Mario Garbuglia. Set. Ferdinando Giovannoni. Cos. Vera Marzot, Piero Tosi. Perf. Ugo Tognazzi, Annie Giardot. Compagnia Cinematografica Champion, 1964.

La Femme de Nulle (The Woman from Nowhere). Dir. Louis Delluc. Art Dir. Francis Jourdain. Perf. Eve Francis, Gine Avril. Cosmograph, 1922.

La Règle du Jeu (The Rules of the Game). Dir. Jean Renoir. Prod. Des. Max Doy. Cos. Coco Chanel. Perf. Marcel Dalio, Nora Gregor. Nouvelles Editions de Films, 1939.

La Sirène des Tropiques (Siren of the Tropics). Dir. Henri Étiévant and Mario Nalpas. Prod. Des. Eugène Carré and Pierre Schild. Perf. Josephine Baker, Pierre Batcheff. La Centrale Cinématographique, 1927.

La Sirène du Mississippi (Mississippi Mermaid). Dir. Francois Truffaut. Set. Claude Pignot. Cos. Yves Saint Laurent. Perf. Catherine Deneuve, Jean-Paul Belmondo. Les Films du Carrosse, Les Productions Artistes Associes, 1969.

Laurence Anyways. Dir. Xavier Dolan. Art Dir. Colombe Raby. Prod. Des. Anne Pritchard. Cos. Francois Barbeau, Xavier Dolan. Perf. Melvil Poupaud, Suzanne Clement. Lyla Films, 2012.

L'Elegance (short). Prod. Sonia Delaunay. Cos. Sonia Delaunay. 1926.

Le Double Amour (Double Love). Dir. Jean Epstein. Art Dir. Pierre Kefer. Cos. Charles Drecoll, Paul Poiret. Films Albatros, 1925.

Le P'tit Parigot (The Little Parisian). Dir. René Le Somptier. Prod. Des. Robert Delaunay, Robert Mallet-Stevens. Cos. Sonia Delaunay. Perf. Marcel Archad, Marquisette Bosky. Luminor, 1926.

Le Vertige (The Living Image). Dir. Marcel L'Herbier. Prod. Des. Pierre Chareau, Robert Delaunay, Sonia Delaunay, Jean Lurcat, Robert Mallet-Stevens. Cos. Jacques Manuel, Sonia Delaunay. Perf. Jaque Catelain, Emmy Lynn. Cinegraphic, 1926.

Les Parapluies de Cherbourg (The Umbrellas of Cherbourg). Dir. Jaques Demy. Prod. Des. Bernard Evin. Cos. Jacqueline Moreau. Perf. Catherine Deneuve, Nino Castelnuovo. Parc Film, 1964.

Letty Lynton. Dir. Clarence Brown. Art Dir. Cedric Gibbons. Cos. Adrian. Perf. Joan Crawford, Robert Montgomery. MGM 1932.

L'Inhumaine (The Inhuman Woman). Dir. Marcel L'Herbier. Art Dir. Claude Autant Lara, Alberto Cavalcanti. Set. Robert Mallet-Stevens (arch), Cos. Paul Poiret. Perf. Georgette Leblanc, Jaque Catelain. Cinegraphic, 1924.

Looking for Langston. Dir. Isaac Julien. Art Dir. Derek Brown. Cos. Robert Worley. Perf. Ben Ellison, Matthew Baidoo, Akim Mogaji. British Film Institute and Sankofa Film and Video, 1989.

Male and Female. Dir. Cecil B. DeMille. Art Dir. Wilfred Buckland. Cos. Paul Iribe, Clare West. Perf. Gloria Swanson, Thomas Meighan. Paramount Pictures, 1919.

Mannequin. Dir. Frank Borzage. Art Dir. Cedric Gibbons. Cos. Adrian. Perf. Joan Crawford, Spencer Tracey. Metro-Goldwyn-Mayer, 1937.

Marie Antoinette. Dir. Sofia Coppola. Prod. Des. K.K. Barrett. Set. Veronique Melery. Cos. Milena Canonero. Perf. Kirsten Dunst, Jason Schwartzman. Columbia Pictures, 2006.

Maurice. Dir. James Ivory. Art Dir. Peter James, Brian Savegar. Prod. Des. Brian Ackland-Snow. Cos. Jenny Beaven, John Bright, William Pierce. Perf. James Wilby, Hugh Grant, Rupert Graves. Merchant Ivory Productions, 1987.

Metropolis. Dir. Friz Lang. Art Dir. Otto Hunte. Cos. Aenne Willkomm. Perf. Brigitte Helm, Alfred Abel. Universum Film, 1927.

Mommy. Dir. Xavier Dolan. Prod. Des. Colombe Raby. Set. Jean-Charles Claveau, Pascale Dechenes. Cos. Francoise Barbeau, Xavier Dolan. Perf. Anne Dorval, Susanne Clement, Antoine Olivier Pilon. Les Films Seville, 2014.

Mon Oncle. Dir. Jacques Tati. Prod. Des. Henri Schmitt. Set. Henri Schmitt. Cos. Jacques Cottin. Perf. Jacques Tati, Jean-Pierre Zola, Adrienne Servantie. Specta Films, 1958.

Monsoon Wedding. Dir. Mira Nair. Prod. Des. Stephanie Carroll. Cos. Arjun Bhasin. Perf. Naseeruddin Shah, Lillete Dubey. IFC Productions, 2001.

My Fair Lady. Dir. George Cukor. Art Dir. Cecil Beaton. Cos. Cecil Beaton. Perf. Audrey Hepburn, Rex Harrison. Warner Bros., 1964.

North by Northwest. Dir. Alfred Hitchcock. Prod. Des. Robert Boyle. Set Henry Grace, Frank McKelvy. Cos. French Klingour, Harry Cress Stanbury. Perf. Cary Grant, Eva Marie Saint, James Mason. Metro-Goldwyn-Mayer, 1959.

Our Dancing Daughters. Dir. Harry Beaumont. Art Dir. Cedric Gibbons. Cos. David Cox. Perf. Joan Crawford, Nils Asther, Johnny Mack Brown. MGM, 1928.

Out of Africa. Dir. Sydney Pollack. Prod. Des. Stephen B. Grimes. Set. Josie MacAvin. Cos. Milena Canonero. Perf. Meryl Streep, Robert Redford. Mirage Enterprises, 1985.

Paris Is Burning (Documentary). Dir. Jennie Livingston. Cast. Venus Xtravaganza, Pepper LaBeija, Dorian Corey, Willi Ninja. Art Matters, 1990.

Pillow Talk. Dir. Michael Gordon. Art Dir. Richard H. Riedel. Set. Russell A. Gausman, Ruby R. Levitt. Cos. Bill Thomas. Perf. Doris Day, Rock Hudson. Arwin Productions, 1959.

Playtime. Dir. Jacques Tati. Prod. Des. Eugene Roman. Cos. Jacques Cottin. Perf. Jacques Tati, Barbara Dennek. Specta Films, 1967.

Prada Candy (short). Dir. Wes Anderson, Roman Coppola. Cos. Prada. Perf. Peter Gadiot, Lea Seydoux. Prada, 2013.

Pretty Woman. Dir. Garry Marshall. Prod. Des. Albery Brenner. Art Dir. Davis M. Haber. Set. Garrett Lewis. Cos. Marilyn Vance. Perf. Julia Roberts, Richard Gere. Touchstone Pictures, 1990.

Princess Tam-Tam. Dir. Edmond T. Gréville. Set. Guy de Gastyne. Cos. Gaston, Philippe Zanel. Perf. Josephine Baker, Albert Préjean. Productions Arys, 1935.

Quantum of Solace. Dir. Marc Forster. Prod. Des. Dennis Gassner. Set. Anna Pinnock. Cos. Tom Ford, Louise Frogley. Perf. Daniel Craig. Olga Kurylenko, Mathieu Amalric. Eon Productions, Metro-Goldwyn-Mayer, Columbia Pictures, 2008.

Queen Christina. Dir. Rouben Mamoulian. Art Dir. Alexander Toluboff. Set. Edwin B. Willis. Cos. Adrian. Perf. Greta Garbo, John Gilbert. Metro-Goldwyn-Mayer, 1933.

Rain. Dir. Lewis Milestone. Art Dir. Richard Day. Cos. Milo Anderson. Perf. Joan Crawford, Walter Hudson. Lewis Milestone Production, 1932.

Rear Window. Dir. Alfred Hitchcock. Art Dir. Joseph McMillan Johnson, Hal Pereira. Set. Sam Comer, Ray Moyer. Cos. Edith Head. Perf. James Stewart, Grace Kelly. Alfred J. Hitchcock Productions, 1954.

Red-Headed Woman. Dir. Jack Conway. Art Dir. Cedric Gibbons. Cos. Adrian. Perf. Jean Harlow, Chester Morris. Metro-Goldwyn-Mayer, 1932.

Roberta. Dir. William A. Seiter. Art Dir. Van Nest Polglasse. Cos. Bernard Newman. Perf. Irene Dunne, Fred Astaire, Ginger Rogers. RKO Radio Pictures, 1935.

Roma Città Aperta (Rome, Open City). Dir. Roberto Rossellini. Prod. Des. Rosario Megna. Perf. Aldo Fabrizi, Anna Magnani. Excelsa Film, 1945.

Rope. Dir. Alfred Hitchcock. Art Dir. Perry Ferguson. Set. Howard Bristol, Emile Kuri. Perf. James Stuart, John Dall, Farley Granger. Warner Bros., 1948.

Sabrina. Dir. Billy Wilder. Art Dir. Hal Pereira. Cos. Hubert De Givenchy. Per. Audrey Hepburn, Humphery Bogart. Paramount Pictures, 1954.

Salome. Dir. Charles Bryant. Art Dir. Natacha Rombova. Cos. Natacha Rombova. Perf. Alla Nazimova. Nazimova Productions, 1923.

Sign of the Cross. Dir. Cecil B. DeMille. Art Dir. Mitchell Leisen. Cos. Mitchell Leisen. Perf. Claudette Colbert, Fredric March. Paramount Pictures, 1929.

Shanghai Express. Dir. Josef von Sternberg. Art Dir. Hans Dreier. Cos. Travis Banton. Perf. Marlene Dietrich, Anna May Wong, Clive Brook. Paramount Pictures, 1932.

Skyfall. Dir. Sam Mendes. Prod. Des. Dennis Gassner. Set. Anna Pinock. Cos. Tom Ford, Jany Temime. Perf. Daniel Craig, Naomie Harris, Javier Bardem, Judi Dench. Eon Productions, Metro-Goldwyn-Mayer, 2012.

Skyscraper Souls. Dir. Edgar Selwyn. Art Dir. Cedric Gibbons. Perf. Warren William, Maureen O'Sullivan. Metro-Goldwyn-Mayer, 1932.

Spectre. Dir. Sam Mendes. Prod. Des. Dennis Gassner. Cos. Tom Ford, Jany Temime. Perf. Daniel Craig, Lea Seydoux, Christoph Waltz. Eon Productions, Columbia Pictures, 2015.

Stolen Holiday. Dir. Michael Curtiz. Art Dir. Anton Grot. Cos. Orry-Kelly. Perf. Kay Francis, Claude Rains. Warner Bros., 1937.

Swing Time. Dir. George Stevens. Art Dir. Van Nest Polglase. Cos. Bernard Newman. Perf. Fred Astaire, Ginger Rogers. RKO Radio Pictures, 1936.

The Affairs of Anatol. Dir. Cecil B. DeMille. Art Dir. Paul Iribe. Cos. Paul Iribe, Clare West. Perf. Gloria Swanson, Wallace Reid. Famous Players-Lasky, 1921.

The Belly of an Architect. Dir. Peter Greenaway. Prod. Des. Ben van Os. Cos. Maurizio Millenotti. Perf. Brian Dennehy, Chloe Webb. Callendar Company, 1987.

The Best of Everything. Dir. Jean Negulesco. Set. Stuart A. Reiss, Walter M. Scott. Cos. Adele Palmer. Perf. Suzy Parker, Hope Lange, Joan Crawford. Jerry Wald Productions and The Company of Artists, 1959.

The Big Sleep. Dir. Howard Hawkes. Art Dir. Carl Jules Weyl, Max Parker. Set. Fred M. Maclean. Cos. Leah Rhodes. Perf. Humphrey Bogart, Lauren Bacall. Warner Bros., 1946.

The Darjeeling Limited. Dir. Wes Anderson. Art Dir. Aradhana Seth. Set. Suzanne Caplan Merwanji, Aradhana Seth. Cos. Milena Canonero (Louis Vuitton). Perf. Owen Wilson, Adrien Brody, Jason Schwartzman. Fox Searchlight Pictures, 2007.

The Favourite. Dir. Yorgos Lanthimos. Art Dir. Caroline Barclay. Set. Alice Felton. Cos. Sandy Powell. Perf. Olivia Colman, Emma Stone, Rachel Weiz. Fox Searchlight Pictures, 2018.

The Fountainhead. Dir. King Vidor. Art Dir. Edward Carrere. Set. William L. Kuehl. Cos. Milo Anderson. Perf. Gary Cooper, Patricia Neal. Warner Bros., 1949.

The Grand Budapest Hotel. Dir. Wes Anderson. Prod. Des. Adam Stockhausen. Set. Anna Pinnock. Cos. Milena Canonero. Perf. Ralph Fiennes, F. Murray Abraham. Fox Searchlight Pictures, 2014.

The Great Gatsby. Dir. Jack Clayton. Prod. Des. John Box. Set. Peter Howitt, Herbert F. Mulligan. Cos. Theoni V. Aldredge (Ralph Lauren). Perf. Robert Redford, Mia Farrow. Paramount Pictures, 1974.

The Great Gatsby. Dir. Baz Luhrmann. Prod. Des. Catherine Murphy. Set Michelle Costello. Cos. Catherine Murphy (Prada, Brooks Brothers). Perf. Leonardo di Caprio, Carey Mulligan, Toby Maguire. Warner Bros., 2013.

The Joy Luck Club. Dir. Wayne Wang. Prod. Des. Donald Graham Burt. Set. Jim Poynter. Cos. Lydia Tanji. Perf. Tamlyn Tomita, Rosalind Chao, Kieu Chinh. Hollywood Pictures, 1993.

The Kiss. Dir. Jacques Feyder. Art Dir. Cedric Gibbons. Cos. Adrian. Perf. Greta Garbo, Anders Randolf, Conrad Nagel. MGM, 1929.

The Life Aquatic with Steve Zissou. Dir. Wes Anderson. Prod. Des. Mark Friedberg. Set. Gretchen Rau. Cos. Milena Canonero. Perf. Bill Murray, Owen Wilson, Cate Blanchett. Touchstone Pictures, 2004.

The Moon is Blue. Dir. Otto Preminger. Art Dir. Nicolai Remisoff. Set. Edward G. Boyle. Cos. Don Loper. Perf. William Holden, Maggie McNamara. Otto Preminger Films, 1953.

The Royal Tenenbaums. Dir. Wes Anderson. Prod. Des David Wasco. Set. Sandy Reynolds-Wasco. Cos. Karen Patch. Perf. Gene Hackman, Anjelica Huston. Touchstone Pictures, 2001.

The Scent of Green Papaya (Mùi đu đủ xanh). Dir. Tran Anh Hung. Prod. Des. Alain Nègre. Cos. Jean-Philippe Abril. Perf. Nu Yên-Khê Tran, Man San Lu. Les Productions Lazennec, 1993.

The Single Standard. Dir. John S. Robertson. Art Dir. Cedric Gibbons. Cos. Adrian. Perf. Greta Garbo, Nils Asther. MGM, 1929.

The Wizard of OZ. Dir. Victor Fleming. Art Dir. Cedric Gibbons. Set. Edwin B. Willis. Cos. Adrian. Perf. Judy Garland, MGM, 1939.

The Women. Dir. George Cukor. Art Dir. Cedric Gibbons, George Gibson. Cos. Adrian. Perf. Norma Shearer, Joan Crawford. MGM, 1939.

The World of Suzie Wong. Dir. Richard Quine. Set. Roy Rossotti. Cos. Betty Adamson. Perf. Nancy Kwan, William Holden. World Enterprises, 1960.

The Young Diana. Dir. Albert Capellani, Robert G. Vignola. Art Dir. Joseph Urban. Cos. Joseph Urban. Perf. Marion Davies, Maclyn Arbuckle. Cosmopolitan Productions, 1922.

Tonight or Never. Dir. Mervyn LeRoy. Cos. Coco Chanel. Perf. Gloria Swanson, Melvyn Douglas. The Samuel Goldwyn Company, 1931.

Top Hat. Dir. Mark Sandrich. Art Dir. Van Nest Polglase. Cos. Bernard Newman. Perf. Fred Astaire, Ginger Rogers. RKO Radio Pictures, 1935.

Twin Beds. Dir. Tim Whelan. Art Dir. John Du Casse Schultz. Set. Edward Boyle. Cos. Rene Hubert. Perf. Joan Bennet, George Brent. Edward Small Productions, 1942.

Under the Red Robe. Dir. Alan Crosland. Art Dir. Joseph Urban. Cos. Gretl Urban. Perf. Robert Mantell, Alma Rubens. Cosmopolitan Productions, 1923.

Une Parisienne. Dir. Michel Boisrond. Prod. Des. Jean Andre. Art Dir (set). Pierre Charron. Cos. Pierre Balmain, Pierre Nourry. Perf. Brigitte Bardot, Charles Boyer, Henri Vidal. Les Films Ariane, 1957.

Valentino Haute Couture F/W 2021: Of Grace and Light (short). Dir. Nick Knight. Set. Andrew Tomlinson. Cos. Valentino. Perf. Erika Lemay, Laetitia Bouffard-Roupe. SHOWstudio, 2020.

Vertigo. Dir. Alfred Hitchcock. Art Dir. Henry Bumstead, Hal Pereira. Set. Sam Comer, Frank McKelvy. Cos. Edith Head. Perf. James Stewart, Kim Novak.

Vogues of 1938. Dir. Irving Cummings. Art Dir. Alexander Toluboff. Cos. Helen Taylor. Perf. Joan Bennett, Warner Baxter. Walter Wagner Productions, 1937.

Way Down East. Dir. D.W. Griffith. Art Dir. Clifford Pember. Cos. Henri Bendel, O'Kane Conway, Lady Duff Gordon, Madame Lisette. Perf. Lillian Gish, Richard Barthelmess. D.W.Griffith Productions, 1920.

Who Are You, Polly Maggoo? Dir. William Klein. Art Dir. Bernard Evein. Cos. Janine Klein. Perf. Dorothy McGowan, Jean Rochefort. Delpire Productions, 1966.

Written on the Wind. Dir. Douglas Sirk. Art Dir. Robert Clatworthy, Alexander Golitzen. Set. Russell A. Gausman, Julia Heron. Cos. Bill Thomas. Perf. Lauren Bacall, Rock Hudson. Universal International Pictures, 1956.

You Only Live Twice. Dir. Lewis Gilbert. Prod. Des. Ken Adam. Cos. Anthony Sinclair, Eileen Sullivan. Perf. Sean Connery, Mie Hamma, Tetsuro Tanba. Eon Productions 1967.

Ziegfeld Girl. Dir. Robert Z. Leonard, Busby Berkeley. Art Dir. Cedric Gibbons. Set. Edwin B. Willis. Cos. Adrian. Perf. Judy Garland, Hedy Lamarr, Lana Turner. MGM, 1941.

Bibliography

Adcock, Michael. 'Remaking Urban Space: Baron Haussmann and the Rebuilding of Paris, 1851–1870'. *University of Melbourne Library Journal* 2:2 (1996): viewed on 13 January 2020, https://museumsandcollections.unimelb.edu.au/__data/assets/pdf_file/0008/1624850/adcock.pdf

Agins, Teri. *The End of Fashion*. New York: HarperCollins, 2009.

Albrecht, Donald. *Designing Dreams: Modern Architecture and the Movies*. New York: Harper and Row 1986.

Anderson, Wes. 'Bar Luce'. *Quaderno Fondazione Prada #8*. Milan: Fondazione Prada, 2016.

Ansen, David. 'Gucci goo'. *Newsweek* (7 December 2009): 23, 68.

Appleton Read, Helen. 'Twentieth Century Decoration'. *Vogue* 73:2 (19 January 1929): 76–7, 100, 106.

Art et Decoration. 'Un décor du film de Marcel L'Herbier'. (Janvier–Juin 1925): 152–4.

Arthur, Paul. 'Film Reviews: *In the Mood for Love*'. *Cineaste* 26:3 (2001): 40–1.

Babuscio, Jack. 'Camp and the Gay Sensibility'. *Queer Cinema, the Film Reader*. Eds. Harry Benshoff and Sean Griffin. London: Routledge, 2004: 121–36.

Bachelor, David. *Chromophobia*. London: Reaktion, 2000.

Bailey, Marlon M. *Butch Queens: Gender, Performance and Ballroom Culture in Detroit*. Ann Arbor: The University of Michigan Press, 2013.

Baird-Murray, Kathleen. *Vogue on Ralph Lauren*. New York: Abrams, 2015.

Barbas, Samantha. *Movie Crazy: Fans, Stars and the Cult of Celebrity*. New York: Palgrave Macmillan, 2000.

Barsacq, Leon. *Caligari's Cabinet and Other Grand Illusions*. New York: Little Brown, 1976.

Basinger, Jeanine. *A Woman's View: How Hollywood Spoke to Women 1930–1960*. Connecticut: Wesleyan University Press, 1995.

Baudrillard, Jean. *Simulations*. New York: Semiotext(e), 1983.

Baum, L. Frank. *The Art of Decorating Dry Goods Windows and Interiors*. Chicago: Show Window, 1900.

Becherer, Richard. 'Picturing Architecture Otherwise: The Voguing of the Maison Mallet-Stevens'. *Art History* 23:4 (2000): 559–98.

Becherer, Richard. 'Past Remembering: Robert Mallet-Stevens's Architecture of Duration'. *Assemblage* 31 (1996): 16–41.

Berthomé, Jean-Pierre. 'Les Décorateurs du Cinema muet en France'. *1895. Mille huite cent quatre-vingt-quinze* 65 (2011): 90–111.

Benjamin, Walter. *The Arcades Project*. Trans. Howard Eiland and Kevin McLaughlin. Cambridge and London: Harvard University Press, 1999.

Benjamin, Walter. 'Paris: Capital of the Nineteenth Century [1939]'. *Perspecta* 12 (1969): 163–72.

Benshoff, Harry M. and Sean Griffin. *Queer Images: A History of Gay and Lesbian Film in America*. Lanham: Rowman & Littlefield, 2006.

Bergfelder, Tim, Sue Harris and Sarah Street. *Film Architecture and the Transnational Imagination: Set Design in 1930s European Cinema*. Amsterdam: Amsterdam University Press, 2007.

Berry, Jess. *House of Fashion: Haute Couture and the Modern Interior*. London: Bloomsbury, 2018.

Berry, Sarah. *Screen Style: Fashion and Femininity in 1930s Hollywood*. Minneapolis: University of Minnesota Press, 2000.

Best, Susan. 'From Representation to Affect: Beyond Postmodern Identity Politics in Feminist Art'. *A Companion to Feminist Art*. Eds. Hillary Robinson and Maria Elena Buszek. New Jersey: John Wiley and Sons, 2019: 405–17.

Best, Susan. 'Rethinking Visual Pleasure: Aesthetics and Affect'. *Theory Psychology* 17:5 (2007): 505–14.

Betsky, Aaron. *Queer Space: Architecture and Same-Sex Desire*. New York: William Morrow and Company, 1997.

Bidou, Henri. 'A l'Exposition Internationale des Arts Decoratifs et Industriels Moderns. Le Décor de la vie modern'. *Vogue* (France) (June 1925): 29–37.

Booth, Hannah. 'Shopping in Bollywood'. *Design Week* (2 May 2002): 19–23.

Booth, Mark. *Camp*. London and New York: Quartet, 1983.

Bourdieu, Pierre. *Distinction: A Social Critique of Judgement Through Taste*. Trans. Richard Nice. London: Routledge, [1979] 1984.

Boym, Svetlana. 'Nostalgia and Its Discontents'. *The Hedgehog Review* 9:2 (2007): 7–18.

Bradshaw, Peter. 'Laurence Anyways- Review'. *The Guardian* (30 November 2012): viewed on 13 January 2019, https://www.theguardian.com/film/2012/nov/29/drama-transgender

British, Pathé. 'Paris Fashions' (1909): viewed on 20 July 2020, https://www.britishpathe.com/video/paris-fashions-4

Breward, Christopher. *The Suit: Form Function and Style*. London: Reaktion, 2016.

Bruzzi, Stella. *Men's Cinema: Masculinity and Mise-en-Scene in Hollywood*. Edinburgh: Edinburgh University Press, 2013.

Bruzzi, Stella. *Undressing Cinema: Clothing and Identity in the Movies*. London: Routledge, 1997.

Buck, Joan Juliette. 'Everybody's All-American'. *Vogue (America)* 182:2 (February 1992): 202–11, 284.

Buck-Morss, Susan. *The Dialectics of Seeing: Walter Benjamin and the Arcades Project*. Cambridge and London: MIT Press, 1991.

Butler, Judith. *Gender Trouble: Feminism and the Subversion of Identity*. New York: Routledge, [1990] 1999.

Butler, Judith. *Bodies that Matter: On the Discursive Limits of Sex*. New York: Routledge, 1993.

Caruso, Joyce. 'Gehry Downtown'. *Artnet* (8 July 2001): viewed on 10 August 2020, http://www.artnet.com/magazine/news/caruso/caruso8-7-01.asp

Chaney, Lisa. *Coco Chanel: An Intimate Life*. New York: Penguin, 2011.

Chapman, Jane. 'The Argument of the Broken Pane: Suffragette Consumerism and the Newspapers'. *Media History* 21:3 (2015): 238–51.

Chapman, Llewella. 'Fitting Fleming's Hero like a Savile Row Suit: The Tailoring of James Bond'. *From Bloefeld to Moneypenny: Gender in James Bond*. Ed. Steven Gerrard. Bingley: Emerald Publishing, 2020: 69–88.

Chatterjee, Deepsikha and Cheri Vasek. 'Bollywood: Cross Pollination between Film Costumes and Fashion'. *Fashion Practice* 12:2 (2020): 219–44.

Chavance, Rene. 'Chez un Cineaste'. *Art et Decoration* (Juillet-Decembre 1927): 43–8.

Cheng, Anne Anlin. 'Skin Fashion: Josephine Baker and Dressing Race'. *Nka: Journal of Contemporary African Art* 37 (2015): 6–15.

Cheng, Anne Anlin. *Second Skin: Josephine Baker and the Modern Surface*. London: Oxford, 2011.

Cheronnet, Louis. 'Boutiques Nouvelles a Paris'. *Art et Decoration* (Juillet–Decembre 1928): 113–20.

Church Gibson, Pamela. *Fashion and Celebrity Culture*. London: Bloomsbury, 2012.

Church Gibson, Pamela. 'The Fashion Narratives of Tom Ford: *Nocturnal Animals* and Contemporary Cinema'. *Fashion Theory* 21:16 (2017): 629–46.

Church Gibson, Pamela. 'From Style Icon to Fashion Victim: Masculinity and Spectacle in the James Bond Franchise'. *Vestoj: The Platform for Critical Thinking on Fashion* 7 (2017): viewed on 5 December 2018, http://vestoj.com/from-style-icon-to-fashion-victim/

Ciufo, Emma. 'Miuccia Prada Unveils Great Gatsby Costumes'. *Harper's Bazaar* (22 January 2013): viewed on 20 August 2020, https://www.harpersbazaar.com.au/fashion/miuccia-prada-unveils-great-gatsby-costumes-7451

Clark, David. 'The Shop Within?: An Analysis of the Architectural Evidence for Medieval Shops'. *Architectural History* 43 (2000): 58–87.

Clarke, David (Ed). *The Cinematic City*. Hoboken: Taylor & Francis, 1997.

Clausen, Meredith L. 'The Department Store: Development of the Type'. *Journal of Architectural Education* 39:1 (1985): 20–9.

Cleto, Fabio. 'The Spectacles of Camp'. *Camp: Notes on Fashion*. Ed. Andrew Bolton. New York: The Metropolitan Museum of Art, 2019: 9–59.

Cleto, Fabio. 'Introduction: Queering the Camp'. *Camp: Queer Aesthetics and the Performing Subject*. Ed. Fabio Cleto. Ann Arbor: The University of Michigan Press, 1999: 1–42.

Cohan, Steve. *Masked Men: Masculinity and the Movies in the Fifties*. Indiana: Indiana University Press, 1997.

Cohen, Arthur (Ed). *The New Art of Colour: The Writings of Robert and Sonia Delaunay*. Trans. David Schapiro and Arthur Cohen. New York: Viking Press, 1978.

Colomina, Beatriz. 'Sex, Lies and Decoration: Adolf Loos and Gustav Klimt'. *Thresholds* 37 (2010): 70–81.

Colomina, Beatriz. *Privacy and Publicity: Modern Architecture as Mass Media*. Cambridge: Cambridge University Press, 1994.

Colomina, Beatriz. 'The Split Wall: Domestic Voyeurism'. *Sexuality and Space*. Ed. Beatriz Colomina. New York: Princeton Architectural Press, 1992: 73–130.

Condello, Annette. *The Architecture of Luxury*. Surrey: Ashgate, 2014.

Conekin, Becky. 'Fashioning Playboy: Messages of Style and Masculinity in the Pages of Playboy Magazine, 1953–1963'. *Fashion Theory* 4:4 (2000): 447–66.

Conor, Liz. *The Spectacular Modern Woman: Feminine Visibility in the 1920s*. Bloomington: Indiana University Press, 2004.

Cook, Pam and Claire Hines. 'Sean Connery is James Bond: Re-Fashioning British Masculinity in the 1960s'. *Fashioning Film Stars: Dress, Culture, Identity*. Ed. Rachel Moseley. London: British Film Institute, 2005: 145–59.

Cornu, Paul. 'L'Art de la Robe'. *Art et Decoration* (Avril 1911): 103–7.

Crewe, Louise. *The Geographies of Fashion: Consumption, Space and Value*. London: Bloomsbury, 2017.

Culver, Stuart. 'What Manikins Want: *The Wonderful Wizard of Oz* and *The Art of Decorating Dry Goods Windows*'. *Representations* 21 (Winter 1988): 97–116.

Daly-Ward, Yrsa. 'Women of the Year: Lashana Lynch on Making History as the First Black Female 007'. *Harper's Bazaar* (3 November 2020): viewed on 23 November, 2020, https://www.harpersbazaar.com/uk/culture/culture-news/a34517814/lashana-lynch-black-female-007-interview/

Daigle, Allain. 'Of Love and Longing: Queer Nostalgia in Carol'. *Queer Studies in Media & Popular Culture* 2:1 (2017): 199–211.

De Beauvoir, Simone. 'Brigitte Bardot and the Lolita Syndrome'. *Esquire* (August 1959): 32–8.

De Mille Presley, Cecilia and Mark A. Vieira. 'The Wickedest Movie in the World: How Cecil B. DeMille Made *The Sign of the Cross*'. *Bright Lights Film Journal* (18 December 2014): viewed 8 January 2020, https://brightlightsfilm.com/wickedest-movie-world-cecil-b-demille-made-sign-cross/#.XhZ9RpIzaS4

Dirix, Emmanuelle. 'Birds of Paradise: Feathers, Fetishism and Costume in Classical Hollywood'. *Film, Fashion and Consumption* 3:1 (2014): 15–29.

Doane, Mary Ann. 'The Economy of Desire: The Commodity Form in/of the Cinema'. *Movies and Mass Culture*. Ed. John Belton. London: The Athlone Press, 1996: 119–34.

Doane, Mary Ann. *Femme Fatales: Feminism, Film Theory, Psychoanalysis*. London and New York: Routledge, 1991.

Doane, Mary Ann. *The Desire to Desire: The Woman's Film of the 1940s*. Bloomington and Indianapolis: Indiana University Press, 1987.

Doane, Mary Ann. 'Film and the Masquerade: Theorising the Female Spectator'. *Screen* 23:3–4 (1982): 74–87.

Downey, Georgina. 'Bathrooms: Plumbing the Canon- the Bathtub Nudes of Alfred Stevens, Edgar Degas and Pierre Bonnard Reconsidered'. *Domestic Interiors*. Ed. Georgina Downey London and New York: Bloomsbury, 2013: 111–28.

Downey, Georgina and Mark Taylor. 'Impolite Reading and Erotic Interiors of Eighteenth Century France'. *Designing the French Interior: The Modern Home and Mass Media*. Eds. Anca I. Lasc, Georgina Downey and Mark Taylor. London and New York: Bloomsbury, 2015: 13–27.

Duff Gordon, Lady. *Discretions and Indiscretions*. New York: Frederick A Stokes, 1932.

Dyer, Richard. *The Culture of Queers*. London and New York: Routledge, 2005.

Eckert, Charles. 'The Carol Lombard in Macy's Window'. *Quarterly Review of Film and Video* 3:1 (1978): 1–21.

Elle (France). 'La Reign Victoria'. (October 2012): 161–7.

Esperdy, Gabrielle. 'From Instruction to Consumption: Architecture and Design in Hollywood Movies of the 1930s'. *The Journal of American Culture* 30:2 (2007): 198–211.

Esquevin, Christian. *Adrian: Silver Screen to Custom Label*. New York: Monacelli Press, 2008.

Evans, Caroline. *The Mechanical Smile: Modernism and the First Fashion Shows in France and America, 1900–1929*. New Haven and London: Yale University Press, 2013.

Evans, Caroline. *Fashion at the Edge: Spectacle, Modernity and Deathliness*. New Haven and London: Yale University Press, 2003.

Faiers, Johnathan. *Dressing Dangerously: Dysfunctional Fashion in Film*. New Haven and London: Yale University Press, 2013.

Fairs, Marcus. 'Armani 5th Avenue by Massimiliano and Doriana Fuksas Architects'. *Dezeen* (23 February 2009): viewed on 10 August 2020, https://www.dezeen.com/2009/02/23/armani-5th-avenue-by-massimiliano-doriana-fuksas-architects/

Farmer, Brett. *Spectacular Passions: Cinema, Fantasy, Gay Male Spectatorships*. Durham: Duke University Press, 2000.

Featherstone, Mike. 'Consumer Culture and Its Futures: Dreams and Consequences'. *Approaching Consumer Culture*. Ed. Evgenia Krasteva-Blagoeva. Cham: Springer, 2018: 1–46.

Featherstone, Mike. 'Luxury Consumer Culture and Sumptuary Dynamics'. *Luxury: History, Culture and Consumption* 1:1 (2015): 47–69.

Featherstone, Mike. 'The Flâneur, the City and Virtual Public Life'. *Urban Studies* 35:5/6 (1998): 909–25.

The Film Daily, 'Leading Stores Exploit Fashions from Roberta' (15 March 1935): 16.

Fischer, Lucy. *Designing Women: Cinema, Art Deco and the Female Form*. New York: Columbia University Press, 2013.

Fisher, Lauren Alexis. 'Inside Fendi's Breathtaking Couture Show at Rome's Trevi Fountain'. *Harper's Bazaar* (8 July 2016): viewed on 24 August 2020, https://www.

harpersbazaar.com/fashion/fashion-week/news/a16573/fendi-couture-show-at-trevi-fountain/

Forest Wilson, Robert. 'The House of Bechoff'. *Vogue (America)* (February 1927): 23–4, 136.

Forest Wilson, Robert. 'The House of Nicole Groult'. *Vogue (America)* (January 1927): 20, 116, 120.

Forest Wilson, Robert. 'The House of Lucien Lelong'. *Vogue (America)*(October 1925): 33–6.

Foucault, Michel. 'Of Other Spaces, Utopias and Heterotopias [1967]'. *Architecture/ Mouvement/Continuite* (October 1984): 1–9.

Frayling, Christopher. *Ken Adam: The Art of Production Design*. London: Faber & Faber, 2005.

Friedberg, Anne. *Window Shopping: Cinema and the Postmodern*. Berkeley: University of California Press, 1994.

Friedman, Alice T. 'American Glamour 2.0: Architecture, Spectacle and Social Media'. *Consumption, Markets and Culture* 20:6 (2017): 575–84.

Friedman, Alice T. *American Glamour and the Evolution of Modern Architecture*. New Haven: Yale University Press, 2010.

Friedman, Alice T. *Women and the Making of the Modern House*. New York: Abrams, 1998.

Fry, Naomi. 'Surface Matters: Todd Haynes's Carol Mistakes Aesthetics for Meaning'. *The New Republic* (13 November 2015): viewed on 5 December 2018, https://newrepublic.com/article/123221/todd-hayness-carol-mistakes-aesthetics-meaning

Gaines, Jane. 'The Queen Christina Tie-ups: Convergence of Show Window and Screen'. *Quarterly Review of Film and Video* 11:1 (1989): 35–60.

Galt, Rosalind. *Pretty: Film and the Decorative Image*. New York: Columbia University Press, 2011.

Giedion, Sigfried. *Space, Time and Architecture*. Cambridge: Harvard University Press 1967.

Glendinning, Miles. *Architecture's Evil Empire: The Triumph and Tragedy of Global Modernism*. London: Reaktion, 2010.

Gray, Christopher. 'From a Mysterious Mansion to a Ralph Lauren Store'. *The New York Times* (7 October 2010): viewed on 19 August 2020, https://www.nytimes.com/2010/10/10/realestate/10scapes.html

Gronberg, Tag. *Designs on Modernity: Exhibiting the City in 1920s Paris*. Manchester and New York: Manchester University Press, 1998.

Gunning, Tom. 'The Cinema of Attraction: Early Film, Its Spectator and the Avant-Garde'. *Early Cinema: Space, Frame, Narrative*. Ed. Thomas Elsaesser. London: BFI, 1990: 56–62.

Gutner, Howard. *MGM Style: Cedric Gibbons and the Art of the Golden Age of Hollywood*. Lanham: Rowman and Littlefield, 2019.

GQ: Gentleman's Quarterly. 'Stetson Shoe Advertisement'. 37:4 (1967): 128.

GQ: Gentleman's Quarterly. 'Trevor Howard: Operation Savile Row'. 36:1 (1966): 96–7.

GQ: Gentleman's Quarterly. 'Monte Christo Advertisement'. 35:1 (1965): 51.

Harper's Bazaar, 'The Rising Tide of White Decors: Lace and Linen in the Boudoir'. 65:26 (1931): 74–5.

Hatherly, Owen. 'Fendi Vidi Vici: When Fashion Flirts with Fascism'. *The Architectural Review* (3 March 2015): viewed on 20 August 2020, https://www.architectural-review.com/essays/fendi-vidi-vici-when-fashion-flirts-with-fascism

Hawkins, Laura. 'Step Up: Dolce & Gabbana's Staircase is Ahead of the Curve'. *Wallpaper** (11 January 2018): viewed on 3 August 2020, https://www.wallpaper.com/fashion/dolce-and-gabbana-marble-design-awards-2018

Heisner, Beverly. *Hollywood Art: Art Direction in the Days of the Great Studio*. London: St James Press, 1990.

Henderson, Susan R. 'Bachelor Culture in the Work of Adolf Loos'. *Journal of Architectural Education* 55:3 (2002): 125–35.

Herzog, Charlotte. 'Powder Puff Promotion: The Fashion Show-in-the-Film'. *Fabrications: Costume and the Female Body*. Eds. Jane Gains and Charlotte Herzog. London: Routledge, 1990: 134–59.

Higashi, Sumiko. *Cecil B. DeMille and American Culture: The Silent Era*. Berkeley: University of California Press, 1994.

Hilderbrand, Lucas. *Paris Is Burning: A Queer Film Classic*. Vancouver: Arsenal Pulp Press, 2013.

Hinds, Hilary. *A Cultural History of Twin Beds*. London: Bloomsbury, 2019.

Hoare, Sarajane. 'Actors Tweeds'. *Vogue* (Britain) (November 1987): 270–6.

Hollander, Anne. *Sex and Suits: The Evolution of Modern Dress*. London: Bloomsbury, [1994] 2016.

hooks, belle. *Black Looks: Race and Representation*. New York and London: Routledge, 2015.

Houze, Rebecca. 'From Weiner Kunst im Hause to the Wiener Werkstätte: Marketing Domesticity with Fashionable Interior Design'. *Design Issues* 8:1 (2002): 3–23.

Howarth, Dan. 'David Chipperfield's Valentino Flagship Store Opens in New York'. *Dezeen* (11 September 2014): viewed on 10 August 2020, https://www.dezeen.com/2014/09/11/david-chipperfield-valentino-flagship-store-fifth-avenue-new-york/

Iannone, Floriana and Francesco Izzo. 'Salvatore Ferragamo: An Italian Heritage Brand and its Museum'. *Place Branding and Public Diplomacy* 13:2 (2017): 163–75.

Iribe, Paul. 'The Audacious Note of Modernism in the Boudoir'. *Vogue* (America) (June 1919): 58–9.

Irigaray, Luce. *This Sex Which is Not One*. Trans. Catherine Porter. Ithaca: Cornell University Press, 1985.

Jackson, Lesley. *The New Look Design in the Fifties*. London: Thames and Hudson, 1998.

Jacobs, Steven. *The Wrong House: The Architecture of Alfred Hitchcock*. Rotterdam: 010 Publishers, 2007.

Jakobsen, Janet. 'Queer is? Queer does? Normativity and the Problem of Resistance'. *GLQ: A Journal of Lesbian and Gay Studies* 4:4 (1998): 511–36.

Jeffers McDonald, Tamar. *Doris Day Confidential: Hollywood, Sex and Stardom*. London: I.B. Tauris, 2013.

Jeffers McDonald, Tamar. *Hollywood Catwalk: Exploring Costume and Transformation in American Film*. New York: I.B Tauris, 2010.

Jones, Angela. 'Queer Heterotopias: Homonormativity and the Future of Queerness'. *Interalia: A Journal of Queer Studies* 4 (2009): 1–20.

Jules-Rosette, Benneta. 'Spectacular Dress: Africanisms in the Fashions and Performances of Josephine Baker'. *African Dress: Fashion, Agency, Performance*. Eds. Karen Tranberg Hansen and D. Soyini Madison. London: Bloomsbury, 2013: 204–216.

Kaiser, Susan B. *Fashion and Cultural Studies*. London and New York: Bloomsbury, 2012.

Kapferer, Jean-Noël. 'The Artification of Luxury: From Artisans to Artists'. *Business Horizons* 57 (2014): 371–80.

Kaplan, Joel H. and Shiela Stowell. *Theatre and Fashion: Oscar Wilde to the Suffragettes*. Cambridge: Cambridge University Press, 1994.

Karaminas, Viki and Adam Geczy. *Fashion and Masculinities in Popular Culture*. London: Routledge, 2007.

Khoo, Olivia. 'Writing about Transnational Cinema: Crazy Rich Asians'. *Writing About Screen Media*. Ed. Lisa Patti. Oxon and New York: Routledge, 2020: 75–8.

Kindo Lopez, Lori. 'Racism and Mainstream Media'. *Race and Media: Critical Approaches*. Ed. Lori Kindo Lopez. New York: New York University Press, 2020: 13–26.

Kirkham, Pat. 'Living in a Modern Way in *The Moon is Blue*: Mid-Century Modern Architecture, Interiors and Furniture'. *Interiors* 10:1–2 (2019): 103–22.

Kirkham, Pat and Sarah A. Lichtman (Eds). *Screen Interiors: From Country Houses to Cosmic Heterotopias*. London: Bloomsbury, 2021.

Klinger, Barbara. *Melodrama and Meaning: History, Culture and the Films of Douglas Sirk*. Bloomington and Indianapolis: Indiana University Press, 1994.

Kosofsky Sedgwick, Eve. *Epistemology of the Closet*. Berkeley: University of California Press, 1990.

Lagerfeld, Karl. 'Karl Chats with Coco'. *Harper's Bazaar* 34:96 (March 2003): 226–9.

Lajer-Burcharth, Ewa and Beate Söntgen. 'Introduction: Interiors and Interiority'. *Interiors and Interiority*, Eds. Ewa Lajer-Burcharth and Beate Söntgen. Berlin and Boston: Degruyter, 2016: 1–13.

Lasc, Anca I. 'The Traveling Sidewalk: The Mobile Architecture of American Shop Windows at the Turn of the Twentieth Century'. *Journal of Design History* 31:1 (2018): 24–45.

Lehmann, Ulrich. 'Language of Pursuit: Cary Grant's Clothes in Alfred Hitchcock's North by Northwest'. *Fashion Theory* 4:4 (2000): 467–85.

Leigh, Helena. 'The Cosmetic Urge'. *Harper's Bazaar* 66 (February 1932): 86, 88, 94.

Leigh, Helena. 'The Cosmetic Urge'. *Harper's Bazaar* 65 (August 1931): 114, 116, 118, 120.

Leigh, Helena. 'The Cosmetic Urge'. *Harper's Bazaar* 64 (July 1930): 100, 102, 104–105.

Leverdière, Shayne and Xavier Dolan. 'Xavier Dolan'. *L'Uomo Vogue* 456 (December 2014): viewed on 1 July 2020, https://www.vogue.it/en/uomo-vogue/cover-story/2014/12/dolan

Lilley, Ed. 'The Name of the Boudoir'. *Journal of the Society of Architectural Historians* 53:2 (1994): 193–8.

L'Illustration. 'Le Pavillon d'Elegance' (Juin 1925): 34.

Lipovetsky, Giles. 'On Artistic Capitalism'. *Crash Magazine* 65, 3 April 2015, available 3 August 2020 from: https://www.crash.fr/on-artistic-capitalism-by-gilles-lipovetsky-crash-65/

Lipovetsky, Gilles. *The Empire of Fashion: Dressing Modern Democracy*. Trans. Catherine Porter. Princeton and Oxford: Princeton University Press, 1994.

Lipovetsky, Giles and Jean Serroy. *L'Ecran Global: Culture-médias et Cinéma à l'âge Hypermoderne*. Paris: Seuil, 2007.

Lipovetsky, Gilles and Veronica Manlow. 'The "Artialization" of Luxury Stores'. *Fashion and Imagination*. Ed. Jo Teunissen. Arnheim: ArtEZ Press, 2007: 154–67.

Loncar, Jena. 'F is for …Fluctuating Symbolism: The Palazzo Civiltà Italiana and Its Shifting Meaning'. *The Routledge Companion to Italian Fascist Architecture: Reception and Legacy*. Eds. Kay Bea Jones and Stephanie Pilat. Oxon and New York: Routledge, 2020: 92–110.

Loos, Adolf. 'Ornament and Crime [1910]'. *Adolf Loos Ornament and Crime: Selected Essays*. Trans. Michael Mitchell. California: Ariadne Press, 1998: 167–76.

Loring, John. *Joseph Urban*. New York: Abrams, 2010.

LVMH. 'Fendi Studios Exhibition Celebrates Close Bond Between Fendi and the Cinema' (30 October 2017): viewed on 20 August 2020, https://www.lvmh.com/news-documents/news/fendi-studios-exhibition-celebrates-close-bonds-between-fendi-and-the-cinema/

Mahdavi, India. 'RED Valentino Sloan Street London'. *indiamahdavi.com* (2016): viewed on 4 September 2020, https://india-mahdavi.com/project/red-valentino-sloan-street/

Mallet-Stevens, Robert. *Le Décor Modern au Cinema*. Paris: Charles Massin, 1928.

Mallet-Stevens, Robert. 'L'éclairage et l'architecture modern'. *Lux* (Janvier 1928): 6–9.

Mallet-Stevens, Robert. *Le Décor de la rue, les magazines, les étalages, les stands d'exposion, les éclairages*. Paris: Les Éditions de Parade, 1927.

Mallet-Stevens, Robert. 'Le Cinema et les arts: L'Architecture'. *Les Cahiers du Mois Cinema* (1925): 16–17.

Mandelbaum, Howard and Eric Myers. *Screen Deco*. Sana Monica: Hennessey and Ingalls, 2000.

Marple, A.M. 'The Impassioned Palate of James Bond'. *GQ: Gentleman's Quarterly* 33:5 (1963): 36, 40, 78, 80, 162.

Massey, Anne. *Hollywood Beyond the Screen*. Oxford and New York: Berg, 2000.

Mattlin, Everett. 'Off the Cuff'. *GQ: Gentleman's Quarterly* 36:3 (1966): 8, 12, 14, 18, 28.

Maynard, Margaret. 'The Fashion Photograph: An Ecology'. *Fashion as Photograph*. Ed. Eugenie Shinkle. London: I.B Tauris, 2010: 54–69.

McCarthy, Fiona. 'Shared Vision'. *Wish: The Australian Magazine* (March 2020): 45–9.

McEwen, Todd. 'Cary Grant's Suit'. *Granta: The Magazine of New Writing* 94 (2006): 119–25.

McNeil, Peter and Giorgio Riello. *Luxury: A Rich History*. Oxford: Oxford University Press, 2016.

Mendes, Silvano and Nick Rees-Roberts. 'New French Luxury: Art, Fashion and the Re-Invention of a National Brand'. *Luxury* 2:2 (2015): 53–69.

Migennes, Pierre. 'De L'Étalage'. *Art et Decoration* (Juliette-Decembre 1929): 97–111.

Miller, Monica L. *Slaves to Fashion: Black Dandyism and the Styling of Black Diasporic Identity*. Durham and London: Durham University Press, 2009.

Mizejewski, Linda. *Ziegfeld Girl: Image and Icon in Culture and Cinema*. Durham and London: Duke University Press, 1999.

Moana Thompson, Kirsten. 'Falling in (to) Colour: Chromophilia and Tom Ford's *A Single Man* (2009)'. *The Moving Image* 15:1 (2015): 62–84.

Moera Hernandez, Coral. 'Patronage, Public Relations and Philanthropy: Fendi for Fountains Case Study'. *Revista de Communication Vivat Academia* 18:133 (2015): 80–124.

Moers, Ellen. *The Dandy: Brummell to Beerbohm*. London: Secker and Warburg, 1960.

Morby, Alice. 'NC Design & Architecture Hides Hong Kong Restaurant behind Grocery Stall'. *Dezeen* (17 February 2016): viewed on 4 September 2020, https://www.dezeen.com/2016/02/17/nc-design-architecture-mak-mak-hong-kong-restaurant-hidden-behind-thai-grocery-stall/

Morgan, Philip. *Italian Fascism: 1915–1945*. London: Palgrave McMillan, 2004.

Morris, Ali. 'Gold Palm Trees Adorn the Monochromatic Interior of Darial Concept store in Barcelona'. *Dezeen* (25 November 2019): viewed on 4 September 2020, https://www.dezeen.com/2019/11/25/darial-store-barcelona-djaba-diassamidze/

Moussinac, Leon. 'Le Décor et le Costume au Cinema'. *Art et Decoration* (Juliette-Decembre 1926): 129–39.

Mulvey, Laura. 'Visual Pleasure and Narrative Cinema'. *Screen* 16:3 (1975): 6–18.

Munich, Adrienne (Ed). *Fashion in Film*. Bloomington: Indiana University Press, 2011.

Museo Salvatore Ferragamo. 'Previous Exhibitions' (2020): viewed on 20 August 2020, https://www.ferragamo.com/museo/en/usa/exhibitions/archive/

Nadoolman Landis, Deborah. *Dressed: A Century of Hollywood Costume Design*. New York: HarperCollins, 2007.

Nagy, Phyllis interviewed by Terry Gross, 'Carol, Two Women Leap into an Unlikely Love Affair'. *NPR Movie Interviews* (6 January 2016): viewed on 2 November 2018, https://www.npr.org/templates/transcript/transcript.php?storyId=462089856

Neale, Steve. 'Masculinity as Spectacle: Reflections on Men and Mainstream Cinema'. *Screen* 24:6 (1983): 2–16.

Nobbs, Karinna, Christopher Moore and Mandy Sheridan. 'The Flagship Format Within the Luxury Fashion Market'. *International Journal of Retail & Distribution Management* 40:12 (2012): 920–34.

Ober Peak, Mayme. 'Every Home's a Stage'. *Ladies Home Journal* 50:7 (1933): 25, 77.

Ogersby, Bill. 'The Bachelor Pad as Cultural Icon'. *Journal of Design History* 18:1 (2005): 99–113.

Okonkwo, Uche. *Luxury Fashion Branding*. London: Palgrave, 2007.

Ostillio, Maria Carmela and Sarah Ghaddar. 'Salvatore Ferragamo: Brand Heritage as Main Vector of Brand Extension and Internationalization'. *Fashion Branding and Communication*, Eds. Byoungho Jin and Elena Cedrola. New York: Palgrave, 2017: 73–99.

Padva, Gilad. *Queer Nostalgia in Cinema and Pop Culture*. Hampshire and New York: Palgrave Macmillan, 2014.

Paulicelli, Eugenia. 'Reframing History: Federico Fellini's Rome, Fashion and Costume'. *Film, Fashion and Consumption* 8:1 (2019): 71–88.

Phelps, Nicole. 'Fall 2016 Fendi'. *Vogue* (8 July 2016): viewed on 24 August 2020, https://www.vogue.com/fashion-shows/fall-2016-couture/fendi

Picardie, Justine. *Coco Chanel: The Legend and the Life*. London: HarperCollins, 2010.

Pine, II, B. Joseph and James H. Gilmore, 'Welcome to the Experience Economy'. *Harvard Business Review*, July–August 1998, available 20 August 2020 from: https://hbr.org/1998/07/welcome-to-the-experience-economy

Place, Janey. 'Women in Film Noir'. *Women in Film Noir*. Ed. Anne Kaplan. London: BFI Publishing, 1992.

Playboy. 'A Playboy Pad: Pleasure on the Rocks, review of John Lautner, Elrod House'. (November 1971): 151–1, 208.

Playboy. 'The Progressive Dinner Party'. (January 1965): 107.

Playboy. 'Playboy's penthouse apartment'. (October 1956): 54.

Postrel, Virginia. *The Power of Glamour: Longing and the Art of Visual Persuasion*. New York: Simon & Schuster, 2013.

Potvin, John. *Deco Dandy: Designing Masculinity in 1920s Paris*. Manchester: Manchester University Press, 2020.

Potvin, John. 'The Velvet Masquerade: Fashion, Interior Design and the Furnished Body'. *Fashion, Interior Design and the Contours of Modern Identity*. Eds. Alla Myzelev and John Potvin. Oxon and New York: Routledge, 2016: 1–17.

Potvin, John. *Bachelors of a Different Sort: Queer Aesthetics, Material Culture and the Modern Interior in Britain*. Manchester: Manchester University Press, 2014.

Rabinovitz, Lauren. *For the Love of Pleasure: Women, Movies and Culture in Turn-of-the Century Chicago*. New Jersey: Rutgers University Press, 1998.

Radner, Hilary. 'Transnational Celebrity and the Fashion Icon: The Case of Tilda Swinton Visual Performance Artist at Large'. *European Journal of Women's Studies* 23:4 (2016): 401–4.

Radner, Hilary. *Neo-Feminist Cinema: Girly Films, Chick Flicks and Consumer Culture*. London: Routledge, 2010.

Rappaport, Erika D. 'A New Era of Shopping: The Promotion of Women's Pleasure in London's West End, 1909–1914'. *Cinema and the Invention of Modern Life*. Eds. Leo Charney and Vanessa Schwartz. Berkeley: University of California Press, 1995: 130–53.

Reed, Christopher. 'Imminent Domain: Queer Space in the Built Environment'. *Art Journal* 55:4 (1996): 64–70.

Rees-Roberts, Nick. 'Fade to Grey: Dolan's Pop Fashion and Surface Style'. *ReFocus: The Films of Xavier Dolan*. Ed. Andre Lafontaine. Edinburgh: Edinburgh University Press, 2019: 209–27.

Rees-Roberts, Nick. *Fashion Film*, London: Bloomsbury, 2018.

Riviere, Joan. 'Womanliness as a Masquerade'. *The International Journal of Psychoanalysis* 10 (1929): 303–13.

Roberts, Mary Louise. 'Samson and Delilah Revisited: The Politics of Women's Fashion in 1920s France'. *The America Historical Review* 98:3 (1993): 657–84.

Robertson Wojcik, Pamela. *The Apartment Plot: Urban Living in American Film and Popular Culture, 1945–1975*. Durham: Duke University Press, 2010.

Rochelle, Hannah and Lucy Pavia. 'What's Now: Big Screen Chic'. *Instyle* (UK) (December 2015): 171–2.

Romano, Elise. 'Aesop Channels Bond in London's Most Instagrammable Store'. *DMARGE* (18 November 2017): viewed on 4 September 2020, https://www.dmarge.com/2017/11/aesop-london-flagship.html

Rosa, Joseph. 'Tearing Down the House: Modern Homes in the Movies'. *Architecture and Film*. Ed. Mark Lamster. New York: Princeton Architectural Press, 2000.

Rose, Steve. 'James Bond: The Enemy of Architecture'. *The Guardian* (4 November 2008): viewed on 22 May 2018, https://www.theguardian.com/artanddesign/2008/nov/04/james-bond-architecture

Roth, Jon. 'Dream House: How Ralph Lauren Created a Retail Revolution on Maddison Avenue'. *Ralph Lauren*, viewed on 19 August 2020, https://www.ralphlauren.com.au/en/style-guide/dream-house

Ruti, Mari. *Feminist Film Theory and Pretty Woman*. London and New York: Bloomsbury, 2016.

Sanders, Joel. 'Introduction'. *Stud: Architectures of Masculinity*. Ed. J. Sanders. New York: Princeton Architectural Press, 1996: 11–25.

Sanders, Joel (Ed). *Stud: Architectures of Masculinity*. New York: Princeton Architectural Press, 1996.

Schimminger, Morgan C. 'Report: Racial Diversity Ticks up Slightly, Size, Age and Gender Representation all Drop for Fashion Month Spring 2021'. *The Fashion Spot* (19 October 2020): viewed on 5 January 2021, https://www.thefashionspot.com/runway-news/858789-diversity-report-fashion-month-spring-2021/

Schleier, Merrill. *Skyscraper Cinema: Architecture and Gender in American Film*. Minneapolis and London: University of Minnesota Press, 2009.

Sepe, Gioria and Alessia Anzivino. 'Guccification: Redefining Luxury Through Art- the Gucci Revolution'. *The Artification of Luxury Fashion Brands*. Eds. Marta Massi and Alex Turrini. Cham: Palgrave, 2020: 89–112.

Shahani, Nishant. *Queer Retrosexualities: The Politics of Reparative Return*. Maryland: Lehigh University Press, 2011.

Shar, Adam. 'Libeskind in Las Vegas: Reflections on Architecture as a Luxury Commodity'. *Critical Luxury Studies: Art, Design and Media*. Eds. John Armitage and Joanne Roberts. Edinburgh: Edinburgh University Press, 2016: 151–76.

Shone, Tom. 'Great Expectations'. *Vogue* (America) (May 2013): 246–55, 314.

Shonfield, Katherine. *Walls Have Feelings: Architecture, Film and the City*. London: Routledge 2000.

ShowStudio. 'Rejecting the White Gaze: Black Photographers in Fashion' (31 October 2020): viewed on 5 January 2020, https://www.showstudio.com/projects/blackhistory-month/panel-discussion-the-future-of-fashion-photography?autoplay=1

Showstudio. 'SHOWstudio and Harrods Present the Future of Fashion'. (18 September 2020): viewed on 3 October 2020, https://www.showstudio.com/news/showstudio-and-harrods-present-future-fashion

ShowStudio. 'Tino Kamal Cry'. (16 November 2019): viewed on 5 January2020, https://www.showstudio.com/projects/cry

ShowStudio. 'A Certain Romance'. (24 October 2019): viewed on 5 January 2020, https://www.showstudio.com/projects/certain-romance;

Smith, Victoria L. 'The Heterotopias of Todd Haynes: Creating Space for Same Sex Desire in Carol'. *Film Criticism* 42:1 (2018): viewed on 2 November 2018, https://quod.lib.umich.edu/f/fc/13761232.0042.102?view=text;rgn=main

Somma, Paola. 'The Palazzo Civiltà Italiana: From Fascism to Fashion'. *The Routledge Companion to Italian Fascist Architecture: Reception and Legacy*. Eds. Kay Bea Jones, Stephanie Pilat. Oxon and New York: Routledge, 2020: 79–91.

Sontag, Susan. 'Notes on Camp [1964]'. *Camp: Queer Aesthetics and the Performing Subject*. Ed. Fabio Cleto. Ann Arbor: The University of Michigan Press, 1999: 53–65.

Sparke, Penny. *The Modern Interior*. London: Reaktion Books, 2008.

Spicer, Andrew. 'Sean Connery: Loosening His Bonds'. *British Stars and Stardom: From Alma Taylor to Sean Connery*. Ed. Bruce Babbington. Manchester: Manchester University Press, 2001: 220–1.

Stern, Radu. *Against Fashion: Clothing as Art*. Massachusetts: The MIT Press, 2004.

Stewart, Janet. *Fashioning Vienna: Adolf Loos's Cultural Criticism*. London: Routledge, 2000.

Stolworthy, Jacob. 'Selfridges to Open in Store Cinema'. *The Telegraph* (4 September 2014): viewed on 28 September 2018, https://www.telegraph.co.uk/culture/film/film-news/11075378/Selfridges-to-open-in-store-cinema.html

Street, Sarah. *Costume and Cinema*. London and New York: Wallflower, 2001.

Street, Sarah. 'The Dresses Had Told Me: Fashion and Femininity in Rear Window'. *Alfred Hitchcock's Rear Window*, Ed. John Belton. Cambridge: Cambridge University Press, 2000: 91–109.

Studlar, Gaylyn. 'Chi-Chi Cinderella: Audrey Hepburn as Couture Countermodel'. *Fabrications: Costume and the Female Body*. Eds. Jane Gains and Charlotte Herzog. London: Routledge, 1990: 159–78.

Sullivan, Robert. 'Dramatic Effect: Reel Talk'. *Vogue (America)* (December 2015): 180, 182.

Sweeny-Risko, Jennifer. 'Fashionable "Formation": Reclaiming the Sartorial Politics of Josephine Baker'. *Australian Feminist Studies* 33:98 (2018): 498–514.

Szegheo Lang, Tamara de. 'The Demand to Progress: Critical Nostalgia in LGBTQ Cultural Memory'. *Journal of Lesbian Studies* 19:2 (2015): 230–48.

Tally, Andre Leon. *The Chiffon Trenches*. London: HarperCollins, 2020.

Tarmy, James. 'The Stair Master: How Peter Marino Turns Simple Steps into Amazing Art'. *Bloomberg* (23 November 2016): viewed on 10 August 2020, https://www.bloomberg.com/news/articles/2016-11-22/amazing-staircase-designs-in-peter-marino-art-architecture

Tasker, Yvonne. *Spectacular Bodies: Gender, Genre and the Action Cinema*. London: Routledge, 1993.

Templar, John. *The Staircase: History and Theory*. Massachusetts: MIT Press, 1998.

Thompson Summers, Brandi. 'Race as Aesthetic: The Politics of Vision, Visibility and Visuality in Vogue Italia's 'A Black Issue'. *QED: A Journal in QLBTQ Worldmaking* 4:3 (2017): 81–108.

Ting, Jasmine Ariel. 'The Crazy Rich Style of *Crazy Rich Asians*'. *Vanity Fair* (14 August 2018): viewed on 23 November 2020, https://www.vanityfair.com/style/2018/08/the-crazy-rich-style-of-crazy-rich-asians

Troutman, Anne. 'The Modernist Boudoir and the Erotics of Space'. *Negotiating Domesticity: Spatial Productions of Gender in Modern Architecture*. Eds. Hilde Heynen and Gulsum Bayder. London and New York: Routledge, 2005: 296–314.

Troy, Nancy J. *Couture Culture: A Study in Modern Art and Fashion*. Massachusetts: Massachusetts Institute of Technology, 2003.

Town & Country. 'Joan Crawford'. (November 1945): 118.

Valentina. 'How Valentina from RuPaul's Drag Race Becomes Fabulous' (23 June 2017): viewed on 5 January 2020, https://www.vogue.com/article/valentina-rupauls-drag-race-hair-makeup

Varnelis, Kazyz. 'Prada and the Pleasure Principle'. *Log* 6 (2005): 129–36.

Vincendeau, Ginette. 'The Old and the New: Bridget Bardot in 1950s France'. *Paragraph* 15:1 (1992): 73–96.

Vogue (America). 'Ralph Lauren Advertisement'. (October 2010): C2 1–7.

Vogue (America). 'Chanel-Her Famous New Dinner Pyjamas'. (November 1965): 116–17.

Vogue (America). 'Lingerie for a New Season'. (October 1932): 98–9.

Vogue (America). 'Miss Crawford of Hollywood Back with the Spoils of Paris'. (October 1932): 64–5.
Vogue (America). 'The Debut of the Winter Mode'. (October 1926): 69.
Vogue (America). 'The House of Jean Magnin'. (March 1927): 52, 170.
Vogue (France). 'L'Escalier des Glaces Chez Chanel'. (August 1931): 41.
Wagner, George. 'The Lair of the Bachelor'. *Architecture and Feminism*. Eds. Debra Coleman, Elizabeth Danze and Carol Henderson. New York: Princeton Architectural Press, 1996: 183–220.
Waldman, Diane. 'From Midnight Shows to Marriage Vows'. *Wide Angle* 6:2 (1984): 34–48.
Wallace, Lee. 'Tom Ford and His Kind'. *Criticism* 56:1 (2014): 21–44.
Wallenberg, Louise. *Fashion and Modernity*. Trans. Rune Engebretsen. London: Bloomsbury, 2019.
Walsh, Claire. 'Shop Design and the Display of Goods in Eighteenth Century London'. *Journal of Design History* 8:3 (1995): 157–76.
Weismann, Helmut. 'Let Architecture Play Itself: A Case Study'. *The City and the Moving Image*. Eds. Richard Koeck and Les Roberts. London: Palgrave Macmillan, 2010: 253–70.
Werth, Leon. 'L'Architecture Intérieure et Mallet Stevens'. *Art et Decoration* (Janvier–Juin 1929): 177–88.
Whitehead, Jean. *Creating Interior Atmosphere: Mise-en-scène and Interior Design*. London and New York: Bloomsbury, 2018.
Whitlock, Cathy. 'Here's Why All the Sets in *Crazy Rich Asians* Look so Authentic and, Well Rich'. *Architectural Digest*, 9 August 2018, available 23 November 2020 from: https://www.architecturaldigest.com/story/crazy-rich-asians-sets
Wigley, Mark. *White Walls Designer Dresses: The Fashioning of Modern Architecture*. Cambridge, MA: MIT Press, 1995.
Williams, Rosalind. *Dream Worlds: Mass Consumption in Late Nineteenth Century France*. Berkeley: University of California Press, 1982.
Wilson, Christina. 'Cedric Gibbons: Architect of Hollywood's Golden Age'. *Architecture and Film*. Ed. Mark Lamster. New York: Princeton Architectural Press, 2000: 121–35.
Wilson, Elizabeth. *Adorned in Dreams: Fashion and Modernity*. London: I.B Tauris, 2003.
Yellis, Kenneth A. 'Prosperity's Child: Some Thoughts on the Flapper'. *American Quarterly* 21:1 (1969): 44–64.
Yotka, Steff. 'Sofia Coppola Goes behind the Scenes at Chanel in a New Documentary'. *Vogue* (10 July 2020): viewed on 20 July 2020, https://www.vogue.com/article/sofia-coppola-goes-behind-the-scenes-at-chanel-in-a-new-documentary
Zoller Seitz, Matt. *The Wes Anderson Collection: Grand Budapest Hotel*. New York: Abrams, 2015.

Index

Note: page numbers in italics refer to illustrations.

Adam, Ken 7, 57, 58, 149
Adam's Rib 22
Adcock, Michael 33
Adrian, Gilbert 3, 18, 21, 35–6, 63, 84, 88, *97*
advertising 14, 18, 31, 50, 53, 80–4, 108–9, 114, 121, 148, 157
  short-film 8, 27, 81, 83, 87–8, 139, 141–2, 146
  see also window shopping
Affairs of Anatol, The (1921) 1, 32
Agent Provocateur 93
All that Heaven Allows (1955) 32, 68
Amarcord (1973) 142
American audiences 14, 19, 20
American consumers 34, 43–4, 60
American Gigolo (1980) 6
And the Ship Sails On 146
Anderson, Wes 82–3, 134, 140–3, *141*, 149
arcades 108, 111–12, 142
Armani 82, 105
Art Deco
  definition 161 n.12
  denigration of 17–18, 43, 65
  furniture 7
  interiors 3, 16, 19, 20, 37–8, *38*, 42–3, 89, 121, 134, 139, 142
Art et Decoration (magazine) 20, 92, 116, 120
art house cinema 8, 13–14, 27, 132
Art Nouveau 1, 3, 7, 55
artification 11, 127, 129, 130, 132–3, 134, 155
Astaire, Fred 98
Au Bonheur des Dames (The Ladies Paradise) (1884) 112
Australia (2008) 134
avant-garde cinema 11, 19, 41, 64, 81, 107, 112, 115–17, 128, 174 n.54
Avedon, Richard 92

Babuscio, Jack 63–4
Bacall, Lauren 31
bachelor
  character 24
  dandy 48–53, 60
  pad 24, 53–60, 153
  queer 69–72
Baker, Josephine 119, 151–2
ballroom subculture 78–80
Bally (shoe company) 119
Balmain 36
Banham, Reyner 53
Bar Luce 140–3, *141*, 144
Barbarella (1968) 4
Bardot, Brigitte 36–7
Barneys 125
The Bath (painting, Stevens, 1873–1874) 33
bathrooms 13, 14, 18, 33–9, 42–3, 75, 138, 156–7
Bauhaus 47
Baum, L. Frank 108–9
Beaton, Cecil 90, 96
Becherer, Richard 119
Bechoff, House of 87
Becker, Judy 66
Beckham, Victoria 91
Bedell Store 122
bedrooms 1, 8, 13, 14, 16–28, 39, 42–3, 54, 55, 56, 59, 76, *138*, 156–7
Beer, Maison 86
Belle de Jour (1967) 5
Belly of an Architect, The (1987) 147
Benjamin, Walter 57, 111
Benshoff, Harry, and Sean Griffin 63
Berkeley, Busby 63, 95, 96, *97*, 122
Berry, Sarah 85, 86
Bertolucci, Bernardo 147
Best, Susan 16, 157
Betsky, Aaron 71, 75

Big Lebowski, The (1998) 58
Big Sleep, The (1946) 30
Blade Runner (1982) 7, 126
Blake, Aston 153
Blanchett, Cate 65, *66, 67, 73, 74*
Block, Pierre 18–19
Bloomingdale's 137
Boccaccio '70 (1962) 145, 146, 147
Body Double (1984) 58
Bollywood 125, 154, 156
Bon Marche, Le 101–2, *102*
Bond, James 9, 41–2, 50–3, *51, 52,* 55, 57–9, 60, 61, 69, 124, 149, 152–3
Bonney, Thérèse 119
boudoirs 1, 8, 13, 16, 18, 21, 24, 28–33, 34, 39, 42–3, 54, 143
Bourdieu, Pierre 11, 88, 89
Bourgoise, Louise 140
boutiques 4, 103, 107, 112, 113–21, 131, 132, 136, *147*, 148
    see also Fendi
Boutique Simultanée *113,* 113–14, 117
Boyd, Ann 138
Boyle, Robert 44, 45
Boym, Svetlana 64
brand
    heritage 81, 91–2, 129, 130–50
    heterotopia 11, 130–6, 143–4, 150, 155
    luxury 11, 28, 102, 127, 129, 130–1, 132, 143–4, 153, 155
Breakfast at Tiffany's (1961) 107, 143
Brioni 51
Brooks Brothers 139
Brosnan, Pierce 51
Browne, Thom 83
Brummell, Beau 47, 50
Bruzzi, Stella 6, 42
Buck, Joan Juliette 136
Bulgari 144
Burberry 83
Butler, Judith 4, 10, 48, 77, 78–9

Callen, Anthea 34
Call Me by Your Name (2017) 7
Callot Soeurs 87
Camille (1921) 1
camp 63–4, 68, 75–9, 83
Campbell, Naomi 94, 151
Carol (2015) 9, 64, 65–7, 72–4, 80, 83, 84, 124

Casino Royale (2006) 51, 61
Castello Cavalcanti (2013) 141
Catelain, Jaque 118
catwalk 10, 77, 79, 83, 89, 125, 146, 151, 156
Cavalcanti, Alberto 116, 142
Cavalli, Roberto 126
celebrity architects *see* starchitects
Chanel, Gabrielle (Coco) 5, *90,* 91–2, 137
Chanel, House of 11, 81, 89–91, 101, 105, 155
Chariots of Fire (1981) 136
Cheng, Anne Anlin 152
cheongsam 26–7
Cheung, Maggie *26*
Chipperfield, David 105
Church Gibson, Pamela 5, 51, 81
Cinderella 92, 96, 99, 134
Cinecitta studios 134
cinema of attractions 125, 174 n.54
class distinction 7, 11, 41, 43, 48, 60, 89, 94–5, 96, 102, 111, 123, 138, 152, 155
Clausen, Meredith 102
Clement, Suzanne 75
Cléo de 5 à 7 (Cléo from 5 to 7) (1962) 111–12
Cleto, Fabio 75
Colomina, Beatriz 43, 56–7
Comer, Sam 3–4
commodification
    of bodies and spaces 11, 80, 155
    of history and nostalgia 11, 129, 136–50, 155
    of women 15, 38–9, 110, 122, 157
Condello, Annette 105
Conekin, Becky 53
Connery, Sean 42, 50, *51*
Conor, Liz 15
consumer culture
    and men 9, 42, 53–60
    reciprocity between cinema and 1, 2–3, 6, 113, 117, 120–1
    and sexuality 8, 9, 80–2, 84
    and women 1, 9, 13, 14–15, 18, 25, 38–9, 84, 109–11
    see also boutiques; department stores; flagship stores; window shopping
Coppola, Francis Ford 82–3
Coppola, Roman 141

Coppola, Sofia 82–3, 91, 143
cosmetics 14, 27–8, 31–2, 34, 109
costume dramas 32–3
Craig, Daniel 51–2, *52,* 152
Crawford, Joan 16, 17, 20, 21, 22, 31, 34, *35,* 35–6, 39, 63
Crazy Rich Asians (2018) 153–4, 155
Cukor, George 21, *29,* 34, *35,* 88
Culver, Stuart 108–9

Dafoe, Willem 142
Dalton, Timothy 51
Dames (1934) 96
dandy, the 47–52, 53, 60, 117–18, 153, 164n18
Dangerous Liaisons (1989) 33
Danse Serpentine (1896) 125
Darjeeling Limited, The (2007) 134, 142
Daughter of the Dragon (1931) 154
Day, Doris *23,* 23–4
De Beauvoir, Simone 37
Dead Poets Society (1989) 136
décor 1, 7, 18, 19, 35, 41, 46, 87, 115–17, 142
    and femininity 24, 27, 30–1, 54, 89
    and masculinity 24, 54
    and queer sensibility 9, 60, 63–5, 70
decoration
    as feminine 1–2, 48, 68
    and masculinity 53, 57, 61
Delaunay, Robert 113
Delaunay, Sonia 11, 100, 107, *113,* 113–14, 117–19, *118*
Delluc, Louis 7, 19
DeMille, Cecil 1, 32, 33–4
Demy, Jacques 123
Deneuve, Catherine 5, 123–4
department stores *see* Barneys; Bedell; Bloomingdale's; Le Bon Marche; Galeries Lafayette; Harrods; Kaufmann; Macy's; Printemps; Samaratain; Selfridges
Desai, Nitin 125
Designer Rugs 139
Devdas (2002) 154
Devil Wears Prada, The (2006) 89
Diamonds Are Forever (1971) 57, 58, *59,* 69
Dinner at Eight (1933) 8, 13, 21–2, *29,* 30, 36, 157

Dior, Christian
    brand 11, 27, 81, 92–3, *93,* 94, 101, 153, 155
    New Look 3, 37
    Tulip-Line 3
Dirix, Emmanuelle 30
display *see* boutiques; department stores; *Exposition des Arts Decoratifs et Industriels Moderns;* flagship stores; stage, the; window shopping
Distant Planet: The Six Chapters of Simona (2019) 132
Doane, Mary Ann 4, 9, 15, 48, 98–9
Doisneau, Robert 90
Dolan, Xavier 65, 75, 76, *77–8,* 77–9, 83
Dolce & Gabbana 103, 146
domestic space 7, 8, 13, 14, 18, 41, 55–6, 72, 149
    see also bathrooms; bedrooms; boudoirs
Doucet, Jacques 118
Dr No (1962) 50, *51,* 57–8
drag *77,* 77–9, *78,* 157
Drecoll, Charles 19, 87
Duchamp, Marcel, *Nude Descending a Staircase, No. 2* (1912) 91, 93
Duff Gordon, Lady (Lucile) 86, 88, 95–6, *95*
Dufrêne, Maurice 18–19
Dulac, Germain 19
Duvivier, Julien 112
Dyer, Richard 65
Dynamite (1929) 34

Eames, Charles and Ray 7, 55
Edwards, Blake *see Breakfast at Tiffany's*
Ekberg, Anita 146
Eckert, Charles 14, 107
Elle (magazine) 36, 91
Elrod, Arthur 58
Elrod House 58–9, *59,* 69
Epstein, Jean 19
Erlich, Leandro 102
Erwin, Hobe 21
Esperdy, Gabrielle 120, 121
Esquevin, Christian 36
Evans, Caroline 85, 87, 90–1
evening gowns 3, 21, 25, 30, 35, 77, 88, 90, 98, 100, 139, 146, 152
Ever After: A Cinderella Story (1998) 134

Evita (1996) 134
experience economy, definition of 130
Exposition des Arts Decoratifs et Industriels Moderns (1925) 18–19, 20, 89, 113, 117, 120, 121, 161 n.12

Faiers, Jonathan 48–9
Fallingwater 44, 58, 60
Far from Heaven (2002) 67
Farmer, Brett 68
Favourite, The (2018) 33
Featherstone, Mike 11, 108, 121, 126, 128
Fellini, Federico 142, 145, 146
female
   autonomy 9, 22–3, 33
   pleasure 16, 30, 33, 37, 39, 157 (*see also* Carol)
   spectatorship 15–16, 28, 98–9, 110 (*see also* window shopping)
femininity
   as mask 4, 37, 48
   performance of 4, 16, 76–7, 157
   traditional 16, 30–1
femme fatale 1, 15, 25, 30–1, *31,* 39
Fendi 11, 99, 129, 142, 143, 145, 146–8, *147*
Ferreri, Marco 132
Fiennes, Ralph 142
Figgis, Mike 93
Firth, Colin 68, *69, 70, 71,* 80
Fitzgerald Suite, The Plaza Hotel, New York 139
Fitzgerald, F. Scott 137
flagship stores 4, 11, 101, 128, 130–1, 155
   Aesop 149
   Fendi 145, 147–8, *147*
   Prada Epicentre 103–4, *104,* 139, *140*
   RED Valentino 149
   Rhinelander Mansion (Ralph Lauren) 136, 137–8
   Salvatore Ferragamo 134–5
   staircases in 103–5
   Tiffany & Co 143
flânerie 111–12
flâneur 111–12, 126
flapper 14, 15, 16
Flavin, Dan 127
Fleming, Ian 53, 57
   see also Bond, James
Fondazione Prada *see under* Prada (brand)

Ford, Tom 51–2, *52,* 60, 65, 68, 69–71, 80–1, 82, 83
Forster, E.M. 82
Foucault, Michel 9, 72, 74, 79, 131
Fountainhead, The (1949) 6–7
Friedman, Alice 43–4, 103, 104–5
Fudong, Yang 81, 141
Fuksas, Massimiliano and Doriana 105
Fuller, Loie 125
Funny Face (1957) 11, 96, 97, *98,* 99

Gaines, Jane 84
Galeries Lafayette 18, 102
Galleria Vittorio Emanuele 142
Galliano, John 94
Galt, Rosalind 2, 154
Garbo, Greta *17,* 17–18, 31, 63, 84, 121, 134
Garcia house 58
Garland, Judy 96, *97,* 109
Gassner, Dennis 57
Gaultier, Jean Paul 126
Gehry, Frank 105, 171 n.46
gender, performance of 4, 10, 16, 31–2, 48, 63–4, 72–8, 153, 156–7
   see also femininity; masculinity
gender roles 15, 14, 77–8, 83–4, 101, 157
   see also femininity; masculinity
Gere, Richard 37, *38*
Gherardi, Piero 145
Gibbons, Cedric 3, 7, 16, 18–19, 20, 36, 120–1
Giedion, Sigfried 60–1, 119
Gilda (1946) 30–1, *31*
Givenchy 94, 96, 97–8, 107, 143
glamour
   architecture and 10, 43–4, 60–1, 99, 103–4, 118–19, 156
   fashion and 5, 21, 31, 81, 88
   of surfaces 11, 121–4
   see also bathrooms; bedrooms; boudoirs; staircases
Glendinning, Miles 148
Godard, Jean-Luc 140
Gold Diggers of 1933 (1933) 30, 96
Goldfinger (1964) 57–8
Goldfinger, Erno 57
Gone with the Wind (1939) 94
GQ: Gentleman's Quarterly (magazine) 50
Grand Budapest Hotel, The (2014) 124, 142, 146

Grand Hotel (1932) 3
Grant, Cary 42, 44, 48–9, *49,* 50
Grant, Hugh 82
Graves, Rupert 82
Great Gatsby, The (1974) 124, 136–7, 138, 139–40, *140,* 144, 153–4
Greenaway, Peter 147
Gronberg, Tag 114
Groult, Nicole 86–7
Guadagnino, Luca 99, *100,* 149
Gucci 11, 129, 132–3, *133,* 134, 143, 144, 176 n.13
Gucci Garden 132–3, *133*

Harlow, Jean 21, *29,* 36, 39
Harper's Bazaar (magazine) 14, 31–2, 90, 97, 152, 156
Harrods 124, 126, 127, 143
Hatherly, Owen 148
Hault, Nicolas 70
haute couture 3, 7, 18, 37, 87, 88, 89, 114, 118–19, 130, 156
Haynes, Todd 65–7, *66, 67,* 68, *73, 74,* 83
Hayworth, Rita 30, *31,* 39
Head, Edith 3–4
Heartbeats (Les Amours Imaginaires) (2010) 83
Heim, Jacques 114
Hepburn, Audrey 96, 97–8, *98,* 99, 107, 134, 143, 146, 152
Hepburn, Katherine 22
Herbst, René 114, 120
heritage films 32–3, 65, 81, 84
Hermès 99, 142
Herzog, Charlotte 85, 89, 95
heterotopias
  brand 11, 130–6, 143–4, 150, 155
  Foucault's definition of 9–10, 72
  queer 64, 72–80, 153, 167 n.13
Hewson, Linda 126
Hinds, Hilary 22
Hitchcock, Alfred 3–4, 9, 41–2, 44–5, *45, 46, 49,* 60, 66
Hogben, Ruth 125
Hollander, Ann 48
hollywood cinema 8, 20, 36
  architecture in 41–2, 44, 69
  fashion in 14, 16, 25, 30, 84, 85, 94–101, 121, 122, 134–5, *135,* 151

interiors in 3, 14, 16–17, 19, 21–2, 25, 32, 33–4, 37–8
  and the Production Code 22, 23, 34, 60, 63
  and representation of non-white bodies, 151–6
  and representation of queer characters 60–1, 65, 69
Hood, Sam 122, *123*
Hope, Frederic 21
Hoult, Nicholas 70, *71,* 81
How to Marry a Millionaire (1953) 31
Hoyningen-Huene, George 92
Hudson, Rock 23–4, 53
Hum Dil De Chuke Sena (1999) 125
Hung, Tran Anh 154

I Am Love (Io sonno l'amore) (2009) 99, *100,* 101, 146, 149
identity
  brand 5, 11, 90, 101, 103, 105, 127, 129–31, 136–7, 144
  feminine 2, 8–10, 16, 18, 25, 27, 31–2, 154
  formation 4, 15
  gay 70–1, 166 n.1
  gender 4, 6, 7, 11–12, 54, 72, 75, 76–7, 79, 151, 157
  heterosexual 77, 82
  homosexual 60, 61, 68, 70–1, 82
  masculine 42, 50
  playboy 9, 24, 50, 52–5, 57–60, 117, 152–3
  queer 2, 61, 64, 70–1, 75, 76, 79–80, 82–3, 154, 166 n.1
  racial 152–3
  sexual 4, 6, 7, 8–10, 15, 25, 27, 32–3, 68, 71–2, 151
Il Conformista (The Conformist) (1970) 147
Iman 151
In the Mood for Love (2000) 8, 13, 25–8, *26,* 149
Instyle (magazine) 83
interiority
  architectural 4
  female characters and 1, 18, 19, 25, 27, 30, 66–7, 72–3, 153
  identity and 2
  male characters and 24, 47, 57, 69–71

International Style 7, 41
Iribe, Paul 1, 32
Isherwood, Christopher 68, 82
Italy in Hollywood (exhibition, 2018–19) 134–5, *135*

Jacobsen, Arne 3
Jacobsen, Janet 64
Jeunet, Jean-Pierre 81
Jourdain, Francis 7, 19–20, 120, 121
Joy Luck Club, The (1993) 153
Julien, Isaac 153

Karaminas, Viki and Adam Geczy 52
Kaufmann's department store 122
Kèfer, Pierre 19
Khoon Hooi 153
Kirkland, Douglas 90
Kiss, The (1929) 17, 31, 121
Klinger, Barbara 95
Knight, Nick 125, 127
Knize gentleman outfitters 55, *56*
Knoll, Florence, furniture 55
Koolhaas, Rem 103, *104,* 140, 171 n.46
Koons, Jeff 127
Kortajarena, Jon 81
Kusama, Yayoi 127

L'Atalante (1934) 7
La Dolce Vita (1960) 142, 145, 146
La Donna Scimmia (The Ape Woman) (1964) 132
La Femme de Nulle (The Woman from Nowhere) (1922) 7
La Règle du Jeu (The Rules of the Game) (1939) 5
La Sirène des Tropiques (Siren of the Tropics) (1927) 119, 151–2
La Sirène du Mississippi (Mississippi Mermaid) (1969) 5
Lacoste 27, 142
Lagerfeld, Karl 91, 92, 94, 148
Lamarr, Hedy 96, *97*
Lanvin, Jeanne 89
Larson, Lola 58, *59*
Laudrée 143
Lauren, Ralph 11, 129, *136,* 136–9, 143, 144, 155
Laurence Anyways (2012) 9, 64, 65, 75, 76–9, *77–8,* 80, 83, 168 n.32

Lautner, John 41, 43–4, 58–9, 69–70, *70*
Le Corbusier 43, 47, 120
Le Double Amour (Double Love) (1925) 19
Leff, Naomi 136
Léger, Fernand 116
Lehmann, Ulrich 49–50, 60
L'Elegance (1926) 114
Le P'tit Parigot (The Little Parisian) (1926) 107, 116, 117, *118*
Le Somptier, René 107
Le Vertige (The Living Image) (1926) 107, 116, 117
Lelong, Lucien, House of 87
Leopard, The (1963) 149
Les parapluies de Cherbourg (The Umbrellas of Cherbourg) (1964) 123
Lethal Weapon II 58
Letty Lynton (1932) 22, 36
Leuchten, Kaiser 46
L'Herbier, Marcel 41, 107, 115, 115–16, 116–17
Life Aquatic, The (2004) 142
L'Inhumaine (The Inhuman Woman) (1924) 41, *115,* 115–16
Lipovetsky, Gilles 11, 85, 102, 129, 148
and Veronica Manilow 130, 136, 176 n.10
Lissenko, Nathalie 19
Livingston, Jennie 79
Looking for Langston (1989) 153
Loos, Adolf 9, 42, 43, 46–8, 50, 52, 55–7, *56,* 60, 61, 152
Louis, Jean 25, 30
Louis Vuitton (brand) 82, 83, 105, 127, 134, 142
Maison Etoile 134
Lucile *see* Duff Gordon, Lady
Luhrmann, Baz *124,* 125, 139
Lumière Brothers 125
Luna, Donyale 151
Lynch, David 81
Lynch, Lashana 152

Macy's 14, 36, 88, 121
Madonna 80
Magnin, Jean, House of 87
Mahdavi, India 143, 149
Mahogany (1975) 89
Maison Beer 86

Maison Mallet-Stevens 118, 121
Maison Myrbor 89
male body *see* Bond, James; dandy, the; masculinity
male gaze, the 15, 36–7, 39, 85, 97–9, *98*, 112
Male and Female (1919) 33, 34
Malin House 58
Mallet-Stevens, Robert 11, 19, 41, 107, 113–21, *115–16, 118*
Manabe, Daito 133
Manilow, Veronica, and Gilles Lipovetsky 130, 136, 176 n.10
Mannequin (1937) 88, 123
Mar-a-Lago 122
Mara, Rooney 65–74, *66–67, 73, 74*
Marchand, Corinne 112
Marchesa 83
Marie Antoinette (2006) 6, 33, 143
Marino, Peter 105
Martin, Catherine *124,* 125, 139, *140*
masculinity
    heroic 9, 39, 47, 48, 61, 112
    and heterosexuality 24–5, 42–4, 47–61, 146
    queer 82, 83
Mason, James 44
masquerade 2, 4, 28, 32, 37, 47–8, 66, 73, 75, 77, 83, 100–1, 156, 157
Mastrioianni, Marcello 145–6
Maurice (1987) 82
Max Factor 31, 157
Maynard, Margaret 93
Maywald, Willy 92, 93
McCartney, Stella 126
McEwen, Todd 50
McNeil, Peter, and Giorgio Riello 130
McQueen, Alexander 125
McQueen, Steve 141
melodrama 19, 25–6, 32, 68–9, 74–5, 81, 82, 99
menswear 80–1, 82–3, 137
Merchant-Ivory 82
Metropolis (1923) 7
Michele, Alessandro 132–3
mid-century modern
    architecture 42, 43, 59, 103
    design 25, 32, 41, 44, 69
    furniture 3
Miller, Monica L. 153

mirrors 21, 28, 29, 30, 32, 33, 37, 59, 73–6, *74,* 89, 90, 91, 92, 98–9, 107, 108, 112, 126, 149
mise-en-scène 1, 2, 3, 5, 10, 11, 29, 42, 66, 68, 70, 88, 102, 117, 120, 128, 129, 137, 139, 149, 157
Miyake, Issey 79, 105
modern
    architecture 41–8, 55, 57–61, 119
    design 17–19, 22, 41, 44–6, 54
modern woman 8–9, 14–16, 22–3, 25, 39, 89, 115
    lifestyle 16, 18, 114, 117, 137
modernism 3, 7, 32, 90–1, 115–17, 121, 147–8
    as evil 41–2, 44–8, 57–8
    as masculine 9, 24–5, 42–4, 47–8, 55, 56–7, 59–61, 68
    as queer, 60–1, 69–72, 74
modernity 18, 43, 44, 111, 114
Mon Oncle (1958) 149
Monroe, Marilyn 31, 134
Monsoon Wedding (2001) 154
Moon is Blue, The (1953) 7
Moore, Julianne 68, *69*
Moore, Roger 51
Mulvey, Laura 9, 15, 16, 37
My Fair Lady (1964) 96, 152

Nagy, Phyllis 73
Neale, Steve 42
Nendo 102
Neutra, Richard 41
Newman, Bernard 3, 88
Newton, Helmut 91
Nicolas, Gwenaël 103
No Time to Die (2021) 152
North by Northwest (1959) 9, 44–50, *45–6, 49,* 52, 58, 60, 61
Nude Descending a Staircase, No. 2 (Duchamp, 1912) 91, 93

Octopussy 53
Okonkwo, Uche 131
Op Art 4
Orientalism 153–4
ornamentation 46–7, 60, 65, 68, 105, 142
Orry-Kelly 88, 121
Our Dancing Daughters (1928) 16, 20
Out of Africa (1985) 136, 155

Palazzo Civiltà Italiana *145,* 145–8
Paltrow, Gwyneth 142, 157
Panton, Verner 4
Paquin, Jeanne 86, 87, 118
Paris is Burning (1990) 79–80, 168 nn.36–7
Parker, Suzy 90
Parks, Trina 58
Party, The (1968) 149
Paulicelli, Eugenia 145
people of colour, underrepresentation of in fashion 151–6
performativity 4, 10, 13, 48, 59, 63, 75, 77–8, 125
Phillips, Arianne 68
Pickford, Mary 134, 135
Pillow Talk (1959) 13, *23,* 23–5, 53
Pine, B. Joseph, and James Gilmore 130
Playboy (magazine) 24, 42, 53–5, 59, 60, 153
playboy identity 9, 24, 50, 52–5, 57–60, 117, 152–3
Playtime (1967) 7
pleasure
    and dressing 82
    and looking 10, 16, 42, 65, 66, 82, 85, 111–12, 126, 154
    and patriarchal attitudes 15–16, 75–6
    and queer desire 61, 64, 65, 68, 82
    and surface 14, 16, 21, 65–72, 76, 84
Poiret, Paul 5, 19, 86, 87, 88, 92, 114, 116, 118–19
Polanski, Roman 141
Polglase, Van Nest 3
Ponti, Gio 142
pop art 4, 127
Potvin, John 4, 54, 60–1, 69, 70
Poupaud, Melvin 75, *77*
Powell, Sandy 66, 83
Prada (brand) 11, 81, 103–4, 124, 140–2, 144, 146, 153
    epicentre 103–4, *104,* 139, *140*
    Fondazione 140, *141,* 143
Prada Candy (2013) 141
Prada Epicentre *see under* Prada (brand)
Prada, Miuccia 139, *140*
Pret-à-Porter (1994) 89
Pretty Woman (1990) 13, 37–9, *38*
Printemps 102
Production Code 22, 23, 34, 60, 63
prostitution 22, 33, 34, 37, 38–9
publicity
    campaigns 80, 83–4, 95
    images 90
Pugh, Gareth 125

Quantum of Solace (2008) 57
Queen Christina (1933) 84, 121
queer
    aesthetics 61, 63–4, 69–72
    audiences 63–4
    cinema 10, 64, 79, 83
    closet 60, 70–1
    commodification 80, 168 n.40
    definition of 166 n.1
    desire 61, 64, 65, 68, 82
    fashionability 80, 82
    heterotopia 64, 72–80, 153, 167 n.13
    kinship 64, 69, 78–9
    masquerade 65–8, 73, 75, 76–80
    nostalgia 9, 64–72
    spaces 65, 71, 75, 76–7

Rabanne, Paco 4
Rabinovitz, Lauren 111
Radner, Hilary 38, 101
Rain (1932) 22
Rambova, Natacha 1
Rear Window (1954) 4
Redford, Robert 136
Red-Headed Woman (1932) 30
Reed, Christopher 65
Rees-Roberts, Nick 6, 77, 83
Rhinelander Mansion 136, 137–8
Riviere, Joan 4
Roberta (1935) 88
Roberts, Julia 37–9, *38*
Roberts, Mary Louise 14
Robie House 43
Roma Città Aperta (Rome, Open City) (1945) 147
Rope (1948) 60
Rosa, Joseph 41
Rose, Steve 57
Ross, Diana 89
Rossellini, Roberto 147
Royal Tenenbaums, The (2001) 142
Ruhlmann, Émile-Jacques 19

Russell, Lillian 21
Russell, Rosalind 35
Ruti, Mari 38

Saarien, Eero 3
Sabrina (1954) 96–7
Saint Laurent, Yves, 5, 27, 79, 83
Saint, Eva Marie 44
Salomé (1923) 1
Salon d'Automne 113
salon, the 56, 86–9, 91, 101, 112, 137
Salvatore Ferragamo 134–5, *135*, 144
Samarataine 102
Sander, Jil 99, 101
scenography 96, 136, 138, 144, 148–9
Scent of Green Papaya, The (Mùi đu đủ xanh) (1993) 154
Schaffer Residence 69, *70*
Schiaparelli, Elsa 21, 88, 92
Schleier, Merrill 6–7
Scott, Ridley 141
screen, the 2, 20, 41, 108, 112, 121–2, 126
Sedgwick, Eve Kosofsky 71
Selfridge, Harry Gordon 109, 110
Selfridges 109–10, *110*, 125, 126, 127
set design 6, 7, 19, 32, 41, 45, 57–8, 115–19, *115*, 121–2, 129, 136, 139, 145
 see also Adam, Ken; Mallet-Stevens, Robert; Martin, Catherine
sexuality
 and consumption 13, 22
 female 13, 16, 21–7, 30–1, 33, 36–9, 43, 54, 152
 male, 23–4, 37, 52, 54–5
 and morality 1, 13, 21–3, 30
 see also camp; dandy; the; drag; playboy identity; queer
Shanghai Express (1932) 30, 154
Shanghai Tang 134
Shearer, Norma 20, 31
Sheats-Goldstein House 58
shop window 84, 107–12, 114, 120, 121–2, 123–4, 125, 126, 127, 148–9, 155
Show Window (magazine) 108
SHOWstudio 125–7, 156
Shwartzman, Jason 141
Sign of the Cross (1932) 34
Silva, Raoul 61
Sinclair, Anthony 42, 50

Single Man, A (2009) 9, 60, 64, 65, 68–72, *69–71*, 74, 80–2
Single Standard, The (1929) 13, *17*, 17–18
Sirk, Douglas 32, 66, 68
Skyfall (2012) 61
Smith, Paul 126
Sontag, Susan 63
space
 private 7, 8, 13, 14, 18, 28, 32, 41, 54–6, 70–2, 148, 149
 public 14, 32, 54, 55, 70–2, 109–12, 148
Sparke, Penny 5, 54
spectacle
 bodies as 9, 10, 11, 42, 111–12
 fashion as 5, 85–6, 125
 see also staircases; window shopping
spectatorship 11, 43, 67, 107–8, 111, 157
 female 15–16, 28, 98–9, 110 (*see also* window shopping)
Spectre (2015) 51–2, *52*, 57
Spicer, Andrew 50
Spiral Staircase, The (1946) 99
spy films 9, 41–2, 44, 48, 60
stage, the 5, 85–9, 152
staircases
 as fashion icon 85–6, 89–94, 152, 169 n.5
 as film motif 94–101
 as statements of luxury fashion 101–5
 symbolic function of 10–11
starchitects 4, 103, 104–5, 140, 171 n.46
Steichen, Edward 92
Stevens, Alfred 33
Stockhausen, Adam 142
Stolen Holiday (1937) 88
suffragettes 110, 127, 155
suit, the 41–2, 47–61, 136, 146, 153, 164 n.18
Swanson, Gloria 34, 134, 135
Swinton, Tilda 99–101, *100*, 142

Tally, André Leon 94
Tati, Jacques 7, 149
Templar, John 92
theatre 5, 87, 88, 102, 103, 108, 109, 122, 130
 see also Ziegfeld Follies
Theatre (magazine) 1
Thompson, Kirsten Moana 68
Tiffany & Co 124, 143

Tonight or Never (1931) 5
Top Hat (1932) 3
Trevi Fountain 145, 146
Troutman, Anne 26, 28
Troy, Nancy 87, 88
Turner, Lana 96, *97*
Twin Beds (1942) 23

Under the Red Robe (1923) 122
Une Parisienne (1957) 8, 36–7
Urban, Joseph 96, 122
Usonian houses 44

Valentino (brand) 83, 105, 125, 146, 149
Valentino, Rudolph 135
van der Rohe, Mies 53
Vandamm House 44–7, *45, 46,* 58
Varda, Agnes 111–12
Vertigo (1958) 4
Viard, Virginie 91–2
Vigo, Jean 7
Villa Necchi Campiglio 99, 101
Villa Noailles 116
Vincendeau, Ginette 37
Vionnet, Madeleine 89, 114
Visconti di Modrone, Violante 7
Vogue (magazine) 14, 20, 21, 32, 82, 83, 86–7, 90, 91, 97, 136, 151, 156
Vogues of 1938 (1937) 88

Wagner, George 44
Waldman, Diane 84

Wallace, Lee 81
Wallenberg, Louise 1
Wallpaper* (magazine) 103
Way Down East (1920) 88
Weiner Werkstätte 55
Whitehead, Jean 10
Who Are You, Polly Maggoo? (1966) 4
Wiley, James 82
Williams, Rosalind 112
Wilson, Elizabeth 15
window shopping 11, 107–8, 111–12, 114
Winged Victory of Samothrace (sculpture, 200BC) 98
Wizard of Oz (book, 1900; film, 1939) 108–9, 121
Wojcik, Pamela Robertson 7, 55, 60
Women, The (1939) 8, 13, 34–6, *35,* 88, 123, 157
Wong Kar-Wai 25–8, *26,* 149
World of Suzie Wong, The (1960) 154
Wormley, Edward 46
Wright, Frank Lloyd 43, 44–5, 53, 58, 103
Written on the Wind (1956) 32

Yamamoto, Yoji 126
You Only Live Twice (1967) 57
Young Diana, The (1922) 32, 122

Ziegfeld, Florenz 95
Ziegfeld Follies 95, 95–6, 122
Ziegfeld Girl (1941) 96, *97,* 122–3, *123*
Zola, Émile 112

www.ingramcontent.com/pod-product-compliance
Lightning Source LLC
Chambersburg PA
CBHW070316230426
43663CB00011B/2150